I0083824

Claiming Citizenship

Claiming Citizenship is an authoritative and vital series published by Zed Books in partnership with the Citizenship Development Research Centre (CDRC).

Each high-quality volume features thoroughly peer-reviewed research from senior experts in their field, which examines the multifaceted issues of citizenship, rights, participation and accountability. The books are global in scope and packed with empirical and original case studies, largely from Southern contexts, bringing voices and materials to debates that have often been dominated by the North. While essential reading for development studies students and researchers, the series will be of interest to a broad range of scholars, activists and practitioners concerned with issues of citizenship.

Available titles

Inclusive Citizenship: Meanings and Expressions, edited by Naila Kabeer

Science and Citizens: Globalization and the Challenge of Engagement, edited by Melissa Leach, Ian Scoones and Brian Wynne

Rights, Resources and the Politics of Accountability, edited by Peter Newell and Joanna Wheeler

Spaces for Change? The Politics of Citizen Participation in New Democratic Arenas, edited by Andrea Cornwall and Vera Schattan Coelho

Citizenship and Social Movements: Perspectives from the Global South, edited by Lisa Thompson and Chris Tapscott

Citizen Action and National Policy Reform: Making Change Happen, edited by John Gaventa and Rosemary McGee

Globalizing Citizens: New Dynamics of Inclusion and Exclusion, edited by John Gaventa and Rajesh Tandon

Mobilizing for Democracy: Citizen Action and the Politics of Public Participation, edited by Vera Schattan P. Coelho and Bettina von Lieres

About the editors

Vera Schattan P. Coelho is a senior researcher at CEBRAP, where she coordinates the Citizenship and Development Group. She has a PhD in social science. Her research interests are public policies, political participation, accountability, democracy and development. She has led various comparative studies in the areas of new forms of citizen participation, social policies systems and democracy.

Bettina von Lieres teaches at the University of the Western Cape in South Africa and at the University of Toronto in Canada. A political scientist by training, her research interests lie at the intersection of development studies and democratic theory, with a particular focus on citizen participation in the global South.

Mobilizing for democracy

citizen action and the politics of public participation

edited by Vera Schattan P. Coelho
and Bettina von Lieres

BLOOMSBURY ACADEMIC
LONDON • NEW YORK • OXFORD • NEW DELHI • SYDNEY

BLOOMSBURY ACADEMIC
Bloomsbury Publishing Plc
50 Bedford Square, London, WC1B 3DP, UK
1385 Broadway, New York, NY 10018, USA
29 Earlsfort Terrace, Dublin 2, Ireland

BLOOMSBURY, BLOOMSBURY ACADEMIC and the Diana logo
are trademarks of Bloomsbury Publishing Plc

First published by Palgrave Macmillan, 2010
Reprinted by Bloomsbury Academic, 2024

Cover designed by Andrew Corbett

A catalogue record for this book is available from the British Library.

A catalog record for this book is available from the Library of Congress.

ISBN: HB: 978-1-8481-3445-4
PB: 978-1-8481-3446-1
ePDF: 978-1-8481-3447-8
ePUB: 978-1-8481-3915-2

Contents

Tables and Figures

Tables

Figures

Acknowledgements

This book represents the outcome of a global collaboration that has taken place over four years under the auspices of the UK Department for International Development (DFID)-funded Development Research Centre on Citizenship, Participation and Accountability (CDRC). A very special thank you goes to John Gaventa, CDRC director, for his wise, astute, generous, humorous and, above all, participatory and inclusive leadership. We are grateful to all the members of the DRC's 'deepening democracy in states and localities' working group for our lively and fascinating transnational discussions, which flourished despite differences in language, research approaches and political backgrounds: Alex Shankland, Andrea Cornwall, Arilson Favareto, Celestine Nyamu Musembi, Chris Tapscott, Duncan Okello, Idaci Ferreira, Jibo Ibrahim, John Williams, Lisa Thompson, Naila Kabeer, Ndodana Nleya, Sam Egwu, Sandra Roque, Simeen Mahmud, Steven Robins and Zander Navarro.

We would like to thank the following colleagues and friends for their generous help in commenting on the manuscript of the book, and for acting as discussants and facilitators at our workshops in Brazil, South Africa and the UK: Andrea Cornwall, David Kahane, Fiona Wilson, Laurence Piper, Jenny Pearce, Marian Barnes, Ben Cousins and Evelina Dagnino. A thank you also to our two anonymous reviewers and, especially, to Stuart Corbridge and Mark Warren for their discerning and helpful comments on how to build more accurately the comparative dimension of our work.

We owe special thanks to Greg Barrett for his boundless patience and time in helping us with background material. Thank you to Karen Brock and Kristen Chew for their incredible editing. In the UK, Joanna Wheeler and the DRC coordination team of Nick Benequista, Graeme McGregor, Georgina Powell-Stevens and Alison Dunn kept the DRC ship afloat, made sure that we all arrived for our meetings and did not forget to develop local policy messages! We also want to thank all the national foundations and donors that supported the research and dissemination work. Lastly, we would like to thank DFID for making possible this global research on democracy.

Muito Obrigada!

Vera Schattan P. Coelho and Bettina von Lieres

Acronyms

ACDS	Associação dos Camponeses para o Desenvolvimento Social (Association of Small Farmers for Social Development)
ACF	Arewa Consultative Forum
ADCM	Associação para o Desenvolvimento da Cultura Mudombe (Association for Mudombe Cultural Development)
ADRA	Acção para o Desenvolvimento Rural e Ambiente (Action for Rural Development and the Environment)
ADSAC	Associação para o Desenvolvimento Social e Ambiente Comunitário (Association for Social Development and the Community Environment)
ANC	African National Congress
ANPP	All Nigeria People's Party
APROCOR	Associação para a Promoção das Comunidades Rurais (Association for the Promotion of Rural Communities)
ARG	Associação dos Residentes de Guapiruvu (Guapiruvu Residents' Association)
ARM	Associação dos Residentes de Mandira (Mandira Residents' Association)
ASA	Association for Social Advancement
BRAC	Bangladesh Rural Advancement Committee
CACS	Conselho de Auscultação e Concertação Social (Council for Social Consultation and Dialogue)
CBO	community-based organization
CCT	City of Cape Town
CDF	Constituency Development Fund
CDRC	Citizenship Development Research Centre
CEBRAP	Centro Brasileiro de Análise e Planejamento (Brazilian Centre for Analysis and Planning)
CEM	Centro de Estudos da Metrópole (Centre for Metropolitan Studies)
CIMI	Conselho Indigenista Missionário (Indigenous Missionary Council)
CLS	*conselhos locais da saúde* (local health councils)
CONSAD	Consórcio de Segurança Alimentar e Nutricional e Desenvolvimento Local (Consortium for Food Safety and Local Development)
CSO	civil society organization
DDC	District Development Committee

DSEI	*distritos sanitários especiais indígenas* (special indigenous health districts)
FUNASA	Fundação Nacional de Saúde (National Health Foundation)
HDI	Human Development Index
ICJ	International Commission of Jurists
IDP	integrated development plan
INEC	Independent National Electoral Commission
IPPG	Inter-Parties Parliamentary Group
JCNARC	Joint Committee of the National Assembly for Review of the Constitution
KANU	Kenya African National Union
KHRC	Kenya Human Rights Commission
KNCHR	Kenya National Commission on Human Rights
LASDAP	Local Authority Service Delivery Action Plan
LATF	Local Authority Transfer Fund
LDP	Liberal Democratic Party
MOAB	Movimento dos Ameaçados por Barragem (Movement of Those Threatened by the Dam)
MP	Member of Parliament
MPLA	Movimento Popular de Libertação de Angola (Popular Movement for the Liberation of Angola)
NACATT	National Civil Society Coalition against the Third Term
NAK	National Alliance Party of Kenya
NaRC	National Rainbow Coalition
NCD	Núcleo de Citadania e Desenvolvimento (Citizenship and Development Group)
NGO	non-governmental organization
NPRC	National Political Reform Conference
NRA	Núcleo Representativo das Associações do Dombe Grande (Federation of Representative Associations of Dombe Grande)
ODSC	Organização para o Desenvolvimento Social (Organization for Social Development)
OPIN	Organização dos Povos Indígenas do Acre, Sul do Amazonas e Noroeste de Rondônia (Organization of Indigenous Peoples of Acre, Southern Amazonas and North-western Rondônia)
PCdoB	Partido Comunista do Brasil (Communist Party of Brazil)
PD	People's Dialogue
PDL	*plano de desenvolvimento local* (local development plan)
PDP	People's Democratic Party
PRONAF	Programa Nacional de Fortalecimento da Agricultura Familiar (National Programme for Supporting Family Farmers)
PROSHIKA	Proshikkhan Shikkha Kaj (Training, Education and Action)

PT	Partido dos Trabalhadores (Workers' Party)
SAHPF	South African Homeless People's Federation
SDI	Slum Dwellers International
SEPI	Secretaria de Estado dos Povos Indígenas (State Secretariat for Indigenous Peoples)
SINTRAVALE	Sindicato dos Trabalhadores na Agricultura Familiar do Vale do Ribeira (Union of Farming Families of the Vale do Ribeira)
SJC	social justice committee
SNM	Samajik Nyay Manch (Association for Social Justice)
SSL	Saúde Sem Limites (Health Unlimited)
SUS	Sistema Único de Saúde (Unified Health System)
UNI	União das Nações Indígenas do Acre e Sul do Amazonas (Union of Indigenous Nations of Acre and Southern Amazonas)
UNITA	União Nacional para a Independência Total de Angola (National Union for the Total Independence of Angola)
UNO	Upazila Nirbahi Officer
UP	Union Parishad
VMx	Victoria Mxenge Housing Federation

Foreword by John Gaventa

How is democracy built and sustained, especially in politically difficult contexts and settings? What is the contribution of collective citizen action to the process?

Answers to these questions need a fresh perspective. For too long, research on democracy has been dominated by the experiences of older, western democracies, and by scholars based in those countries.

This book is different. To our knowledge, it is one of the few volumes on democracy to draw largely from scholars who are deeply rooted in the experience of relatively young democracies, all of which are non-western. These new case studies of citizen mobilization for democracy, from Angola, Bangladesh, Brazil, India, Kenya, Nigeria and South Africa, provide a fresh perspective on how democracy is built and sustained, and on the role of citizen action in the process.

While many studies on democracy in such settings focus on the process of building formal democratic institutions – elections, parliaments, the executive and the judiciary – these studies begin from a different viewpoint. Rather than starting with the problem of how to build western-style democratic institutions, the first authors ask how citizens engage, mobilize and participate to make their voices heard in their own societies. In turn, they argue, taking a citizens' perspective leads to important insights into how citizen mobilization contributes to developing more inclusive and accountable institutions, as well as to the deepening of democratic cultures and the skills of citizen engagement themselves.

Through these chapters we realize that citizen mobilization for democracy is more than lining up at the ballot box in periodic elections; it can also mean participation in community associations, such as we see in Kenya, Angola or Bangladesh. It can mean involvement in social movements to obtain rights and justice, as seen in the movements of indigenous people in the Brazilian Amazon, in Nigeria's struggles to protect and reform the political process, or in South Africa's movements of homeless people. In other instances, it involves participation in formal governance processes, whether for ensuring social justice in India, health rights in Brazil or changing the way politics is done in

Kenya. In all of these, citizen mobilization for democracy is an active process of ongoing engagement and action.

While the case studies give compelling evidence of the contribution of such bottom-up forms of citizen action to realizing democratic ideals, they are not idealistic or romantic about the process. Over the last two decades, much work on democracy in developing societies has assumed the importance of associational civil society, still influenced perhaps by Alexis de Tocqueville's famous book *Democracy in America*, first published in 1838 when American democracy itself was still young. While also calling attention to the importance of associations, this book challenges the assumption that these are always good for democracy – arguing that we must also examine the nature and activities of the associations and social movements themselves. While pointing to the importance of citizen engagement in democracy building, the authors also are aware of the risks of elite capture, manipulation and uses of citizen mobilization for non-democratic ends. And while urging us to look beyond a thin notion of democracy which is based only on citizens electing their political representatives, they also challenge us to examine the issue of representation *within* civil society organizations as well. In so doing, they point to the fact that democratization is rarely a linear and steady path. It is complex, full of reversals, and often contradictory – offering a messiness which confounds the search for simplistic formulas or blueprint approaches for how democracies in differing settings are both attained and sustained.

This book is the last in the series on *Claiming Citizenship*, published by Zed Books in collaboration with the Development Research Centre on Citizenship, Participation and Accountability (Citizenship DRC), a network of some sixty researchers and practitioners working in twenty countries, hosted by the Institute of Development Studies, University of Sussex. (For further information see www.drc-citizenship.org.) Funded by the Department for International Development in the UK, with additional support from the Rockefeller and Ford Foundations, this innovative ten-year programme ends in 2010. Through its decade of research, the programme has produced eight volumes in this series, which together have included over 100 original case studies on citizen action. Together these volumes provide deeply grounded, empirical insights into the meanings of inclusive citizenship (Kabeer, 2005), the politics of knowledge, science and citizen action (Leach, Scoones and Wynne, 2005), the politics of rights and accountability (Newell and Wheeler, 2006), the dynamics of citizen participation in 'new' democratic arenas (Cornwall and Coelho, 2007), citizenship and social movements (Thompson and Tapscott, 2010), citizen action and national policy reform (Gaventa and McGee, 2010), globalization and citizen action (Gaventa and Tandon, 2010), and now this final volume on how citizens mobilize for democracy.

The Citizenship DRC research network has been unique in several respects. Rather than focusing simply on research in the traditional sense, it sought also to use its research (as well as the research process) to influence policy and practice, as well as to strengthen our own capacities as a highly diverse group of interdisciplinary scholars and activists. By working together over a period of years, we developed a 'bottom-up' and iterative approach to building the research programme, through which research questions were collectively identified, explored through interaction and engagement with concrete cases, discussed and theorized, and re-explored. In the process, we also were able to build a culture of collaboration across vastly differing contexts – be they south–south and south–north, or institutional, political or disciplinary – and to learn to engage as scholars-practitioners with the issues and problems we sought also to study. In this sense, our research in this project was not only about 'mobilizing for democracy', but also reflected a unique way of mobilizing ourselves to construct knowledge for and about the process of democratization.

As the overall coordinator of the Citizenship DRC's work, I am deeply grateful to Vera Schattan Coelho and Bettina von Lieres, who served as co-convenors and co-editors of the stream of work reflected in this volume, as well as to each of the contributors. They have brought enormous skill, perseverance and commitment to the task. I am also grateful to have been able to participate in the deeply collaborative and energetic conversations of the democracy researchers whose work is reflected in this volume. Our brainstorming of the project in Brazil, and midway reflections in both Sussex and South Africa, gave an opportunity for fascinating learning together. While the editors in their own acknowledgements have thanked others who helped on this volume (p. ix), I also wish to thank Zed Books and each of its staff, from the editors to the marketers, for supporting the production of this series. Thanks go especially to Robert Molteno and Anna Hardman, who saw and encouraged the possibilities of the first four volumes, and later to Susannah Trefgarne and Tamsine O'Riordan, who did the same for the last four.

Finally, my thanks go to all of the researchers in our network, as well as to our donors, for making the work of the Citizenship DRC possible. It has been an exciting journey, always under construction, never quite ending, simultaneously full of possibilities and challenges – much, we have discovered, like citizenship itself. While our formal programme will come to an end, our work as individuals will continue, often through new channels, strengthened I hope by what we have produced and how we have produced it. Through their ongoing commitment, I am confident that our network will contribute in some small way to the deepening of the knowledge and practice of democratic citizenship in years to come.

John Gaventa
Development Research Centre on Citizenship, Participation and Accountability
Institute of Development Studies
July 2010

1 · Mobilizing for democracy: citizen engagement and the politics of public participation[1]

VERA SCHATTAN P. COELHO AND
BETTINA VON LIERES

Introduction

What are the conditions under which citizen mobilization strengthens democratic institutions and cultures? In exploring that question, this book introduces eleven original empirical case studies of how different forms of citizen mobilization have generated democratic outcomes in seven countries of the global South. It highlights the limitations of one-size-fits-all approaches to addressing the challenges of building democracy, and it demonstrates how the prospects for achieving democratic outcomes depend on a combination of forms of mobilization and distinctive political and institutional contexts.

Drawing on the case studies, the book's focus is on what we call 'mediated citizen mobilization', in which marginalized citizens rely on mediators or interlocutors either to trigger or to shape their strategies. The case studies examine three forms of mediated citizen mobilization: associations, social movements and citizen involvement in formal governance mechanisms.

The case studies provide examples of citizen mobilization that has had democratic outcomes in political contexts that vary significantly in terms of constitutional and legal frameworks, state capacities and histories of citizen mobilization. Each of these contextual factors leaves distinctive traces of how citizens and their organizations mobilize for democracy, and also shapes the choice of forms of mobilization. Sometimes, in fragile states or emerging democracies, the most important outcomes of engagement are the construction of democratic citizenship, the capacity to press for rights, and the deepening and expansion of the practices of democratic participation. Where there is a longer history of citizen mobilization, there is a better chance of larger-scale gains – such as the crafting of new agendas for citizen participation or sustained access to economic resources, rights and accountable institutions.

In focusing on the importance of the forms of citizen mobilization and the political context, this book contributes to the debate on democracy building. While international studies devote increasing attention to citizen mobilization and its potential contribution to deepening democracy (Gaventa and McGee, 2010; Björkman and Svensson, 2009; Hossain, 2009), there is still little echo of this debate in the mainstream political and developmental approaches to democracy.

Carothers (2009) defines the political approach to democracy building as centring almost exclusively on building and strengthening representative institutions, such as competitive elections, an independent judiciary and a strong legislature (following Dahl, 1971; Manin, 1997; Przeworski, 1999). By contrast, the developmental approach involves 'a broader notion of democracy, one that encompasses concerns about equality and justice, and the concept of democratization as a slow, iterative process of change involving an inter-related set of political and socio-economic developments' (Carothers, 2009: 5; also Gerrits, 2007; Youngs, 2008).

This book complements these approaches by arguing, through empirical research, that democracy is not built by political institutions or developmental interventions alone. Taking a broader societal view, the chapters explore the conditions under which citizen mobilization has successfully contributed to the articulation of citizens' concerns, the promotion of democratic change, and the pressuring of states to act more accountably and democratically.

We begin this introductory chapter with reference to studies that discuss the challenges of deepening democracy through citizen mobilization. These include the complexities of political representation, the competing claims of political legitimacy and the trade-offs between long-term and one-off democratic gains.

In addition to these problems, we point to the lack of comparative research into how citizen mobilization plays out in different political contexts, and we describe the framework within which we have compared citizen mobilization across contexts.

The next section presents a review of the case studies, organized around the three different forms of mobilization under consideration. We conclude by calling attention to the importance of citizen mobilization for the project of deepening democracy.

Deepening democracy through citizen mobilization

This book engages with the 'deepening democracy' approach in current debates on democracy – a strand that, put simply, focuses on the 'contemporary project of developing and sustaining more substantive and empowered citizen participation in the political process than what is normally found in liberal representative democracy alone' (Gaventa, 2006b: 7; see also Fung and Wright, 2003; Dryzek, 2000).

Scholars and activists who take this approach argue that citizenship should mean far more than just the enjoyment of legal rights and the election of representatives. Many of them view citizenship as involving the building of broad coalitions and mobilization with the potential to frame new agendas and to provide a counterbalance to state power by encouraging citizens to voice their demands, to advocate for special interests and to play a 'watchdog' role (Dagnino et al., 2006; Appadurai, 2002; Edwards and Gaventa, 2001). For others, deepening democracy involves being heard by the state and participating directly in deliberation and decision-making on political and policy issues (Cornwall and Coelho, 2007; Mansbridge, 2003; Avritzer, 2002; Warren, 1992); or else having direct relations with government institutions, as opposed to relations that are brokered by powerful patrons or relations that are characterized by detachment (Houtzager and Acharya, 2010).

In short, the deepening democracy approach highlights the importance of citizen engagement in shaping the opportunities for wider democratic change. Within this approach, however, there is a growing body of literature that focuses on the challenges inherent in getting citizens involved in democratic change.

A first set of challenges concerns a tendency by some commentators to automatically equate the growth of civil society organizations (CSOs) with increased democratization. Lewis (2004) and Houtzager and Acharya (2010), among many others, call attention to the fact that there is often nothing inherently democratic about CSOs and movements. They focus attention on the possible disjunctures between the practices of democracy, as advocated by CSOs, and the everyday realities of clientelism, patronage and authoritarian local politics experienced by their members and ordinary citizens. Several cases highlighted in this volume show empirically how citizens' mobilizations are, to varying degrees, shaped not only by the organizations that mediate them, but also by existing local power dynamics. These cases demonstrate the need for a better understanding of how different modes of rule, authority and political culture interconnect and cut across one another in practice; how and why they last; and how they affect emerging forms of citizen mobilization.

From this perspective a second set of challenges embraced by the authors in this book concerns the task of specifying the conditions under which groups and associations not just mediate but actually produce the democratization of public politics. As Heller states:

Just as a vibrant civil society can promote trust and cooperation, it can also promote particularism that fosters rent-seeking lobbies and exclusionary identities. (Heller, 2000: 498)

In this sense, a much clearer understanding is still needed about the conditions under which a plurality of civil society associations and movements converges to deepen democracy.[2] Several of our authors discuss the degree to which the mobilizations they analyse have built alliances, accessed state resources and gained a voice inside political institutions, and whether this has contributed to meaningful change in the institutions or in state responsiveness.

A third set of challenges concerns the representativeness and legitimacy of those CSOs that engage the state's authority over (and its monopoly on) decision-making (Urbinati and Warren, 2008; Brown, 2008; Ebrahim, 2003). Lavalle et al. (2005) address the complex relationship between CSOs and political representation, arguing that CSOs often fail to ask in whose name they speak and act, or by what mechanisms they are authorized to act and are held to account.[3] Several of our chapters highlight the complexities of such mediated political representation.

These challenges highlight the complex political dynamics involved in citizen mobilization: asynchronous forms of political authority, the challenges of seeking long-term democratic gains and the democratic legitimacy of those that speak in the name of minorities and marginalized citizens. In addition to these three cross-cutting problems, this book is animated by a fourth challenge that is less salient in the literature: given these constraints, how do the diverse forms of citizen engagement shape the possibilities for deepening democracy in different political contexts?

While there is a vast literature concerning citizen mobilization and its associated outcomes and constraints, there is very little comparative empirical research into how different forms of mobilization perform in a variety of political contexts. This shortcoming appears clearly in a systematization of the literature conducted by Peruzzotti (2008). He identified potential 'layers' of political involvement by citizens, each of which is expected to deal with specific challenges and to be capable of making a range of contributions to the political process. The first layers – covered in this volume by associations and social movements – play the role of 'constitutive' mediation, which implies the acquisition of political consciousness, awareness and knowledge of citizenship and rights. The next layers – covered in our cases by citizen involvement in formal governance arenas – have been labelled 'representative mediation' and are more directly linked to processes of political representation.[4] The authors of this book tackle the lack of empirical research into the capacity of these different forms of engagement to bring about the expected outcomes in different political contexts. In doing so, they look at how different forms of mobilization intersect with political contextual differences to produce democratic outcomes.

Next we provide a brief description of the analytical categories used to frame this comparative work.

As was discussed above, our case studies have been grouped around three distinct forms of mobilization that have already been well described in the literature: associational and NGO-driven mobilization; social movement mobilization; and citizen involvement in formal political institutions, including in spaces for participatory governance. These categories were placed on a spectrum running from constitutive forms of political mediation (associations and social movements) to representative forms of political mediation (participation in formal governance structures).

To explore how different forms of mobilization played out in different political contexts, we classified the contexts, following an aggregation of democracy indices and indicators produced by the Polity IV project, Freedom House and the Economist Intelligence Unit. According to this aggregation, countries were clustered into two groups related to the characteristics of their political regime.[5] These are shown in Table 1.1.

Despite the different variables used to calculate the indices (which include the competitiveness of the political system, the constraints on the chief executive and political rights and liberties), Brazil, India and South Africa were consistently clustered at the high end of democratic state functioning. All three are middle- to upper-middle-income states with strong democratic institutions, are relatively decentralized and have a variety of sites for citizen participation (including formal political participation, various participatory governance mechanisms and relatively strong civil societies). In terms of human development within this cluster, Brazil performs particularly well; it is followed by South Africa and then India. Brazil and South Africa have had persistently high levels of income inequality, though this is a feature that is slowly beginning to change in Brazil.

At the opposite end of the spectrum, the political indicators of Angola and Nigeria show similar patterns. These are relatively unaccountable states, where there are fewer opportunities for citizens to make their voices heard in the democratic arena. In addition, both (though particularly Angola) are considered relatively 'fragile' states according to

TABLE 1.1 Selected countries classified by type of political institutions

Democratic institutions	Polity IV[1]	Freedom House[2]	EIU[3]
Stronger	India (9)	Brazil ('free')	South Africa (31)
	South Africa (9)	South Africa ('free')	India (35)
	Brazil (8)	India ('free')	Brazil (41)
↔	Kenya (7)	Bangladesh ('partly free')	Bangladesh (91)
	Nigeria (4)	Kenya ('partly free')	Kenya (103)
	Angola (-2)	Nigeria ('partly free')	Nigeria (124)
Weaker	Bangladesh (-6)	Angola ('not free')	Angola (131)

Notes: 1. Polity IV data track political regime characteristics of countries across the world each year. Data pertaining to political regime are collected for each country before an annual country score is given based on a scale from -10 (strongly autocratic) to 10 (strongly democratic). 2. Freedom House data track annual developments in democratic consolidation and political freedom using various indicators of political rights and civil liberties. Countries are evaluated based on their score across these indicators and given a 'freedom status' of either 'free', 'partly free' or 'not free'. 3. The Economist Intelligence Unit's (EIU) Index of Democracy provides an annual 'snapshot' of democracy across the world, based on countries' performances on a range of indicators pertaining to democratic quality, good governance and political participation. Countries are scored, ranked (out of 167 countries) and classified as either 'full democracy', 'flawed democracy', 'hybrid regime' or 'authoritarian regime'.

a number of measures, including their ability to deliver advances in human development. Bangladesh and Kenya – the other two countries that appear in this volume – tend to move between the extremes of this spectrum and to have less stable outcomes across political and social variables. The quality of democracy in those two countries is somewhat mixed, as is their performance in terms of basic human development indicators.

With respect to democratic outcomes, we look particularly at those with the potential to address the kind of deficits pointed out by Luckham et al. (2000): hollow citizenship, weak horizontal accountability and lack of vertical accountability. The democratic outcomes in our case studies have already been analysed by Gaventa and Barrett (2010) as part of a wider body of research into citizen engagement and participation.[6] Although we took their work as a point of departure, we ended up with a somewhat different classification of outcomes, identifying three broad categories.

The first set of outcomes covers those that concern building citizenship, particularly when citizens gain a greater awareness of their rights and empowered self-identities, and new capacities for political participation. The second set includes outcomes where particular practices of participation and collective action have built new citizen agendas on access to rights and services. The third set focuses on strengthened procedural accountability, working towards the construction of inclusive political processes that enhance the systems of checks and balances between society and government. Achievements in the first two categories help to tackle issues of hollow citizenship and weak horizontal accountability, while achievements in the third category deal with a lack of vertical accountability.

This analytical framework made possible a comparison of how different forms of citizen mobilization concerned with deepening democracy tackled the challenges described in this section in the seven countries that made up our universe. We now turn to the cases.

Citizen mobilizations in the global South

We present eleven case studies that explore particular strategies of citizen mobilization in the seven countries of the global South listed in Table 1.1. First, we discuss examples of the three forms of mediated citizen mobilization discussed in the introduction. We go on to examine how citizens and associations have developed different styles of activism and have chosen their preferred forms of mobilization in two contexts.

Mediated mobilization

Associational mobilization: constructing citizenship Relationships between development and human rights NGOs and wider associational networks that work with poor populations are explored in case studies from Kenya, Bangladesh and Angola, where socio-economic inequalities and lack of political accountability are widespread. They focus on democratic outcomes related to an extension of a rights-based understanding of citizenship, improved welfare outcomes, promotion of formal political participation, and policy changes.

In Chapter 2, Nyamu Musembi surveys 500 respondents in Kenya, half of whom had received training from NGOs working with empowerment programmes at the local level, and half of whom had not. In Chapter 3, Kabeer and Mahmud study six Bangladeshi organizations that range from narrowly focused microfinance NGOs to organizations focused on social mobilization. From these six organizations, they select two from opposite ends of the spectrum (where they expected differences in likely impacts to be most pronounced). They interviewed 600 respondents from communities in which these two organizations have worked. In Chapter 4, Ferreira and Roque describe how they worked with a federation of fifteen local associations in Angola, the majority of which represented small-scale farmers, while a few offered civic education services.

These three chapters show how, in the context of fragile democratic institutions and strongly centralized states, both rural and urban NGOs and the associational networks they spawn can make a difference in fostering civic virtues, in teaching political skills and in nurturing a growing ability and willingness on the part of grassroots leaders to check abuses of power at the local level. Both Nyamu Musembi and Kabeer and Mahmud also report that NGO members are more likely to vote and to stand as candidates in elections. In the realm of welfare outcomes, Ferreira and Roque report increases in the capacity of small-scale farmers' associations to protect the livelihoods of their poor members.

In response to current literature asking for evidence of the capacity of associations to stimulate democratic attitudes (Finkel, 2002; Bratton et al., 1999), these chapters bring strong empirical support to the thesis that associations can make a difference in building democratic citizenship by increasing people's knowledge of their rights and by bolstering their capacity for political action. While the existence of associations does not, in itself, lead to democratization, their everyday practices and deliberate programmatic interventions can and do contribute to shaping active citizenship at the grassroots level.

The findings also support the notion that the nature of CSOs matters to the democratic outcomes they can achieve. Kabeer and Mahmud and Ferreira and Roque highlight the links between the political visions and values that organizations hold and the different capacities they promote. While farmers' associations and microcredit NGOs stress economic and technical support for their constituencies, civic associations stress mobilization and awareness building. Nyamu Musembi and Kabeer and Mahmud found strong evidence that respondents involved in empowerment programmes in Kenya and in grassroots mobilization in Bangladesh, respectively, were more involved in organizing public protests or campaigns on any issue. According to Nyamu Musembi, this 'reinforces the conclusion that the respondents trained in political empowerment are more likely to challenge abuses of power' (Chapter 2, this volume). Their data also reveal a greater involvement in local politics, with respondents reporting more interactions with politicians and local bureaucracies, as well as more participation in local institutional spaces.

Despite these positive outcomes, there is a strong message in these three chapters about the limited capacity of the associational mobilization to influence the broader democratization process or public policies. While they recognize that channels have been opened and that there has been some success in promoting dialogue between active citizens and local government, the interactions seem to have had a very limited impact in changing the nature of the broader political system. These results are explained by the authors as being related to the absence, in countries such as Kenya, Angola and Bangladesh, of robust, institutionalized channels for citizen–state interaction, linking local and national politics. As a result, political participation tends to be sporadic in nature and of limited effectiveness, while gains from it are difficult to consolidate and sustain.

Social movements: contesting political authority and building state responsiveness While the chapters in Part One focus more on the democratic outcomes of citizen mobilization mediated by organized civil society groups such as NGOs and CSOs, the cases in Part Two each describe citizen mobilizations led by social movements, which also rely extensively on associations. In Chapters 5 and 7, Shankland and Robins present cases from Brazil and South Africa, where (in both cases) the context is of a relatively strong state. The authors show how social movements can shape democratic possibilities for citizen engagement in the public sphere by initiating important policy changes, in order to broaden access to health and housing for marginalized groups. Democratic gains through social movement mobilization are also evident, however, in contexts with more fragile democratic institutions. In Chapter 6, Ibrahim and Egwu present a case from Nigeria – a political context with relatively unaccountable political institutions, but a long history of citizen mobilization. They show how social movement mobilization can achieve important democratic outcomes associated with changes in electoral policy.

Shankland's chapter examines the experience of the indigenous peoples of Acre State in the Brazilian Amazon in dealing with tensions over health services in the two decades since Brazil's return to full democracy. His case study traces the changes in direction taken by the indigenous peoples' movement, which has shifted from placing an emphasis on rights-claiming mobilization outside the state, to direct participation in the management of outsourced government health services, and back again.

While there have been significant gains associated with the increased formal recognition by the state of indigenous peoples' movements (and also with their greater political participation), the evidence remains mixed on whether there has been much of a transformation in the material conditions under which Acre's indigenous peoples live or in the level of fulfilment of their constitutional right of access to health services that are both medically effective and respectful of cultural differences. The redistribution of resources towards indigenous health and well-being has fallen short of what might have been expected – particularly in view of a perverse process of redistribution within the indigenous minority that has actually increased internal inequality and reinforced unequal patterns of political recognition.

Ibrahim and Egwu examine the political trajectory of the 'anti-third term' campaign in Nigeria – a broad-based social movement that involved MPs, civil society, opposition parties and the popular masses. It succeeded in bringing together a wide range of actors, who went on to forge long-term alliances and who continue to advocate democratic reform in political parties. This case demonstrates how alliance-based strategies generated a significant – albeit short-term – reshaping of regimes of citizenship in Nigeria by opening up new possibilities for civil society action and guaranteeing citizens' political rights.

Robins discusses the South African Homeless People's Federation (SAHPF), an organization of poor urban women that was involved in a wide range of activities, including savings clubs, housing and land issues, income-generation projects, community policing and HIV/AIDS intervention. The SAHPF was a globally connected social movement that used sophisticated strategies of 'cross-border activism' and global networking to create horizontal relations of trust and solidarity. It was also effective in attracting donor and state funding and in building houses for marginalized groups.

Robins draws attention to the disjuncture between the official ideology of the organization and the everyday ideas and practices of the rank-and-file members of the SAHPF in Cape Town. He shows how the horizontal, non-party-political, non-hierarchical, democratic ideology of the organization came to clash with party-political patronage networks and leadership cliques that had developed among the grassroots housing activists in some of Cape Town's townships. As Robins points out, however, despite these tensions the forms of social capital developed through SAHPF rituals of daily savings and 'horizontal exchange' can contribute towards the emergence of self-reliant communities.

The democratic outcomes described in these three cases are uneven. Their possibilities are shaped by the wider cultures and practices of political authority in each context, as well as by the specific choices of tactics and strategies of the social movements themselves. Nevertheless, all three cases do suggest positive democratic outcomes in relation to recognizing and influencing broader political agendas, enhancing state responsiveness and amplifying access to rights and public policies.

While recognizing these achievements, the authors also draw attention to the limitations of social movements in changing the political cultures of citizen engagement. The way social movement leaders interact with politicians (and often with their own constituencies) can be somewhat undemocratic, even when they rely on their own organizations to nurture a sense of democratic citizenship in their participants. The South African and Brazilian cases also call attention to the fact that, while social movements can successfully promote new agendas and facilitate access to rights and services, they can also simultaneously reinforce distributive inequalities among marginalized groups.

Citizen involvement in formal governance mechanisms In the past decade there has been great interest in the possibilities of public involvement in formal mechanisms of governance, and a number of different approaches and techniques to allow the participation of ordinary citizens have been suggested and implemented (Fung, 2004; Fishkin and Farrar, 2005; Gastil and Levine, 2005). More recently, the literature on participatory democracy has turned its attention to such problems as 'elite capture', technocratic bias and the lack of vibrant social forces engaging in participatory spaces. Recognition is mounting that, while many new participatory governance experiments have led to considerable increases in citizen participation in local and national decision-making, they have rarely reached down to the most marginalized communities. Questions have also been raised about the ability of participatory institutions to perform in political contexts that lack vibrant associations and social movements (Cornwall and Coelho, 2007; Ansell and Gash, 2008).

Drawing on this literature, the authors in this volume highlight the challenges of citizens to enter institutionalized participatory spaces, to tackle power asymmetries and to be involved in the policy decision-making processes. They draw attention to the fact that even the participatory governance literature remains very focused on institutions, and that more emphasis needs to be given to the role of citizen mobilization in supporting vibrant institutions.

Three chapters focus on citizen engagement in formal governance mechanisms. In Chapter 8, Mohanty presents a case from India, and in Chapter 9, Coelho and colleagues present a second case from Brazil. Both these settings are characterized by well-functioning democratic institutions, and the chapters examine the role of citizen mobilization in shaping participatory governance. In Chapter 10, Okello presents a second case from Kenya, which examines the role played in articulating changes in public policies by individuals who were socialized in CSOs, but subsequently entered government after the return to multiparty democracy in 1992.

Despite differences in context, all three cases show positive outcomes achieved by mobilized citizens in terms of political inclusion and building political processes that are better prepared to transmit to government innovative agendas forged in the realm of civil society, concerning the welfare and dignity of *dalits* (lower-caste people) in India, access to health care in Brazil and the democratization of public policy in Kenya.

Mohanty studies the dynamics of social mobilization and participation in *panchayats*, a level of local government formed in rural areas following a constitutional amendment in 1992. She analyses the *dalit* mobilization spearheaded by local CSOs, and concludes that substantial gains have been made in ensuring the redistribution of resources to *dalit* communities in areas such as housing, water, electricity and transport infrastructure. According to Mohanty, the pursuit of social justice in *panchayats* has been predicated on two principles – affirmative action that promotes *dalit* participation, and social inclusion through increased engagement with welfare planning and provision. Despite these gains, Mohanty suggests that the *panchayat* itself has remained largely closed, resisting the acceptance of *dalits* as equals. She argues that 'striving for dignity is a piece of radical political imagining that does not exist in the vocabulary of the state or of formal democracy, but the *dalits* have articulated this concept in their quest for social justice' (Chapter 8, this volume).

Coelho et al. describe their research into local health councils, a mechanism of public involvement in health governance introduced by the 1988 Brazilian Constitution. They examine the relationship between social mobilization and citizen involvement in the decision-making process of health policy, looking at local health councils in six peripheral metropolitan areas with different histories of social mobilization. The three councils located in areas with a history of strong social mobilization are characterized by greater inclusion and participation, and by diverse networks, especially between and among politicians, political institutions, health units, public health managers, associations and participatory forums. These councils have also drawn up a diverse range of accountability-enhancing planning proposals and monitoring activities. This suggests that strong performance on indicators related to planning, monitoring and innovation is dependent on the presence of previous mobilization.

In contrast to studies that highlight the shortcomings of participatory forums (Sumathi and Sudarsen, 2005), both these cases show marginalized actors successfully entering formal governance spaces and helping to build processes that allow the transmission of new agendas into the political process. These cases suggest that the combination of efforts – mobilization and participation – strengthens the capacity of those marginalized groups already linked to broader struggles to connect with politicians and public service managers and, as a result, to make welfare gains. Nevertheless, as the cases also show, these successes have not precluded episodes when these spaces have been 'captured' by more organized groups, or when local clientelistic and authoritarian dynamics have held sway.

Okello looks at what happened after the 2002 general elections in Kenya, when civil society actors mobilized directly for the party that won the election. This led to a number of civil society leaders entering government and trying to move the country towards a progressive culture of politics, identifying key themes central to the democratization of the state: constitutional reform, human rights, accountability and anti-corruption measures. Okello argues that there was a clear intellectual contribution from civil society actors to this progressive agenda, and that this needs to be recognized in spite of ongoing operational limitations. Various individuals have positively influenced decisions and operation within government itself, and new laws, institutions, philosophies and practices have been initiated. However, Okello also points out that, once in power, some ex-civil society leaders did not behave any differently from traditional politicians in dispensing ethnic-based patronage or in circumventing accountability.

All three cases are testimony to the pathways that have been opened up in recent years to facilitate the entry and participation of mobilized citizens in formal governance mechanisms, serving as channels for the communication of citizen agendas upwards in the policy process. Nevertheless, as the cases suggest, it is when participatory mechanisms in formal governance coincide with citizen mobilization – whether in the form of associations or social movements – that the effectiveness of these pathways is ensured.

Where and how to participate?

Our final two chapters look at citizens' styles of activism, as well as their choices surrounding the strategies for mobilization, in order to understand how the different contexts of mobilization shape the styles of activism that will emerge (Snyder and Mahoney, 1999).

In Chapter 11, Thompson and Nleya explore the ways in which individual citizens in South Africa understand their democratic citizenship and choose different strategies for engagement. Their chapter focuses on the findings of a survey of 300 citizens of Khayelitsha township in Cape Town, who were interviewed about governance and service delivery. They explore the diversity of the political strategies that ordinary citizens employ to make democratic demands, including for better services. They show how citizens make use of a range of different strategies to strengthen the practices and efficacy of participation, which in turn can help to build a responsive state that delivers adequate services.

The case highlights the centrality of residential street committees, a highly localized and decentralized network of anti-state engagement that existed under apartheid. These committees are complemented by a wide range of other organizational forms and strategies, which include both protests and formal channels of representation, such as the province-wide ward committee system. They also make contact with politicians and bureaucrats and take part in associations and social movements.

In Chapter 12, Favareto and colleagues focus on the styles of activism and the choices of political engagement among four different local organizations in the Ribeira Valley, an area of south-eastern Brazil characterized by environmental protection and populated by poor traditional communities. Their chapter looks at the different styles of activism employed by movements and organizations involved in community mobilization around social conflicts related to access to land, natural resources and public policies. The case shows that associations and social movements often develop markedly different styles of activism and position themselves very differently in relation to the wider participatory governance environment, even when functioning in the same sort of institutional framework.

The authors show how styles of activism are shaped by the past political experiences and historical trajectories of individual citizen leaders, in particular the norms and cultural habits informing their activism; the state, which frames the group's opportunities and claims; and the nature of the networks and ties that these organizations establish through their histories.

Both Thompson and Nleya and Favareto and colleagues show how a diversity of connections and networks linking state and society can enhance citizens' opportunities for mobilization. They show that the transformation of the polity depends on the dynamics in play between the structural determinants of collective action and the choices made by the groups, which they vividly describe and analyse in the cases.

Looking across the cases

The cases we present in this book analyse the challenges and the specific contributions that different forms of citizen mobilization make to deepening democracy in various political contexts. They describe mobilizations that have faced various kinds of constraint. Despite these constraints, they have achieved impressive outcomes in terms of building citizenship, crafting new agendas, accessing rights and services and promoting more accountable policy processes. We now return to the issues we raised earlier, and point to four findings about the relationship between historical trajectories that shape context, the choices made by citizens about forms of mobilization, and the democratic outcomes they have been able to achieve.

First, we looked at the ability of these forms of mobilization to promote democratic outcomes. As noted above, we departed from Gaventa and Barrett's (2010) categorization of democratic outcomes, choosing instead to define three key categories: the construction of citizenship, state responsiveness to citizen demands for rights and services, and greater inclusion in policy processes and decision-making. Looking across our case studies, we classified the outcomes reported from each form of mediated citizen mobilization – associations, social movements and citizen involvement in formal governance mechanisms – according to these three categories. The results are shown in Figure 1.1.

As we can see, 90 per cent of the outcomes achieved by associations are related to the construction of citizenship, and in particular how citizens gain a greater awareness of rights and an increased capacity for action. The first three chapters show how associations have played a key role in fostering a greater knowledge of rights and in building up their members' confidence and capacity to participate politically. Ferreira and Roque, for example, report how increases in the membership of associations in Angola resulted not only in material improvements in the livelihood of association members brought about by credit schemes, but also in an increased sense of citizenship, self-esteem and capacity to intervene in public life. A member of the federation of local associations that they studied told the authors:

> One of the biggest achievements of my experience with the association is to have become aware that I am somebody like any other person; that I am seen as a person as much as a police officer is; that I am considered

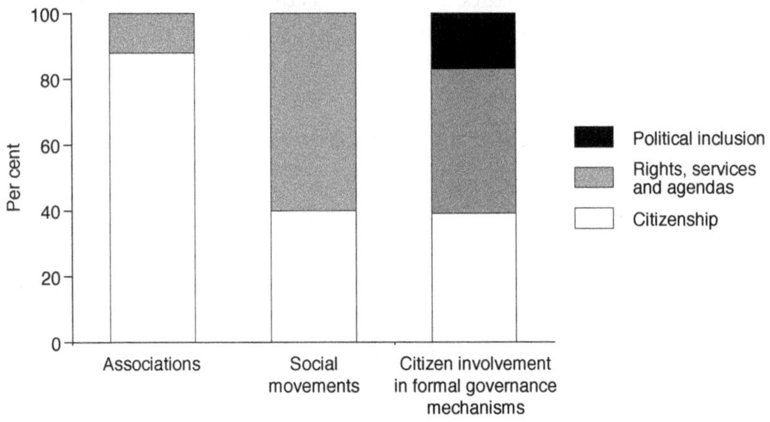

Figure 1.1 Democratic outcomes by form of mobilization

> as a person as much as a prominent person is. This means that I have the same status as somebody who holds a prominent position [in society]. My rights are similar to those of this other person. If there is something that goes against my dignity, I can place the complaint with an official entity that will respond to my concern. (Chapter 4, this volume)

Social movements, in turn, contributed to building citizenship; but, as the cases show, they have also been particularly well equipped to press successfully for state responsiveness. Some 58 per cent of the outcomes achieved by social movements relate to the state's responsiveness to citizens' demands for rights, services and agendas. The cases presented in Chapters 5, 6 and 7 show important contributions to strengthening the state's responsiveness to citizens' demands in Brazil, Nigeria and South Africa. In Nigeria, for example, the coalition of organizations that formed a movement against the president's tenure extension bid succeeded in developing a new citizen agenda for participation in electoral policy; while in South Africa, members of the SAHPF spoke of how organizing as a federation – and as members of a social movement–NGO partnership – had assisted them in accessing the state housing subsidies and in increasing their confidence in formulating citizen claims on the state.

Finally, the examples of citizen involvement in formal governance present a more balanced profile of outcomes and make a unique contribution to strengthening inclusive policy processes. Coelho and colleagues, for example, show how, by joining in participatory councils, well-organized representatives from health movements could achieve greater political inclusion and better responsiveness to their demands.

Second, it is important to bear in mind that both the forms of mediated citizen mobilization that showed the greatest capacity to promote state responsiveness – social movements and citizen involvement in formal governance mechanisms – are characterized by a prior history of citizen mobilization. Social movements acted and delivered when they were backed up by associations; and the effective delivery of democratic outcomes by participatory governance mechanisms was closely related to the presence of associations and social movements.

Third, the chapters in this book collectively call attention to the fact that the meaning and relevance of the democratic outcomes achieved through citizen mobilization depend on the context in which the outcomes are achieved. In weaker democracies, associational forms of mobilization have proved to be very important in producing democratic outcomes associated with the construction of citizenship: new knowledge of rights, new identities as citizens and new capacities for practices of political participation. In the context of stronger democracies, outcomes are more likely to be associated with access to resources, rights and accountable institutions. While social movements and citizen engagement in formal governance mechanisms have also been observed in weaker democracies, they have been organized around classical representational issues, such as elections in the Nigerian case. By contrast, in stronger democracies, social movements have focused on issues associated with the building of more accountable states and inclusive policy processes.

Finally, *fourth*, it is important to consider that these democratic outcomes are sometimes uneven and are by no means the result of linear processes of democratization. The trajectories of citizen mobilization often involve gains and reversals, especially in political contexts where there are competing forms of political authority, such as rights-based authority and clientelism. Citizen mobilization often involves complex negotiations with these alternatives. In addition, citizen mobilization sometimes entrenches institutional solutions that favour the 'organized marginalized' – those whose claims are mediated through CSOs – as opposed to less organized citizens with weaker links to civil society and state actors. As Shankland argues in the case of the Brazilian indigenous peoples, the gains of the indigenous health movement have not been distributed equally among the poor and the marginalized.

Democratic outcomes are often mediated by these kinds of political complexities, and a key theme that runs through all the chapters is the difficulty of evaluating such outcomes. Democratic gains should not be regarded in purely institutional or procedural terms; nor should they be thought of purely in terms of social justice and economic outcomes as they are heterogeneous and must be defined and articulated with reference to their distinctive contexts.

Final remarks

The case studies that follow vividly illustrate the fact that democracy is not built through political institutions or developmental interventions alone. Citizens and their mobilizations can make a difference – by articulating concerns, developing capacities for political engagement, mobilizing for democratic change and pressuring states to act more accountably through democratic policy processes.

In developing these cases, the authors have departed from the literature on diverse forms of civil society organization and institutional innovation. While the debates on the roles of associations, social movements and more formal forms of participation in governance institutions all served as starting points for their research, it soon became clear that a more integrated analytical approach was needed – one that explored the particular contribution of each of these forms of citizen mobilization to the deepening of democracy, separately and in combination with others, in differing contexts.

The chapters provide strong evidence of the particular ability of associations to build citizenship, of social movements to successfully press for state responsiveness, and of engagement in formal governance processes to contribute to the building of accountable policy processes. In settings with weaker democracies, associational forms of citizen mobilization have been extremely successful in producing democratic gains associated with the building of new identities and capacities around democratic citizenship. In stronger democracies, social movements and engagement in formal governance have been more successful in introducing new political agendas and struggles for rights, as well as in fostering more inclusive policy processes.

However, while our cases suggest different patterns of citizen mobilization in settings with weaker and stronger democracies, they also call for more research both on the mechanisms that combine the different forms of citizen mobilization, and on the different democratic outcomes generated by these combinations. Together, the chapters point out the crucial role that civil society mobilization plays in building the political structure – the institutions and cultures – for citizen involvement in politics, a crucial aspect of the deepening democracy project.

The cases in this book paint a rich picture of how the historical trajectories that shape political context, together with the choices made by citizens of the forms of mobilization, contribute to generating specific democratic outcomes. The authors call for greater attention to be paid by researchers and practitioners to the crucial role that citizen mobilization and the politics of public participation can play in building and deepening democracy.

Notes

1 A first draft of this introduction was discussed at the Hauser Center, Harvard Kennedy School; we want to thank David Brown, Alnoor Ebrahim, Archon Fung, Jane Mansbridge, Martha Chen, Xijin Jia, Oonagh Breen and Sherine Jayawickrama for their useful comments. The arguments were then reworked and discussed at the 'Participation and Mobilization' seminar organized by the Citizenship Development Research Centre (CDRC) and the Brazilian Centre for Analysis and Planning (CEBRAP) at the University Research Institute of Rio de Janeiro. We want to thank Marcus Figueiredo, Leonardo Avritzer, John Dryzek, Evelina Dagnino, Kathryn Hochstetler, Argelina Figueiredo and Jorge Romano as well as all the DDSL team for their comments and guidance. Special thanks are due to John Gaventa, Mark Warren, Andrea Cornwall, Celestine Nyamu Musembi and Greg Barrett for their detailed and discerning comments.

2 A related and important issue is that the 'inflation' of collective actors and forms of political engagement – such as protests, social participation, litigation and lobbying – poses additional problems of coordination for the political system, and may serve to deepen democracy at the expense of restricting the prospects of economic development (Plattner, 2004; Coelho and Favareto, 2009).

3 For more on this topic, see Manin (1997) and Urbinati and Warren (2008).

4 Interest groups and political parties are included in this category of representative mediation.

5 www.systemicpeace.org/inscr/inscr.htm; www.freedomhouse.org/uploads/fiw10/FIW_2010_Tables_and_Graphs.pdf; http://graphics.eiu.com/PDF/Democracy%20Index%202008.pdf (accessed 4 February 2010).

6 Gaventa and Barrett (2010) analysed a sample of 100 cases – including those in this volume – of citizen engagement and participation in twenty countries. The case studies were carried out between 2001 and 2009 within the framework of the Development Research Centre on Citizenship, Participation and Accountability (www.drc-citizenship.org/). The authors organized and coded the various democratic and developmental outcomes that occurred as a result of citizen participation into four categories, with nine sub-categories. They then looked at how outcomes were distributed across the sample. We use the chapters from this volume as a subset of their sample and analyse cases using our own coding system, based on state-regime type, mobilization strategy and outcomes.

PART ONE

Associational mobilization: constructing citizenship

2 · Have civil society organizations' political empowerment programmes contributed to a deepening of democracy in Kenya?

CELESTINE NYAMU MUSEMBI[1]

Introduction

This chapter evaluates whether the political empowerment programmes undertaken by civil society organizations (CSOs) at the local level have translated into a deepening of democracy in Kenya. It is part of a wider study (Okello, this volume) that has assessed fifteen years of civil society engagement in political reform since multiparty politics began in 1992. It concludes that the record is mixed: CSO political empowerment programmes score high in terms of fostering civic virtue, teaching political skills and nurturing a growing ability and willingness on the part of grassroots communities to check abuses of power at the local level. However, the programmes gain only an average score in terms of their contribution to enhancing the autonomy and sustainability of grassroots associational life, and rate very low on their contribution to an improvement in the quality and equality of representation of interests in local governance.

In Kenya, as in most of sub-Saharan Africa, the early 1990s saw the start of a significant investment of donor resources to support civil society political activism, which translated into the development of a virtually new 'human rights and governance' CSO sector. A survey of non-profit organizations found that, up until 1980, only one organization had described itself as doing 'civic and advocacy' work. Over the next ten years, under a repressive single-party system, no organization would describe itself in these terms. However, between 1991 and 2001, six organizations described themselves thus. This figure understates the exponential growth of organizations in the sector during this period, as many new organizations did not seek formal registration in their own right, preferring to take cover as a programme within an existing organization (Institute for Develoment Studies, 2007: 6; Mutunga, 1999).

At the national level, political activists – along with other actors in broader civil society, including religious organizations and professional societies – have taken part in articulating a macro-political reform agenda. This alliance of forces was key in challenging the one-party state. CSOs have also contributed to the strengthening of democracy at the national level (Okello, this volume). At the local level, a significant number of organizations in this CSO sub-sector have also invested in the grassroots political empowerment initiatives that are the focus of this chapter.[2]

Framing research questions on 'deepening democracy': how do we know what we are looking for?

In order to examine these grassroots political empowerment initiatives properly, we must make explicit what we consider to be indicators of deepened democracy. This is an inescapably contextual and subjective (even normative) exercise. We developed evaluative questions, guided by the literature on civil associations and their contribution to the process of democratization. Archon Fung usefully groups into six categories the types of contribution that civil associations are said to make towards enhancing democracy (Fung, 2003: 515). He bases the categories on a selection of the arguments from the literature on associations and democracy:

1. Intrinsic value: that the very existence of associative life enhances democracy by virtue of expressing the freedom of association.
2. Fostering civic virtue and teaching political skills.
3. Offering resistance to power and checking government.
4. Improving the quality and equality of representation of interests.
5. Facilitating public deliberation.
6. Creating opportunities for citizens and groups to participate directly in governance.

Using Fung's list as a point of reference, we generated the following evaluative questions for the study:

1. Have CSO-initiated political empowerment programmes enriched associational life at the grassroots level?
2. Have CSO initiatives fostered civic virtue and taught political skills at the grassroots level?
3. Have CSO initiatives played a role in checking abuse of power at the local level?
4. Has CSO intervention improved the quality and equality of representation of interests in local governance?
5. Have CSOs played a role in facilitating public deliberation and creating opportunities for direct participation in governance?

Methodology: sample design, sampling procedures and site selection

The study surveyed 500 purposively selected respondents, half of whom had received training through CSO-initiated grassroots political empowerment programmes and half of whom had not.[3] Identifying trained respondents proved to be less straightforward than we had hoped. First, we identified organizations working at the grassroots level. We first consulted the Paralegal Support Network (PASUNE), formed belatedly in 2003 to bring some coordination to the myriad initiatives in community-based paralegal training conducted by CSOs at the grassroots level between 1992 and 1999. From PASUNE we obtained a partial database of the community paralegal workers trained by each of the network's members.

We then approached member organizations individually to supplement this information, as well as organizations that were not members of PASUNE but that we knew from previous research (Nyamu-Musembi and Musyoki, 2004) to be involved in grassroots political empowerment work. We also asked the trained respondents of grassroots political empowerment programmes whether they knew of other people who had received similar training.

In selecting the non-trained respondents, we targeted people who could be considered 'peers' of the trained respondents in terms of age, gender, income and educational level. For the sake of balance, in each district we drew the non-trained respondents from the same geographical locality and situation as the trained respondents. If we interviewed a school teacher who was trained as a community paralegal worker, for example, we would find another school teacher who was not. This enabled us to minimize the significance of any differentiating factors (gender, age, income and level of education) other than the key variable, namely having been trained through a CSO-initiated political empowerment programme.

From the information available to us, we established that there had been CSO-led political empowerment initiatives in twenty-five districts;[4] we drew our sample from ten of these. In selecting the study districts, we took into account the need to represent as many of the country's regions as possible, organizational diversity (so as not to concentrate excessively on the initiatives of one organization) and balance in approaches to political empowerment.[5]

Data collection was by means of a semi-structured questionnaire. In addition to the survey, we also conducted key informant interviews with leaders of selected CSOs, and we examined their programme records.

Civil society's contribution to democratization in Kenya: exploring the debate

Stephen Ndegwa has sought to answer much the same question as this study: 'how ... NGOs, as part of civil society, contribute to democratization in Africa and what conditions facilitate or inhibit their contributions' (1996: 1). From the outset, Ndegwa treats with scepticism the optimism contained in what he terms the 'civil society–political liberalization' thesis espoused by – among others – Diamond (1989), which he describes as 'problematic at best' (Ndegwa, 1996: 2). Diamond argues that solutions to the problem of lack of democracy in Africa will come not from reforming the state, but from civil society, which he sees as a crucially important factor at every stage of democratization:

> The greater the number, size, autonomy, resourcefulness, variety and democratic orientation of popular organizations in civil society, the greater the prospects for some kind of movement away from rigid authoritarianism and towards semi-democracy and eventually democracy. (Diamond, 1989: 25)

Ndegwa concludes that non-governmental organizations (NGOs) are not necessarily imbued with qualities that oppose undemocratic governments, and therefore any claim that they are central to furthering and consolidating democracy must be interrogated thoroughly in each specific context (Ndegwa, 1996: 6).

Ndegwa's second conclusion provides our current study's entry point into this debate. He concludes that an NGO makes a more durable contribution to deepening democracy through its work at the grassroots level – whether or not this work is labelled 'political empowerment' – than through overt political activism at the macro level. Ndegwa notes that the predominant trend in the 1990s was for NGO political activism at the macro level not to be complemented by initiatives at the grassroots level. He concludes that the potential of NGOs to alter state–society relations is therefore limited, and whatever democratic gains they make from such macro-level engagement are unlikely to be sustainable (ibid.: 4, 22). Grassroots communities that are empowered as independent political actors, capable of engaging the state in their own right (as opposed to relying on an intermediary) are the benchmark for assessing contributions by NGOs to deepening democracy (ibid.: 24).

The reason for the 1990s disconnect between macro-level political activism and grassroots organizing, in a nutshell, is that overt political mobilization was triggered by growing opposition to the one-party state and by the accompanying repression of political and civil freedoms. The framing of this struggle against the one-party state at the macro-political level was couched around the need to overhaul the constitution and redesign institutions of governance to allow for more political freedom. Focused on the formal demise of the one-party state, this framing did not adequately create a link between political repression, economic decline and the deleterious impact of their interaction on people's livelihoods. For this reason, mobilization at the national level by organized civil society groups such as NGOs and mainstream churches did not really connect with mobilization at the grassroots level, which was largely formed along 'community development' or poverty alleviation lines. The former focused on civil and political rights, while the latter acknowledged the climate of repression but articulated its struggle largely in terms of social and economic rights (Mutunga, 1999; Nyamu-Musembi and Musyoki, 2004).

We agree with Ndegwa that grassroots political empowerment is crucial to sustaining any democratic gains, and must be central in any evaluation of CSO contributions to democratic consolidation. What Ndegwa does not acknowledge in his study, however, is that there were CSO initiatives aimed explicitly at grassroots political empowerment, albeit not so many at the time of his study. These and subsequent initiatives made since the end of one-party rule are the subject of our current study. Ndegwa does not propose any criteria for assessing empowered independent grassroots political engagement. Neither is he explicit about what ideal is sought in altered state–society relations at the grassroots level. Our study draws on the spirit of Ndegwa's conclusions and on the questions derived from Fung's categorization above to take stock of CSO-initiated political empowerment interventions at the grassroots level.

Findings

The study's findings are organized around the five evaluative questions spelt out in the introductory section.

Have CSO-initiated political empowerment programmes enriched associational life at the grassroots level?

CSO political empowerment programmes have tended to work through community-based groups. A CSO might identify an existing group working on a social welfare issue (such as the needs of widows and orphans) and then train its members in issues of rights and governance, using women's and children's rights as an entry point to a broader curriculum.

A second approach would be for the CSO to identify individuals who, after receiving training, can be encouraged to set up a community-based group to deliver services such as paralegal assistance. This was a common model for all the CSOs involved in the study: individuals were identified through existing institutions, such as churches or professional bodies – and most commonly through teachers' associations.

The majority of community groups working on issues of rights and governance were formed by one or other of these approaches, and a significant number can, therefore, trace their roots to CSO-initiated political empowerment programmes. Of the 250 respondents who had received training, 160 indicated that they had organized into community-based groups to pursue the objectives of the political empowerment programmes. Of these, only 22 per cent indicated that their groups had already been in existence prior to the CSO intervention, while 58.2 per cent stated that their groups had been formed on the initiative of a CSO. Thus, evaluating the institutional legacy of CSO intervention at the grassroots must be central to this study. In assessing the quality of CSO contribution to associational life at the grassroots level, we discuss the survey's findings on the survival rate of groups, and whether groups exhibit the capacity for autonomous political action.

Sustainability The study worked with two indicators of sustainability: the first is degree of group solidarity (measured by regularity of meetings), and the second is the extent to which a group is financially self-sustaining. Of the 250 trained respondents, 160 belonged to community groups organized around the objective of community political empowerment. Meanwhile, of the 250 non-trained respondents, 145 belonged to community groups with varied objectives, mostly to do with livelihood concerns. The tables below compare the characteristics relevant to assessing group sustainability across the two categories of respondent.

Table 2.1 shows the degree of face-to-face interaction, indicated by the regularity of meetings. Responses on the regularity of interactions reveal whether a group is truly active or exists only on paper, by virtue of registration. While 93 per cent of non-trained respondents were in

TABLE 2.1 Regularity of group meetings (%)

	Trained respondents who belong to groups (N=160)	Non-trained respondents who belong to groups (N=145)
At least once per month	55.6	93.1
Quarterly	12.5	4.8
Occasionally	31.9	2.1

groups that met at least once a month, the corresponding figure among trained groups was 55.6 per cent. The study took irregular or infrequent meetings to be a sign of weak solidarity among the members, suggesting that a group was inactive or even defunct. This suggestion was backed up by qualitative evidence, which showed that some of the trained respondents' groups had cycles of activity, coming to life intermittently in response to some opportunity (such as a sub-contract from a CSO) or to conduct civic education preceding a national election.

Our data suggest that, on the whole, groups organized through the political empowerment initiatives of CSOs exhibited weaker solidarity than community-based groups concerned with livelihoods.

TABLE 2.2 Main source of group funding (%)

	Trained respondents who belong to groups (N=160)	Non-trained respondents who belong to groups (N=145)
Members' contributions	64.3	75.1
Group-managed income-generating projects	7.7	50
The CSO that helped to found the group	45	46.9
Other external sources	14	31.3

Table 2.2 paints a rather paradoxical picture: the assessment made by trained respondents of their groups' reliance on external funding suggests that they were less dependent on external funding than were non-trained respondent groups. Yet non-trained respondents' groups, reflecting a seemingly greater reliance on external funding, were many times more likely than trained respondents' groups to initiate income-generating projects to fund the group, and significantly more likely to rely on member contributions.

If the trained respondents' groups are not so reliant on external funding, yet rely even less on member contributions, and hardly at all on income-generating projects, just what are their sources of funding? This apparent paradox is, in fact, consistent with the funding environment of the human rights and governance NGO sub-sector at the time of the study, and with qualitative data gathered through key informant interviews.[6] Donor funding for this sub-sector dropped off sharply after the Kenya African National Union (KANU) lost power in the 2002 elections, as the new government was viewed favourably by donors. Governance and human rights-related activities were to be funded largely under the government's Governance, Justice, Law and Order Sector Reform Programme, funded by a consortium of donors. Due to a disagreement over the framework for civil society participation in the programme, many organizations pulled out and received no funding. Grassroots political empowerment programmes suffered severe cutbacks – and all against an existing background of reduced funding in the wake of the Inter-Parties Parliamentary Group (IPPG) agreement of 1997.[7]

The common story of almost all the trained respondents who belonged to groups involved in political empowerment programmes was that, in the initial period, they got financial support from the 'founding' CSO, but that this ceased at the end of the programme period or when the pilot phase was over.[8] Although, in theory, a group's activities were then supposed to be sustained through local fund-raising initiatives, many groups had not successfully made this transition at the time of the study. This is what leads to the paradoxical picture: they were not 'dependent' on external funding sources (because these sources had dried up), but at the same time they had not established self-financed alternatives, such as income-generating projects.

With regard to membership contributions, although the table suggests that the majority of trained respondents saw their group as relying significantly on membership contributions, the picture that emerges from the qualitative data is that the groups were struggling to meet such basic expenditure as the rent on their premises, since payment of membership contributions was irregular and inadequate. Indeed, the only groups that had a geographical address (i.e. that operated offices) were those that were still receiving some support from a CSO.

What, then, does this tell us about the contribution of CSO-initiated grassroots political empowerment programmes? The point of forming or supporting local groups was that the individuals and groups trained would then become agents of change in their localities – the classic trickle-down model. The realization of this objective has been patchy, with weak solidarity among the trained respondents and lack of financial sustainability constituting the biggest problems. However, this finding only tells us that there is little or no formally organized activity to 'spread the message'. As we discuss below, the data suggest that, at an informal level, most respondents trained in political empowerment are working individually as agents of change.

Capacity for autonomous political action Given the central role of CSOs in establishing and supporting local groups, we are dealing with community-based associations that are not, on the face of it, an expression of autonomous organizing at the grassroots level. To a certain extent, CSOs were building on already existing mobilization at the grassroots level, but there was also some 'manufacturing' of local civil society going on.

Generally speaking, therefore, CSOs contributed to the pluralization of associational life at the grassroots level. Thanks to their interventions, the terms 'political empowerment', 'rights awareness' and 'working for social justice' have joined the catalogue of objectives around which rural associational life is organized. However, the question of whether or not the groups thus created or supported are capable of undertaking autonomous political action was indirectly answered in the negative by our data. If the groups do indeed have autonomous capacity for political action, they should be in a position to engage with new issues that emerge once the CSO has wound up its programme in the area.

We asked about two recently introduced (and much discussed) devolved funds for local development projects – the Constituency Development Fund (CDF)[9] and the Local Authority Transfer Fund (LATF)[10] – including whether groups had been involved in monitoring the use and management of these funds in their communities. Any group engaged in grassroots political activism and rights awareness in contemporary Kenya would be hard pressed to ignore the glaring gaps in accountability in both funds, aggravated by a very narrowly conceived role for citizens. These deficiencies have been widely discussed in the media. However, there was very low involvement in any monitoring work to do with these new policy initiatives: the vast majority of the trained respondents were not involved in any monitoring initiative. This was not for any lack of awareness about the CDF and the LATF: only 17.2 per cent of trained respondents said they were involved in initiatives to do with monitoring the use and management of CDF funds, though 95.6 per cent of them were aware of the CDF. Meanwhile, 21.6 per cent were involved in initiatives to monitor the LATF, though 91.2 per cent were aware of the fund.

Political empowerment programmes appear not to have produced dynamic local groups and individuals capable of taking independent political action in response to evolving challenges of governance at the local level. It appears that, outside the context of a project, local groups on the whole find it difficult to sustain their energy to respond to new challenges without the injection of resources by CSOs.

In the context of grassroots associational life in Kenya, any discussion of the autonomy of local groups must also include their autonomy from politicians. Groups at the grassroots level have long been tied into 'vote-bank politics', and have been used by politicians for their own ends. Among those respondents trained in political empowerment, 11.3 per cent of those in a group indicated that their group had been approached by a political party for support (compared to 7.6 per cent of non-trained respondents). Among the 'goodies' on offer from politicians in exchange for a group's political support are the nebulous promise of 'development' and the more tangible pledge of financial assistance to the group, often in the form of a guarantee that a group's proposals to the CDF will be funded.

When the question asked replaced 'political party' with 'political candidate', the figures rose quite significantly – to 17.5 per cent for trained groups and 22.8 per cent for non-trained groups. When we asked whether the group had ever taken a decision to offer support to a political party or candidate, 23.8 per cent of trained respondents answered in the affirmative, as against 17.2 per cent of non-trained respondents. Conversely, 33.8 per cent of trained respondents said their groups had decided not to support a particular party or candidate, compared to 22.1 per cent of non-trained respondents.

It seems quite contradictory that trained groups should appear more willing to associate with politicians, yet at the same time be more likely to take measures to protect the group's non-partisan status. There are two explanations for this. The first is that, in many cases, the groups were supporting one of their own for office: a significant number of the trained respondents from political empowerment programmes have either stood or intend to stand for political office, and there is anecdotal evidence that many politicians at the local and national level can trace their roots to these groups. The second explanation is that a number of trained groups may have passed resolutions declaring their non-partisanship because that is what was expected of them by virtue of their training from the CSO. The reality of their practice may, therefore, diverge from their non-partisan stance on paper.

There is nothing in our data to suggest that groups that have benefited from CSO political empowerment programmes are any less susceptible to vote-bank politics. If anything, their significant interest in placing 'one of their own' in political office indicates that they would have little interest in working towards eliminating political patronage from grassroots associational life.

Have CSO initiatives fostered civic virtue and taught political skills at the grassroots level?

Among the virtues that associations are presumed to imbue in their members are respect for others, tolerance, respect for the rule of law, willingness to participate in public life and self-confidence. When individuals have these virtues, democracy becomes more robust (Fung, 2003: 520). Virtues are difficult to measure: the closest that we got was to enquire about willingness to participate – and actual participation – in public life.

We started with the most basic and most formal: participation in the electoral process. Almost all the trained and non-trained respondents were registered to vote (99.6 per cent and 92.4 per cent, respectively). Then we enquired about actual participation in voting, taking as points of reference the most recent general elections (2002) and a 2005 national referendum to adopt a new constitution. We found that, among trained respondents, 91.2 per cent had voted in both the 2002 general elections and the 2005 referendum. Among non-trained respondents, 83 per cent had voted in the 2002 general elections and 84.8 per cent in the 2005 referendum. The difference is significant enough for us to conclude that CSO political empowerment programmes do play a role in shaping people's attitudes to participation in the electoral process.

Moving to a less formal assessment of willingness to participate in public life, we enquired into involvement in community public life, working with a broad list of activities as indicators. The findings are reflected in Table 2.3.

It is clear that the respondents trained in political empowerment are

TABLE 2.3 Participation in community public life (%)

Activity	Trained respondents (N=250)	Non-trained respondents (N=250)
Organizing fund-raising for community projects	78.4	51.2
Arbitration of disputes before chief, assistant chief or village headman	85.9	46.8
Leadership in clan, kin group, 'hometown association', welfare association, burial society	42.4	17.6
Leadership in church or other religious community	64.4	46.8
Accompanying people to government offices to assist them	90.8	58
Giving people information on how to access government institutions and services	94.4	58
Drafting letters and other documents for people needing assistance	78.4	40
Serving as a civic education instructor	80.3	23.2

very active in serving their communities, engaging in activities that are, on the whole, public spirited; therefore they can be said to manifest civic virtue. Can CSO programmes take credit for this? It is significant that 76 per cent of trained respondents listed 'leadership training' as one of the topics covered in the curricula of the CSO political empowerment programmes. This tells us that CSOs did intend to pass on civic virtues that would create community leaders. When we asked the trained respondents whether they had already been playing these community roles before they took part in the programme, 47 per cent replied in the affirmative. This suggests that, for more than half of them, active involvement in community life coincided with the training, which is a significant success. In answering this question, some did differentiate among the activities. They said, for instance, that while they were already involved in activities such as fund-raising for community projects and church leadership, it was only after taking part in the programme that they began to accompany people to government offices, draft letters and documents for them, or take part in dispute arbitration.

The literature tends to treat the fostering of civic virtue and the teaching of political skills separately. The latter places an emphasis on people being able to do things that are important for political action, such as running meetings, writing letters or making speeches. We decided to focus on the extent to which trained respondents exhibited – or felt that they had acquired – the political skills necessary to seek political office, hold leadership in political parties and other bodies, and serve on local public committees. The notable figures are that 11.6 per cent of trained respondents had been candidates for election in cooperatives or professional associations, as opposed to 2.4 per cent of untrained respondents; 6.8 per cent had stood for local council office, as opposed to 1.6 per cent of untrained respondents; and 20.4 per cent intended to stand in the then approaching 2007 general elections, as opposed to 8.8 per cent of untrained respondents. The comparison does establish the fact that the trained respondents have more confidence in their political skills and their ability to compete in the political process.

Regarding involvement in party politics, we found that 41.6 per cent of trained respondents were members of a political party or parties,[11] compared to 30.4 per cent of non-trained respondents; 28.4 per cent of trained respondents described themselves as active in party politics, compared to 20.8 per cent of non-trained respondents; and 12.4 per cent of trained respondents were in leadership positions in their political parties, compared to 8.4 per cent of non-trained respondents. The variances are significant enough to suggest that political empowerment education does make a difference to one's self-perception as a political actor.

We had expected to find significantly higher levels of involvement among the trained respondents (compared to those who had not been trained) on local committees that manage recently devolved earmarked development funds, as well as on older bodies such as the District Development Committees (DDCs), established in 1983. As Table 2.4 shows, with the marginal exception of community-initiated committees managing public amenities, this was not the case. The figures show a large difference between the high rate of participation among trained respondents in the community-constituted committees (where positions are filled through a public nomination process) that manage public amenities such as schools, hospitals and community water projects, and the low rate of participation in constituency-based committees that manage devolved funds, which are staffed by appointment through the local MP.

When it comes to the constituency-based committees, the chances of being appointed do not vary much between those who have taken part in political empowerment programmes and those who have not. The absolute discretion of the MP in making these appointments is a key explanatory factor; political loyalty (rather than competence) is what informs the process. Unlike the public amenity committees, the constituency funds committees pay sitting allowances to members, and are therefore seen as a way of rewarding political allies. A second explanation could simply be numbers: positions on constituency-based committees are rather limited, with each committee being staffed by no more than twenty people. Therefore the participation rate – even in a random sample of constituents – is more likely than not to reflect low percentages.

However, if we read these figures alongside those for participation on the DDC and on the LATF committee, there is some suggestion that the political-discretion explanation carries considerable weight: the rates of participation on these two committees – whose numbers are also limited – show much more significant variance between trained and non-trained respondents than is seen in the constituency-based committees. The explanation lies in the process for constituting these committees, where there is much more room for public input. The ward representatives on the LATF are chosen at an annual meeting between council officials and residents to design the Local Authority Service Delivery Action Plan (LASDAP). Local residents are represented through community-based civil society groups, since the system relies on a stakeholder consultation model. The DDC operates at the various administrative levels: sub-location, location, division and district. At each level, the administrator in charge convenes a meeting of 'local leaders' and consults on the formation of the committee. The figures in Table 2.4 suggest that these processes allow some room for merit, knowledge and skill to be taken into account, in contrast to the unabashed political patronage that characterizes recruitment to constituency-based committees. Indeed, many trained respondents remarked that, in fact, participation in political empowerment programmes diminished one's chances of ever serving on a constituency-based committee, since the politicians will work hard to ensure that well-informed people, who are likely to question them, do not get to be appointed to the committees in the first place.

TABLE 2.4 Service on public committees (%)

Type of committee	Trained respondents (N=250)	Non-trained respondents (N=250)
Constituency Development Fund	7.6	4.8
Constituency Bursary Fund	5.2	2.4
Constituency AIDS Control Fund	6	4.4
Local Authority Transfer Fund	14.8	6.4
District Development	25.2	8
Any public school, hospital or other amenity	65.6	38.8

Have CSO initiatives played a role in checking abuse of power at the local level?

That CSOs have played a key role in challenging abuse of power at the national level is well known (Ndegwa, 1996; Mutunga, 1999), but contributions at the grassroots level are less well documented. It is worth noting that the earliest CSO political empowerment programmes – in the early 1990s – were designed with precisely this goal in mind. The Catholic Justice and Peace Commission's programmes, for instance, complemented 1980s programmes that had trained people in active non-violence and fostered their ability to analyse and challenge their oppression (Nyamu-Musembi and Musyoki, 2004). It was thought that if a critical mass of people knew their rights as citizens, and possessed sufficient knowledge of the legal and institutional procedures to follow in challenging violations of those rights, there would be a groundswell of resistance to the excesses of one-party rule.[12]

Our study took two aspects of the survey data as an indication of the contribution made by CSO interventions in checking abuse of power at the grassroots level. As part of a series of questions on engagement with government institutions and officials, we asked respondents whether they had ever, individually or collectively, confronted (as opposed to petitioned) their MP or councillor on any issue. Among the trained respondents, 20 per cent said they had confronted their councillor, and 9.2 per cent said they had confronted their MP. Among non-trained respondents, the figures were 9.6 per cent and 2.8 per cent, respectively. The issues over which the respondents had confronted the politicians included delay in responding to proposals submitted to local devolved funds committees, corruption and land grabbing, biased allocation of funds, and stalled projects. Clearly, the trained respondents are considerably more engaged in challenging abuses of power than are their untrained peers.

Even so, these figures also show that a majority of trained respondents are not active in challenging abuse of power. This is partly explained by the qualitative data: among the challenges identified by paralegal community workers was the absence of institutional backing or cover following the departure of the CSOs that trained them. This obliges them to pick their battles, in the full knowledge that, without institutional cover, they will be left exposed to the consequences of challenging local power.

The second aspect of the survey data that relates to checking abuse of power came from a question on whether respondents had ever been involved in organizing a public protest or campaign on any issue. Of the trained respondents, 50.8 per cent said 'yes', compared to 25.2 per cent of non-trained respondents. This reinforces the conclusion that the respondents trained in political empowerment are more likely to challenge abuses of power.

'Overcoming fear' was cited repeatedly in an open-ended discussion on what individual trained respondents considered to be the greatest benefit to have emerged from the programmes.

Has CSO intervention improved the quality and equality of representation of interests in local governance?

Civil associations are seen as an additional channel (besides voting, lobbying and direct contact with officials) by which citizens can articulate their interests to those people who make policy and laws (Fung, 2003: 524). They have the ability to exercise a collective voice on behalf of their members' interests, enhancing their chances of being heard.

They are also better positioned than are individuals to take advantage of invited spaces for stakeholder participation.

In the Kenyan context, local-level politics are defined by political patronage. Access to government services, officials and institutions is (more often than not) defined by one's relationship to specific individuals within the system. The study took the position that reliance on political patronage is a mark of lack of equality of representation of interests, because those without connections or those unable to mobilize enough resources to acquire such connections are inevitably excluded. It also results in poor-quality representation, since decisions made do not reflect the best use of resources. One illustration of this is the proliferation of uncompleted projects that are typically spread throughout a constituency or local authority – a reflection of the tug-of-war among various 'strongmen', minor patrons on the CDF committee or the local council competing to please its respective clients.

It would be a tall order to expect local associations produced by CSO interventions to be able to counter this deeply entrenched culture of politics. However, the study took the position that any indication that the trained respondents were challenging this culture would reflect positively on the political empowerment programmes. The study, therefore, worked with the following hypotheses on this issue:

1 That clientelistic or patronage-based relations between people and their political leaders and government officials do not promote deepening of democracy.[13]
2 That such clientelistic and patronage-based relations ought to be replaced by relations anchored in entitlement on no other grounds than one's right as a citizen.
3 That the creation of institutional spaces for local-level citizen participation in Kenya since the late 1990s marks the beginning of an institutional alternative to clientelistic or patronage-based access to the state at the grassroots level, and is therefore a step in the direction of deepening democracy.
4 That awareness and utilization of these institutional spaces by grassroots communities is a proxy indicator of progress towards a citizenship-based model in engaging the state at the local level.
5 That the trained respondents involved in political empowerment programmes were more likely to be engaging in these institutional spaces than non-trained respondents.

Our findings suggest a much more mixed and nuanced picture. The creation of institutional spaces for citizen participation (specifically

LASDAP and the opportunity to present proposals to the CDF) and the accompanying discourse on equal access for all citizens have done little to replace client-based, personalistic modes of engagement. Table 2.5 shows that trained respondents were more aware of these new institutional spaces than were non-trained respondents, and were also more likely to attend consultative forums with their local authorities and to be involved in presenting proposals to local committees managing devolved funds.

TABLE 2.5 Awareness and use of institutionalized spaces for representation of interests (%)

Knowledge and utilization of local authority transfer fund	Trained respondents (N=250)	Non-trained respondents (N=250)
Knows about fund	91.2	53.2
Attended LASDAP meeting	52.4	44.8
Involved in proposing projects	50	32

At a glance, therefore, one of our hypothesis was confirmed – respondents involved in political empowerment programmes are more likely to know about and to use these institutional spaces than is the average person. But does this suggest an emerging alternative to clientelistic modes of presenting concerns and interests to local officials? Our findings suggest not. While the trained respondents were using institutionalized channels to articulate their interests, they were also more involved in petitioning for the *personal* intervention of the local MP (42.4 per cent of trained respondents, compared to 33.2 per cent of non-trained respondents) or a local councillor (61.4 per cent of trained respondents, compared to 47 per cent of non-trained respondents). Just over 20 per cent of the requests made by trained respondents to their local MP were for personal, family or group benefit, rather than in the wider public interest.

There are structural and cultural reasons for this state of affairs. First of all, structural reform to create institutionalized avenues for citizens to access the state and present their interests has not changed the prevailing political culture, with its expectation that political leaders or office holders must respond to personal problems. Consequently, the creation of CDF and bursary programmes has done little to shorten the queues outside the Parliament Road offices and MPs' constituency homes. Second, people who approach the state through institutional channels still employ the personal approach as insurance against the risk of institutional failure. People have little reason to expect that institutional channels will work efficiently (let alone fairly) – a situation that is aggravated by the absence of established procedures for appeal and by the fact that decision-makers are not required to give reasons for their decisions. Third, institutional channels themselves become 'privatized' by the patrons for further leverage, as an MP may already have made promises to certain groups long before the proposal comes before the committee.

What we have ended up with, therefore, is a hybrid or 'syncretic' system. The narrative of equal representation of interests for all citizens coexists with the predominant patron–client model of engaging with the state. Without a change in this predominant culture of politics, the creation or strengthening of civil associations at the grassroots level – whether through a CSO political empowerment programme or by some other means – is unlikely to bring about improvement in quality and equality of representation. CSO interventions in the form of political empowerment programmes have obviously equipped trained respondents with the knowledge of how a system of entitlement-on-the-basis-of-citizenship should work; but the data suggest that the trained respondents have simply multiplied their options for representation of their interests, rather than transformed them. CSO-led mobilization at the grassroots level has, therefore, made little contribution on this front. It is clear that a larger investment in transforming the culture of politics is necessary before improvement in quality and equality of representation can be realized.

Have CSOs played a role in facilitating public deliberation and creating opportunities for direct participation in governance?

It has been argued that associations are most valuable to the democratic process when they are more directly engaged in governance and facilitate direct citizen participation in governance (Fung, 2003: 528). Fung and Wright's work puts forward the concept of 'empowered participatory governance'. Governance is empowered in the sense that citizens take part in forums that are not merely consultative but actually carry a decision-making power that feeds directly into policy formulation (Fung and Wright, 2001; 2003) and citizen participation is facilitated rather than mediated by associations.

Fung and Wright (2003) emphasize that, in order to contribute to deepening democracy, direct citizen participation in governance should not be an end in itself. Rather, it should yield alternative, more democratic, ways of organizing the political and administrative machinery. As can be seen from the above discussion on patronage, the mere utilization of governance forums by citizens does not translate into expanded democratic space or the democratization of practices of engagement between citizen and state. Democratization can be achieved only if citizens actually use these spaces to transform the practice or culture of governance.

So, in the context of our study, we need to ask two questions. First, have CSO interventions facilitated direct citizen participation in governance? Second, do the results of this intervention at least bear the potential to transform the practice of governance at the local level?

We acknowledge that, while CSOs can play a role in pressuring for the creation of forums that enable direct citizen participation in governance, this depends as much on high-level political commitments to institutional reforms. There has been little such political commitment in Kenya's local governance, and so there are very few examples of direct citizen participation in governance to cite. Even LASDAP and CDF are limited – especially the former, as it is merely consultative and only goes as far as problem identification. CDF committees afford very limited representation of citizens and, most importantly, they do not remedy the flawed accountability model at the national level, in which MPs act as the authorizing, spending and monitoring and evaluation authority all rolled into one.

In the absence of good examples of direct citizen participation in governance, we asked instead whether the groups that had benefited from CSO political empowerment programmes were relatively better equipped to engage direct with governance institutions. Did they exhibit more interaction with government institutions than other community-based groups? Frequency of interaction with government officials and institutions does not, in itself, tell us anything about the quality or content of interactions, or their potential to transform the practice of governance. The presumption made here is that such groups have more opportunity to influence what goes on in official spaces than do community-based, self-help groups, which tend to be more insular or narrowly focused on group interests.

We asked whether a group's work brought it into contact with specified government officials and institutions. We drew up a broad list, ranging from the lowest level of village headman and assistant chief through to the higher political offices of councillor and MP. We found that interaction is most intense at the lowest levels and diminishes higher up the chain. For example, while over 93 per cent of respondents said that their work brought them into contact with the chief and assistant chief, 60 per cent registered contact with the district commissioner, and only 23 per cent registered contact with the provincial commissioner. Contact with political offices yielded interesting results: 65 per cent for the council as an institution, as compared to 81.3 per cent for the councillor as an individual, and 61.3 per cent for the MP.

Most remarkable were the responses to the follow-up question: 'Who usually initiates contact?' Among the trained respondents who belonged to groups, 97.5 per cent indicated that their group officials were the ones who usually initiated contact with the government institution or official in question. Only 16 per cent said that contact was usually initiated by the government institution or official. (There is some overlap here, as some indicated both.) Incidentally, even the relatively few non-trained respondents' groups that do interact with government institutions do so predominantly on their own initiative, as Table 2.6 shows. This result is significant, because it tells us that, generally speaking, local groups are setting their own agenda in their interaction with government institutions and officials, whatever the substance of that agenda may be. At the very least, the data show a greater degree of engagement among trained respondents' groups. This further confirms that those groups that have benefited from political empowerment programmes find themselves in a more advantageous position than those that have not been through such programmes. They can turn their closer engagement with government officials and their relative ability to access higher levels of government into an opportunity to set an agenda that reflects

TABLE 2.6 Engagement with government (%)

Group's work brings it into contact with:	Trained respondents' groups (N=160)	Non-trained respondents' groups (N=145)
Local council	65	49
Village headman	90.6	69.7
Assistant chief	93.1	68.3
Chief	93.8	70.3
District Officer	83.8	51
District Commissioner	60	35.2
Provincial Commissioner	23.1	20
Line ministry officials	65	43.4
Member of Parliament	61.3	41.4
Councillor	81.3	54.5

democratic ideals. In this way, they can potentially influence the way in which the government institutions in question operate.

However, even assuming that the groups do succeed in setting such an agenda in their engagement with government, it would be naïve to expect such an agenda on its own to result in a transformation of the culture of the institutions in question. LASDAP furnishes an example. In a previous study on democratizing local governance[14] we found that the LASDAP process has been pigeonholed into an island of participation in an overall local government culture that does not seriously entertain the idea of giving local residents any reasons for decisions; still less does it value their input into the design of projects that have an impact on them. From the officials' perspective, there was simply no indication that participatory processes such as LASDAP have the potential to gradually transform mainstream local government towards a culture of transparency and accountability.

There are clearly structural limitations to what CSOs can do to facilitate direct citizen participation in governance.

Conclusion

Can we then say that fifteen years of CSO political empowerment programmes at the grassroots level in Kenya have resulted in a deepening of democracy? Responses to our five review questions suggest a mixed picture. On the first question, we concluded that CSO intervention has, without a doubt, pluralized grassroots associational life, increasing the number of citizen groups at the local level and the range of issues around which they are organized. However, setting up local groups as the primary vehicle for community political empowerment does not produce community-based groups that are capable of independent political action. The groups have also proved to be unsustainable, due to weak solidarity among their members and a lack of financial resources independent of the intervening CSO. The greatest potential for the realization of the objectives of the programme lies not in these groups but in the individual resourcefulness of trained respondents embedded in community public life. The sole man or woman trained as a community paralegal worker, accompanying someone to a government office, ready to ask officials questions, does much more to alter citizen–state relations than do the rarely convened community workshops on rights to services, which depend on donor funds.

The answer to the second question – whether CSO initiatives have fostered civic virtue and taught political skills at the grassroots level – is a resounding 'yes'. Participants in political empowerment programmes are more likely to be registered to vote, more likely to vote, more likely to be active in party politics and more likely to offer themselves as candidates for both formal electoral processes and positions in associations, such as cooperatives and professional bodies. The trained respondents proved active in serving their communities through their involvement in the committees that manage public amenities and in fund-raising for community projects, as well as in presiding over informal institutions of governance. Political patronage, however, curtails their involvement in key local committees that control devolved funds, since politicians have overwhelming control over those committees.

The answer to the third question – whether CSO intervention has played a role in checking abuse of power at the local level – is also 'yes'. This role is well recognized at the national level, and our findings show that the local level has experienced a growing ability and willingness to challenge abuse of power.

The fourth question – whether CSO intervention has improved the quality and equality of representation of interests – leads inevitably to a negative response. The study found that trained respondents were more knowledgeable than non-trained respondents about institutionalized channels for engaging the state and accessing state resources at the grassroots level, and that they were more likely to be utilizing institutional channels than the average person. However, there is no basis for the optimistic view that the channels can even begin to function as an alternative to clientelistic, patronage-based channels. This is because the trained respondents are also more likely than are non-trained respondents to seek out the personal attention of politicians for their own private benefit. Representation is far from being equalized.

Finally, on the question of whether CSOs have played a role in facilitating public deliberation and in creating opportunities for direct citizen participation in governance, CSO intervention has placed the trained respondents' groups in a position of advantage in their dealings with government officials and institutions. They are generally able to have closer engagement than are non-trained respondents' groups, and in particular they register a greater ability to engage with higher levels of government. They are able to take the initiative and to set the agenda in engaging with government institutions and officials. However, the issue of finding room for direct citizen participation in governance would require high-level political commitment to structural reforms, and it is not in the power of CSOs to deliver this. This leads to the overall conclusion that CSO intervention in the form of political empowerment programmes at the grassroots level can contribute to the deepening of democracy, but that the specific ability of CSOs to facilitate direct citizen participation in governance is seriously constrained by the absence of structural reform guaranteeing citizens such a direct role.

Overall, the study's findings have led us to a significant conclusion on the structure–agency question. The predominant approach employed by CSOs in grassroots political empowerment is training, with the underlying assumption that the individuals trained will act collectively to trigger societal change. Consequently, there is an expectation that behaviour change and accumulated action on the part of individual citizens will transform political institutions and establish democratic habits. The most positive evaluation of the impact of grassroots political empowerment programmes relates to what those who have been involved in the programmes are able to do as individual citizens. However, the findings also render very stark the structural limitations of what individuals, whether or not they are associationally active, can do to change such features of the political culture as clientelism or intolerance of direct citizen participation in governance. Such institutional transformation would require collective action on a larger scale, bringing together a critical mass of committed individuals strategically positioned within government institutions, and a strategic alliance of powerful organizations that articulate broad interests rather than narrow sectarian demands.

Notes

1 The author acknowledges the excellent research assistance provided by Geoffrey Manduku Nyambane and Peter Otienoh, and the generosity of all the people we interviewed, as well as invaluable advice from Peter Houtzager on the design of the survey.

2 In this chapter, the term 'grassroots political empowerment programmes' is used to refer to community-level initiatives of organized civil society (non-profit) groups working in the area of human rights and governance. The initiatives that are the focus of this chapter involve the training of individuals and groups to serve as community-based paralegal workers, human rights monitors or civic educators. This chapter examines the grassroots political empowerment programmes of sixteen organizations: ActionAid, Catholic Justice and Peace Commission, Centre for Governance and Development, Centre for Law and Research International, Education Centre for Women in Democracy, International Federation of Women Lawyers, International Commission of Jurists, Kituo cha Sheria (Legal Advice Centre), League of Kenya Women Voters, Legal Resources Foundation, Kenya Paralegals Association, Stichting Nederlandse Vrijwilligers (SNV – Foundation of Dutch Volunteers), Women's Action Forum for Networking, Women's Resource Centre and Development Institute, Pathfinder, Coalition on Violence Against Women.

3 Those who had participated

in programmes were identified first, followed by the control group of those who had not.

4 At the time the study was designed (October 2006), Kenya had seventy-five districts.

5 In the 1990s, the focus was on paralegal training, but after the 1997 elections this shifted towards engagement in such policy processes as decentralization of development funds (interview with Morris Odhiambo, Executive Director, Centre for Law and Research International, Nairobi, 6 September 2006).

6 Interviews with Mr Kasina, Coordinator, Kitui community paralegal programme, Kitui, 5 December 2006; Monica Mbaru, Acting Executive Director, International Commission of Jurists, Kenya Chapter, Nairobi, 27 September 2006; Jedidah Wakonyo, Executive Director, Legal Resources Foundation, Nairobi, 11 September 2006; Benson Mutiso, Coordinator, Makueni Paralegal Community Association (MAPACA), Makueni, 27 November 2006; Johnstone Mutavuta, Board Member, MAPACA, Kibwezi, 29 November 2006; Richard Kaka, Member, MAPACA, Kibwezi, 29 November 2006.

7 The IPPG agreement was a package of minimal reforms negotiated by the political parties to persuade opposition and civil society groups to abandon their threatened boycott of the 1997 elections. The reform package is seen as having resulted, unwittingly, in a false sense of security among foreign donors, making them feel that it was no longer a priority to invest in the types of grassroots political empowerment initiatives that were justified in an explicitly repressive climate.

8 In 1999/2000, CSOs such as the International Commission of Jurists (Kenya Chapter) and the Legal Resources Foundation invested in 'phase-out training', as a prelude to handing over the initiative to independent management by the community-based groups. The programmes ran into financial difficulty as soon as the CSOs' financial support was scaled back or discontinued altogether. The financial crisis was deepened by a failure to pay membership dues, tied to low morale among the paralegals, who were no longer receiving allowances through the CSOs (interviews with Mr Kasina, Ms Mbaru, Ms Wakonyo, Mr Mutiso, Mr Mutavuta and Mr Kaka).

9 The CDF was created by a 2003 law that placed 2.5 per cent of national revenue under the direct control of Members of Parliament and required them to set up a committee at the constituency level to manage the fund. While the Act spells out certain categories of people (women, men and youth) who must be represented on the committee, it does not stipulate a process for staffing it. Most MPs, therefore, engage in very opaque dealings that subvert the stated intention of the law.

10 The LATF was set up by a 1998 Act of Parliament, and requires 5 per cent of national revenue to be allocated to local authorities (municipal and county councils). In 2001, guidelines were issued requiring citizen participation in local authorities' decision-making on how to spend the funds. The disbursement of 40 per cent of the funds was made conditional upon a local authority's preparation of a Local Authority Service Delivery Action Plan (LASDAP), prepared in consultation with local residents. Implementation of the LASDAP

guidelines commenced only in 2003. Participation is envisaged only at the point of problem identification and up to the time a project is conceived, but not in the implementation, monitoring or evaluation of the project.

11 We found that it was not uncommon for one person to hold party membership cards for two or more parties; registration alone is clearly not evidence of party loyalty.

12 Interview with Morris Odhiambo, Executive Director, Centre for Law and Research International, Nairobi, 6 September 2006.

13 That clientelist or 'personalistic' approaches to engagement in governance are inherently undemocratic is taken for granted in influential writings, for example White (1998).

14 The study 'Democratizing Local Governance in Kenya: with Lessons from Ghana, Tanzania and Uganda' (2004–05) was part of the Learning Initiative on Citizen Participation and Local Governance (see www2.ids.ac.uk/logolink/index.htm). It was conducted in four districts of Kenya, and its findings were used in community-level civic education in the run-up to the 2005 constitutional referendum.

3 · Microfinance and social mobilization: alternative pathways to grassroots democracy?

NAILA KABEER AND SIMEEN MAHMUD[1]

Civil society and democracy: theoretical perspectives

Ideas about civil society have become an increasingly important strand in the current discussions within the international development community about democracy and good governance. Many of these ideas are rooted in western political and philosophical traditions and have been imported (not always successfully) into the international development discourse. There are, of course, competing conceptualizations of civil society within this broader literature, with competing implications for state–society relations. These can be broadly divided into liberal and radical traditions (Elliot, 2006; Lewis, 2004). As might be expected, it is largely conceptualizations drawing on the mainstream liberal traditions that have been favoured in the transfer to development contexts.

Within traditional liberal theory, civil society is seen as the realm of voluntary associations, and exists in the space between state, market and family. There is a strong normative tendency within this tradition: the view that civil society is a 'good thing' (Lewis, 2004). The work of Tocqueville has been particularly influential within this tradition.[2] He stressed principles of voluntarism, community spirit and independent associational life that characterized civil society as an important counterbalance to the state's domination of society. More recently, the work of Putnam (1993a, b) promotes the idea of civil society as the 'social capital' of a nation, generating horizontal relationships of trust and reciprocity and capable of being harnessed for collective action in the interests of the wider society. He contrasts this with the vertical patron–client relationships that characterize kin-based communities and that promote a bounded form of morality, the privileging of narrow self-interest over the collective good.

Such ideas have underpinned a great deal of the more positive discussions about civil society that are a feature of the international development discourse. However, a further strand was added to these discussions, with the rise in the 1980s of the neoliberal agenda within the international donor community. Its critique of the rent-seeking state and its privileging of private initiative led to public sector reforms designed to reduce the state's role in both the economy and service delivery and to promote market forces. Where markets failed to emerge or were characterized by imperfections, civil society organizations (CSOs), particularly development non-governmental organizations (NGOs), were seen as the next best alternative.

Civil society thus occupies two, somewhat different, roles in the international development agenda. CSOs have become an integral part of the donor-led 'good governance' agenda, based on assumptions about the 'elective affinity' between civil society and democracy (Betteille, 2000). Within the (frequently justified) neoliberal critique of bloated, inefficient and corrupt states, a proliferation of organized, voluntary and autonomous associations is viewed as critical to the task of building and consolidating the democratic sphere. In addition, it has become an integral part of the privatization agenda, representing a preferred alternative to state provision wherever the markets are either lacking or failing.

There is an alternative radical tradition in the literature on civil society – one that has been heavily influenced by the work of the Italian philosopher Antonio Gramsci and others. This tradition depicts civil society as a sphere comprising organizations that are separate from (but enmeshed with) the power structures of the state and market, and in which competing ideas about state and society struggle with one another (Davis and McGregor, 2000; Lewis, 2004). There is nothing inherently democratic about these organizations. Instead they are characterized by varying degrees of co-optation into existing power structures, and hence act in varying degrees to challenge or uphold the existing social order.

The question that these debates raise, therefore, is whether the nature of CSOs matters to their outcomes. Putnam (1993a, b), for instance, recognized that some associations are more productive of the values that support good government than are others; however, as Elliot (2006) points out, this was a minor caveat to his major theme of celebrating the positive contribution CSOs make to democracy, thanks to the social capital they produce: according to Putnam, such contributions could arise from purely social groups or sports clubs, as well as from associations that set out to promote democratic values. Similarly, Rosenblum (1994) argues that what prepare citizens for democracy are not the values held by associations, but the plurality of associations with permeable boundaries, as well as the ability of people to opt out of them.

Others, however, have argued that the vision and values of organizations matter to their achievements on the democratic front. Those influenced by the work of Freire (1972) have stressed the need to build the organizational capacity of the poor and dispossessed, in order to enable them to mobilize politically for their rights as citizens. More recent arguments suggest that promoting the role of NGOs in service provision (as an alternative to the state) risks undermining their capacity to deliver on the governance front. On the one hand, unlike governments, NGOs are not authorities that can legitimately be expected to uphold the rights of poor people (Moore and Putzel, 1999). On the other hand, their service delivery function dilutes their capacity to maintain a watchdog function and to hold governments accountable. However, such arguments are valid only in certain contexts. In the context of Bangladesh, the alternative to NGOs is not a reasonably responsive and well-functioning state, but a highly corrupt and predatory one.

The NGO sector in Bangladesh

The aim of this chapter is to explore some of these questions from the perspective of the NGO sector in Bangladesh. Recent estimates suggest that around 22,000 NGOs are currently operating in the country. Most are extremely small and local in their activities. Our concern is with registered development NGOs: although there are only around 2,000 of these, they constitute a prominent and very visible strand of civil society in Bangladesh, and one that is far more active in the everyday lives of the country's poorer citizens than other strands of civil society. It has been estimated that they operate in more than 78 per cent of villages in what is still a largely rural society, and directly benefit around 35 per cent of the total population.

The NGO sector has undergone substantial change since the country's independence from Pakistan in 1971. Many NGOs were founded in the difficult years following the war of independence, and they adopted a radical approach to social change. They were influenced by the structural analysis of socio-economic inequality that is exemplified in some classic studies from that period (BRAC, 1983; Arens and van Beurden, 1977; Village Study Group, 1975). They were also inspired by the work of Freire (1972), with its emphasis on the 'conscientization', organization and mobilization of poor and dispossessed groups. Most relied on funds from international NGOs and foundations that shared their vision of social justice: Oxfam, the Ford Foundation, Canadian University Service Overseas, War on Want, Swallows, Action Aid and Diakonia.

By the end of the decade, NGOs had begun to undergo a series of changes. The onset of military rule in 1976 had led to a gradual narrowing of the civil society space for radical politics. NGOs that received funding from foreign donors were required to register with a newly created 'NGO Bureau', which allowed the government to make life difficult for those whose activities it wished to curtail. Some began to tone down their radical agenda. This was not reversed even after the restoration of democratic rule in 1991. The end of the Cold War saw an increasing preoccupation on the part of the official donor community with problems of governance and with the need to build civil society both as a training ground for democracy and as an alternative service provider.

While official donor support for the NGO sector expanded, its focus came to be largely on the organizations' service provision role. The percentage of total foreign aid disbursed to Bangladesh that went direct to NGOs rose from 6 per cent in 1990 to 18 per cent in 1995, and remained around this level in subsequent years (Thornton et al., 2000). While the availability of large-scale official aid led to a rapid proliferation of NGOs, the decline in the availability of funds from international NGOs (which had operated on a relatively equal footing with national NGOs) and the increasing reliance of national NGOs on official donor agencies altered the relationship both between NGOs and donors and between different NGOs.

Much of the increased donor funding has come to be concentrated on an elite group of NGOs, which have moved into a league of their own in terms of size, budget and staffing (Devine, 2003). In fact, in the period 1999–2000, the three largest NGOs – the Bangladesh Rural Advancement Committee (BRAC), the Association for Social Advancement (ASA) and Proshikkhan Shikkha Kaj (PROSHIKA – Training, Education and Action) – received more than 72 per cent of all donor funds to the NGO sector. As Devine points out, the pattern of favouring the large NGOs has reflected the pressures on donors 'to scale up successful development operations, reduce burdensome transaction costs, decrease NGO reliance on donor money and initiate a process that would secure financial sustainability' (2003: 230). Funding decisions have been based on technical criteria, such as efficiency, added value, cost-effectiveness and performance, and have sought to impose a 'logical framework' structure on the way NGOs plan their activities. The concern with financial sustainability has led to a growing concentration on microfinance services within the NGO community, accompanied by the abandonment of social services and, to an even greater extent, the social mobilization activities.

Some of these changes in NGO orientation are tracked by Devine (2003). He notes that, between 1989 and 1999, the amount that was spent on microfinance by the eleven largest NGOs put together rose from 29 per cent of total expenditure to 38 per cent, and the proportion spent on economic support services increased from 27 per cent to 34 per cent. Meanwhile, the share that went on social services declined from 33 per cent to 22 per cent, and on social mobilization – from 11 per cent to 6 per cent. A recent World Bank study found that over 80 per cent of NGOs surveyed were engaged in the delivery of microfinance, while around 50 per cent provided social services (World Bank, 2006).

We can see, therefore, that there has been a considerable homogenization of the NGO sector in Bangladesh, particularly since the 1990s – driven partly by the technical demands of donor funding. The government has also contributed to this homogenization through the establishment of the Palli Karma-Sahayak Foundation, a large fund intended to promote microfinance organizations along the lines of the now internationally renowned Grameen Bank model. Such homogenization of strategies has also brought about a homogenization of vision, with the abandonment of the radical vision of social equality that drove NGO activity in the early years, and the promotion instead of market-based opportunities as the basis for social inclusion and citizenship.

The hypothesis behind our research is that different organizational models have different outcomes. This was motivated by the findings of an earlier qualitative study of citizenship narratives among the working poor in Bangladesh. This suggested that such organizations as were purposely designed to promote the identity and practice of citizenship among the working poor were far more likely to report such outcomes than were organizations that were narrowly tailored to the provision of microfinance (Kabeer with Haq Kabir, 2009). At the same time, we expected that the microfinance organizations might perform better on developmental outcomes. Our analysis of outcomes therefore included indicators generally associated with poverty reduction (such as assets, income, health-seeking behaviour, financial skills), indicators that sought to capture changes in participation in the community and in the political and policy domain, and indicators of knowledge and attitudes that would point to a growing sense of citizenship. These outcome indicators only partly reflected specific organizational goals; they also reflected our own attempts to capture the kinds of change at the grassroots level that, we believe, would contribute to improvements in the state of governance in Bangladesh.

Survey methodology and description of sample

This chapter provides a preliminary analysis of a larger study of NGOs in Bangladesh that was designed to explore their role in the promotion of democratic values and practices in Bangladeshi society and the extent to which differences in their visions and strategies have affected their contribution to this goal. As Thornton et al. (2000) have pointed out, NGOs can, on the basis of their visions and strategies, be placed on a continuum, with the more narrowly focused microfinance organizations at one end, organizations focused on social mobilization at the other end, and organizations that provide social services (often in combination with microfinance) occupying an intermediate position. The six NGOs selected for the research project represented different points on this continuum: ASA and Grameen Bank are at the minimalist, microfinance end of the spectrum, while Nijera Kori and Samata are at the purely social mobilization end. The intermediate organizations are PROSHIKA (which combines microfinance with social mobilization) and BRAC (which combines microfinance with social service provision and legal training).

Our methodological strategy for establishing change was to compare indicators measuring knowledge, attitudes and practices reported by 'new' and 'old' members of an NGO, on the assumption that any evidence of major differences between the two groups can be attributed to the length of their membership of these organizations. In consequence, new members are used as a control group in this study. Impact attribution strategies of this kind are, of course, methodologically fraught (as indeed are most efforts to assess causality in the social sciences). In view of the fact that we are at a preliminary stage in our analysis and have not used multivariate statistical techniques (something we plan to do at a later stage) to control for differences in the backgrounds and individual characteristics of members of different NGOs, we have limited our analysis to two organizations at opposite ends of the continuum, where we would expect differences in likely impacts to be most pronounced. We have selected ASA to represent the minimalist microfinance end of the continuum and Samata to represent the social mobilization end.

ASA is a national NGO that covers all sixty-four districts of Bangladesh and over 72,000 villages. In 2008, it had a total membership of 6.86 million people, of whom 65 per cent were women. The total number of organized groups was 237,000. Though they do receive individual loans for business purposes, men are not organized into groups by ASA. ASA group membership is thus entirely made up of women.

Samata is a much smaller NGO. It operates in seven districts of south-west and north-west Bangladesh, covering 2,226 villages. It organizes both men and women into (same sex) groups. In 2008, the total number of groups was around 11,000, and total membership was 200,000, of whom 55 per cent were women.

TABLE 3.1 Differences in organizational approaches

Indicators	Samata	ASA
Group dynamics		
Group formation	Yes	Yes
Size of group	10–20	15–35
Sex composition of group	Male and female	Only female
Frequency of meeting	Weekly	Weekly
Group fund	Yes	No
Group federation	Yes	No
Livelihood support		
Skills training	No	No
Savings facility	Yes	Yes
Microcredit	No	Yes
Social services (health, education)	No	No
Mobilization		
Training on rights	Yes	No
Training on collective action	Yes	No
Joint group activity	Yes	No
Leadership building	Yes	No
Support for collective action	Yes	No

The data come from a 2007 questionnaire survey of 100 'new' and 200 'old' members, randomly selected from each of the six NGOs in the study. 'New' members had joined within the last six months, while 'old' members had joined at least five years previously. In order to minimize variations in background factors that might be due to geographical location, the study was carried out in the south-west region of Bangladesh, where all six NGOs had branches. From the list of old and new branches in each area, we randomly selected two old and one new branch, and from each branch we randomly selected 100 members. Because of differences in their group formation strategy (see above), the entire ASA sample was made up of women, while the Samata sample was evenly divided between the sexes.

Some of the differences between the organizational approaches of ASA and Samata are shown in Table 3.1. Both organizations have group-based strategies, meet on a weekly basis and promote savings by group members. However, attendance is not compulsory for ASA members. ASA provides microcredit services to its members, but Samata maintains an attitude of hostility to NGO provision of credit, on the grounds that it would reproduce old relationships of dependency in a new form. Samata allows its groups to retain control over their savings in the form of group funds, and to take loans from the group fund. The savings of members of ASA are generally kept with the organization. Samata provides rights-awareness training to its members. ASA does not provide such training, but, when the occasion arises, its groups may hold discussions on such issues as dowry, child marriage and so on. Samata also provides training in protests and campaigns, joint group activity and leadership, and has built up a federation of its groups into larger structures or 'people's organizations'. Samata provides support for collective action to access services and *khas* (government) resources.

Table 3.2 provides a description of the individual and household characteristics of our respondents. There is not a great deal of difference in their age profiles: new members of these organizations are mainly in their thirties, while old members tend to be in their forties. Very few of their households are headed by women. Far more of the new members of Samata are likely to be unmarried compared to other categories of marital status. While the majority of respondents in both organizations are from the Muslim majority population, ASA has a relatively high percentage of non-Muslims – mainly Hindus – among its older members. This is because these members were drawn from two Hindu-dominated

TABLE 3.2 Socio-economic profile of respondents

Indicator (%)	Samata New	Samata Old	ASA New	ASA Old
Mean age (years)	32 (33)	43 (40)	35	38
Female household head (%)	2 (4)	2 (4)	4	4
Religion				
Muslim (%)	98 (96)	100 (100)	97	67
Marital status				
Married	78 (82)	95 (93)	95	95
Single	18 (10)	2 (0)	0	0
Widowed, separated	4 (8)	4 (7)	5	6
Level of education				
No schooling	52 (54)	64 (58)	62	63
Up to Class 5	28 (22)	24 (30)	26	21
Up to Class 10	17 (24)	9 (10)	10	16
Secondary school certificate or higher	3 (0)	4 (2)	2	2

Note: Figures in brackets show the female percentage.

areas. Levels of education are quite low: in both organizations, around two-thirds of respondents have no formal schooling. Beyond that, levels of education vary, with Samata reporting slightly higher levels among its members (particularly new members) than ASA. Finally, given the patriarchal constraints that restrict women's economic, political and social options in Bangladesh, we would expect any changes wrought in members' lives to be weaker for women than for men. Since Samata respondents (both old and new) were equally divided between men and women, while ASA members were mainly women, we have included separate estimates for women in brackets.

In the rest of the chapter, we report some of the changes that membership of these organizations has brought to their members' lives. The survey included a series of questions relating to respondents' capabilities and behaviours, knowledge and practice, and values, attitudes and perceptions. These all have a bearing on the kind of society that the organizations are seeking to build. Our interpretation of 'impact' is based on differences reported in various outcome indicators between the new and the old members of each organization. Clearly, other differences between old and new members (such as the differences in age, education, etc.) may also affect these outcomes and will be taken into account in a subsequent paper.[3]

Three sets of changes are explored: changes relating to individual livelihood capabilities, access to public resources and community participation; formal political knowledge and participation; and beliefs, attitudes and perceptions relating to identity, citizenship and social change. Where impacts are evident for both organizations, we take this to be indicative of generic impacts associated with NGO membership, regardless of particular organizational strategy. Where impacts are evident for one NGO but not the other, we take this as organizationally specific evidence of change.

Livelihood capabilities, access to public resources and community participation Our first set of findings related to a range of individual skills and capabilities that are likely to serve respondents well in their daily lives. These include health-related skills and capabilities (the ability to make up an oral saline solution to treat diarrhoea and to recognize pneumonia in small children); economic capabilities (knowing how to open a bank account, calculate the interest payable on a loan, sign a document and use a mobile phone); and political capabilities (the ability to bargain for a fairer return on labour, to file a court case and to voice opinion freely and without fear).

TABLE 3.3 Individual skills and capabilities

Indicator	Samata			ASA		
	New (%)	Old (%)	T-value	New (%)	Old (%)	T-value
Health-related capabilities						
Make oral saline	67 (72)	75 (93)	-1.46	73	83	-1.92
Recognize pneumonia	53 (60)	73 (85)	-3.52	58	65	-1.18
Economic capabilities						
Open bank account	12 (10)	27 (20)	-2.90	6	8	-0.48
Calculate interest on loan	48 (34)	44 (44)	0.74	25	35	-1.76
Use mobile phone	33 (24)	30 (28)	0.53	10	20	-2.11
Sign documents	68 (72)	77 (80)	-1.68	50	64	-2.34
Political capabilities						
Bargain for fair returns to labour	85 (76)	77 (72)	1.63	57	65	-2.30
File court case	26 (10)	42 (29)	-2.63	28	26	0.46
Voice opinion without fear	82 (84)	96 (96)	-3.94	65	65	0.00

Note: Figures in brackets show the female percentage.

TABLE 3.4 Participation in community life and decision-making

Indicator	Samata			ASA		
	New (%)	Old (%)	T-value	New (%)	Old (%)	T-value
Others come for advice	61 (60)	92 (94)	-7.04	71	71	0.09
Accompany others[1]	42 (38)	61 (57)	-3.16	48	51	-0.41
Provide information on government service	66 (60)	89 (91)	-4.85	60	60	0.08
Attended *shalish*	53 (28)	80 (69)	-5.05	26	21	0.06
Participated in *shalish*	15 (4)	41 (27)	-4.69	2	2	0.00
Member of local committee[2]	5 (2)	15 (11)	-2.56	0	2	-1.42
Enhanced voice[3]	5 (6)	81 (78)	-17.70	0	18	-4.67

Notes: Figure in brackets is female percentage; 1. to health centre, bank, court, etc. 2. school committee, *masjid/mandir* committee, bazaar committee, etc. 3. speak out against violence against women, corruption, religious fanaticism, injustice, harassment, etc.

Table 3.3 shows that the majority of members, old and new, of both ASA and Samata are able to make up oral saline, and somewhat fewer are able to recognize pneumonia. While there does appear to be some evidence of impact, this does not vary a great deal by organization. While Samata members generally perform better than ASA members in terms of economic capabilities, it is only among women members that membership appears to have had an impact. In the case of ASA, economic capabilities are generally lower, but they do show evidence of the impact of membership.

With respect to political capabilities, we find that the main evidence of impact among Samata members relates to knowledge of how to bring a court case and the ability to express opinions freely and without fear. This holds true for both women and men. Among ASA members, impact largely relates to bargaining for fairer returns to labour.

Table 3.4 deals with impacts on relationships within the community. Depending on the kind of training and the exposure provided, membership of an NGO can become a conduit to information about legal matters and about the wider world. As a result, within their communities NGO group members become a source of advice and information on a variety of matters. Furthermore, while poor and marginalized sections of the community are rarely permitted to participate in local decision-making committees that are responsible for the governance of local institutions (such as mosques and temples, bazaars, schools and the informal dispensing of justice), a number of NGOs have sought to change this. Many are active in the informal justice systems of village communities, with their members attending and often participating in the proceedings. In some contexts, they have become a significant enough force at the local level to be approached by others to participate in dispensing justice – and even to initiate their own alternative forms of justice. Some NGOs have also encouraged their members to become more involved in local decision-making committees. Indicators measuring the extent to which ASA and Samata are engaged in these activities are presented in Table 3.4. The results suggest that organizational strategies make a discernible difference to the kind of impacts reported.

Older members of Samata, both women and men, were far more likely than new members to be approached for their advice and opinion; they were also more likely to provide others with information and support in relation to accessing government services. They were more likely to be active in informal justice proceedings, attending (as well as participating actively in) *shalish* (local dispute resolution).

Older members of Samata, men as well as women, were generally more likely than newer members to have participated in at least one committee, and were also more likely to have engaged with these committees than were older members of ASA. They were also more likely to be engaged in a wider range of committees than were ASA members: not only did they participate in school, mosque and temple committees (in which some ASA members were also involved), but they were also on committees for *khas* land and water management, in which ASA members were not involved at all.

The positive impact of Samata membership on levels of community participation was evident for both men and women.

Finally, the table tells us that, while older members of both organizations were much more likely to speak out against various forms of injustice than were their newer members, the difference was much larger in the case of Samata for both men and women.

Knowledge and participation in the political domain Table 3.5 deals with the impact of group membership on knowledge and participation in the political domain. We explored levels of political knowledge, interaction with local administration and elected representatives, voting and participation in elections, and exercise of voice and collective agency against injustice. The first indicator is an aggregated measure of political knowledge (knowledge of *shorkar* or government) and ranges from 0 to 7. It measures the respondent's ability to correctly name key political figures and organizations: the chief adviser of the caretaker government in power at the time, the last prime minister, a political party, the local Union Parishad[4] (UP) woman member, the UP chairman, the ward member and the last MP. The average score among older Samata members was 6, compared to an average of 4 among older ASA members. Older Samata members were also more likely to give correct answers than were new members, while there was little difference in the case of ASA members. It should be noted that Samata's impact was evident for both male and female members: indeed it was more marked for female members.

The next set of indicators relate to interactions with locally elected representatives (UP members) and members of the local administration (Upazila Nirbahi[5] Officers – UNOs). The interactions included visiting the UP and UNO offices, talking to the UNO or UP chairman or member, being called for discussion by them, and making demands on them. Here, too, it is evident that differences in organizational strategy have a marked bearing on the impacts reported. Older members of Samata were generally more likely to report these interactions than were newer members (this applied to female Samata members as well as male). Duration of membership of ASA did not appear to have this impact. Furthermore, older members of Samata were more likely to report these interactions than were older ASA members, providing further evidence that membership of Samata strengthened the relationship between its members and local representatives of the state. Once again, this impact was weaker and less consistent among female Samata members. It is worth noting that most respondents in the survey had far more interaction with elected representatives than with government administrators.

The next set of indicators relates to actions taken to protest against injustice through participation in campaigns, demonstrations and various forms of collective action. We have already noted that membership of Samata markedly increased the likelihood that its members (female as well as male) would speak out against injustice. It is therefore not surprising that older Samata members are also more likely than new members to engage in collective action against various forms of injustice, and that this was the case for both men and women. Collective action over rights to land was the most frequently reported, followed by action in favour of women's rights. Access to government services featured least frequently. Women were somewhat less active than men on most issues except women's rights (although male participation was also high on that score). There is very little evidence that ASA membership had any impact on the likelihood that its members would engage in such collective action, and indeed participation in protest was close to zero among its membership, both old and new.

The final set of indicators measures political participation: whether or not respondents voted in local and national elections, stood in local elections, campaigned in them, made their own decision about how they would vote and encouraged others to vote. We also compared what qualities our respondents valued in their candidates. The results suggest evidence of a generic NGO effect for some of our participation indicators. Older members of both organizations were more likely than new ones to have voted in the last national and local elections, with this pattern holding for both men and women in Samata.

However, older Samata members (both male and female) were considerably more likely than new members to have campaigned in the last local election, to have encouraged others to vote and to have made their own decision how to cast their vote. This impact was not evident for ASA members. It is interesting to note that among the members of both organizations – old and new, male and female – honesty was the quality most valued in candidates who stood for election. This may

TABLE 3.5 Indicators of political awareness and participation, by organization and by type of membership

Indicator	Samata			ASA		
	New (%)	Old (%)	T-value	New (%)	Old (%)	T-value
Knowledge of *shorkar*[1]	5.37 (4.76)	6.29 (6.17)	-6.21	4.52	4.70	-0.93
Interaction with local government						
Visited UP[2]	42 (32)	73 (59)	-5.36	42	39	0.50
Visited UNO[2]	2 (0)	12 (11)	-2.93	0	5	-2.16
Comfortable talking to UP	85 (80)	94 (89)	-2.56	88	94	-1.63
Comfortable talking to UNO	25 (16)	38 (30)	-2.56	22	24	-0.29
Consulted by UP[3]	28 (6)	70 (63)	-7.51	2	3	-0.51
Made claim on UP	46 (36)	80 (69)	-6.36	45	43	0.33
Made claim on UNO	2 (0)	38 (32)	-7.24	0	3	-1.75
Protest						
Ever participated in protest[4]	4 (2)	90 (84)	-25.94	1	2	-0.64
For *khas* resource	2 (2)	84 (73)	-21.15	0	0	
For government service	0	15 (10)	-4.10	0	1	0.04
For women's rights	2 (0)	59 (66)	-11.32	1	0	0.01
Against violence	0	25 (24)	-5.68	1	0	0.01

Participation in election						
Voted in last national election	69 (66)	94 (95)	-6.17	82	92	-2.43
Voted in last UP election	71 (68)	94 (95)	-5.54	88	96	-2.64
Campaigned in UP election	29 (12)	46 (30)	-2.78	1	7	-2.26
Encouraged others to vote	66 (58)	87 (88)	-4.41	51	55	-0.65
Own decision to vote[5]	22 (6)	37 (33)	-2.56	18	18	0.00
Prefers honest[6] candidate	62 (62)	83 (82)	-4.11	65	72	-1.24
Prefers pro-poor candidate	30 (22)	50 (53)	-3.35	39	33	1.11
Prefers candidate who delivers[7]	31 (24)	30 (31)	0.18	27	25	0.47

Notes: Figures in brackets show the female percentage; 1. mean number of correct answers out of 7 2. went to see UP chairman/member or UNO for some purpose 3. called by UP chairman/member to discuss some local concern 4. took part in any protest or movement – e.g. resources, services, injustice, violence against women, corruption, etc. 5. did not discuss with anyone who to vote for 6. truthful, not corrupt, unbiased, good character 7. equal rights for citizens/men/women, no religious fundamentalism, good people are elected, democracy is strengthened, bring good government to power, etc.

TABLE 3.6 Attitudes to social justice

Indicator	Samata			ASA		
	New (%)	Old (%)	T-value	New (%)	Old (%)	T-value
Agreed that:						
The rich should have more rights than the poor	10	6	-2.34	9	6	-0.28
Elected representatives do not have to listen to the people	10	2	-2.84	1	3	0.80
A husband can beat his wife for not listening to him	58	37	-3.60	72	48	-3.96
It is not a problem if political leaders who do good for the country pocket some public money	6	2	-1.88	14	16	0.10
It is good for the army to be deployed if the law and order situation is bad	91	91	-1.03	84	85	0.78
It is necessary for pregnant women to go for a medical check-up	100	99	1.23	97	100	-1.78
Girls should continue with school even after marriage	83	92	-2.20	61	68	-1.11
Women should have their own income	99	98	0.64	97	99	-0.87
It is good for women to have control over their income	83	82	0.21	82	84	-0.44
Fate is determined by birth	32	35	-0.43	39	43	-0.66
They aspire to a better life for their children	55	79	-4.44	66	70	-0.70

reflect a verdict on the widespread corruption that characterizes politics in Bangladesh. Candidates who were pro-poor were generally preferred over those who delivered, presumably because those who delivered could not be relied on to deliver to the poor.

Attitudes towards political rights and social justice In this final section of data analysis, we report on the responses to a series of questions that dealt with attitudes to issues of rights, social justice, politics and perceptions of change. Table 3.6 reports on how members of ASA and Samata responded to questions to do with various aspects of social and political justice.

By and large, the findings are extremely positive among the members of both NGOs. On questions of gender, members of both NGOs, old and new, agreed that pregnant women should be given medical check-ups, that women should have an income, and that they should have control over it. How genuinely these beliefs are held is, of course, another matter, given that men continue to dominate household decision-making; but the widespread expression of these beliefs suggests that it is no longer considered socially acceptable to support certain forms of gender discrimination. Duration of membership of Samata does seem to have some effect on members' views about whether girls should continue with their education, even if they get married. Older Samata members are more likely than new ones to believe that they should. They are also more likely to believe this than older ASA members. There is little evidence of any impact in ASA. While there appears to be considerable support among both new ASA and Samata members for the statement that husbands can beat their wives for not listening to them, in both cases the levels of support were much lower among older members of the organizations. In any case, support was generally lower among Samata members.

There were uniformly high levels of support for the statement that the army should be brought in when there was a breakdown in law and order. Once again, this is a comment on the state of politics in recent years in Bangladesh. It reflects the comparisons that people drew between, on the one hand, the violence in the lead-up to the planned 2007 national elections and the chaos that threatened to engulf the country, and, on the other, the relative stability that had prevailed since the army stepped in and installed a 'caretaker government'.

With respect to other political issues, agreement with the statement that 'the rich should have more rights than the poor' was generally low (10 per cent or less) and declined overall with duration of membership

TABLE 3.7 Knowledge of rights and citizenship

	Samata			ASA		
	New (%)	Old (%)	T-value	New (%)	Old (%)	T-value
Knowledge of rights						
Knows meaning of rights	59 (44)	90 (92)	-6.56	73	78	-0.86
Defined as 'claim to social justice/equality'[1]	39 (30)	63 (64)	-3.94	29	41	-2.04
Defined as right over things[2]	6 (8)	10 (8)	-1.03	30	24	1.12
Citizenship						
Heard term citizen	89 (86)	98 (99)	-3.43	66	67	-0.17
Self as citizen	96 (92)	100 (100)	-2.88	74	72	0.37
All equal citizens	78 (70)	92 (89)	-3.33	52	54	-0.33

Notes: Figures in brackets show the female percentage; 1. fair/just/own claim, just due, everyone has equal rights, freedoms, right to speak, justice, humanity, citizens' rights, women's rights 2. family, husband, children, property.

of both organizations. Agreement with the statement that 'elected representatives do not have to listen to the people' was even less common. Levels of agreement with the statement that 'it is not a problem for political leaders to be corrupt if they do good work' were also generally low, but were somewhat higher among ASA members.

Agreement with the statement that 'fate is determined by birth' was lower among older Samata members (35 per cent) than among older ASA members (43 per cent), suggesting that Samata group members are relatively non-fatalistic. However, while membership of Samata appeared to have little impact on this attitude, membership of ASA appeared to reduce it. A related indicator is the extent to which respondents hope for a better future for their children. We find that, while the percentage of older members who hoped for a better future for their children did not differ a great deal between the two organizations, duration of membership of Samata increased such hopes – an effect not seen in the case of ASA.

Table 3.7 reports on knowledge and attitudes relating to rights and citizenship. When it comes to knowing what rights mean, the impact of duration of membership is evident among Samata members: although fewer new Samata members said they knew what rights meant than did new ASA members, there was a marked increase in the percentage who knew among older Samata members. Meanwhile, there was little evidence of change among ASA members. Samata members were also more likely to interpret rights in terms of claims to social justice, equality, freedom of expression, women's rights (and so on) than were ASA members; and while duration of membership increased the likelihood of this interpretation among both groups, the impact was stronger among Samata members. ASA members, on the other hand, were more likely to interpret rights in terms of familial relationships and property, although the percentages supporting this interpretation declined somewhat over time.

The contrast between the two organizations is also striking in terms of their views on citizenship. Compared to ASA members, a higher percentage of Samata members (both old and new) had heard of the term 'citizen'. There was also evidence of a marked increase in knowledge over time among Samata members, but little evidence of such an impact among ASA members. Samata members – old and new, male and female – were more likely to regard themselves as citizens, and there was some increase among older members, particularly women. They were also likely to express the belief that all citizens were equal, and the percentages increased with duration of membership. Very little change was observed among ASA members.

TABLE 3.8 Perception of change by organization and type of membership

	Samata			ASA		
	New (%)	Old (%)	T-value	New (%)	Old (%)	T-value
Perception of changes in own status since joining						
Respect in village	11	93	-23.62	3	57	-10.45
Respect from UP	5	76	-15.59	0	10	-3.32
Respect from UNO	0	17	-4.51	0	2	-1.42
Perception of improvement in community in last 10–15 years						
Access to economic opportunities	87	100	-5.45	99	94	2.01
Access to social services	89	100	-4.51	97	97	0.22
Violence against women	85	98	-4.49	60	67	-1.20
Fairness in justice system	55	94	-8.93	44	52	-1.22

The final set of responses, shown in Table 3.8, relate to perceptions regarding individual and social changes since joining the NGO. For both organizations, older members were far more likely than newer members to believe that they were regarded with more respect in their village since they had joined their respective organization, but the impact is considerably stronger among Samata members. Older Samata members are also far more likely than newer ones to believe that they were respected by elected UP members. Some change was also evident among ASA members, but it was considerably smaller. Older Samata members were also more likely than new members to say that they believed they were respected by UNOs, but the impact was smaller. Almost no ASA members expressed this view.

In terms of changes in the wider community over the last ten to fifteen years, the views expressed were generally positive, although this is more the case for some changes than for others. ASA members appear extremely positive about improvements in economic opportunities (over 90 per cent), though there is some decline among older members. Newer Samata members are less positive (87 per cent) but become much more positive over time (100 per cent). A similar pattern prevails with respect to accessing social services. However, there is a noticeable difference between the two organizations as far as violence against women and the quality of the justice system are concerned. Samata members are far more positive about changes in the incidence of violence against women and appear to become more so over time (85 per cent rising to 98 per cent). ASA members are less positive, and there is little difference between old and new members. Samata members are also generally positive about improvements in the justice system, and become more positive over time (rising from 55 per cent to 94 per cent). ASA members are generally less positive, and there is little difference between old and new members.

Interpreting the findings

We have distinguished in this chapter between two categories of change associated with membership of NGOs. The first is a 'generic' NGO mobilization effect – examples of changes that appear to occur across NGOs, regardless of their specific organizational approach and strategies. Various examples of this were: acquisition of certain basic health and economic capabilities/skills; community participation in informal spaces through acting as a source of advice, information and support to other villagers; reduction in support for husbands beating their wives; increase in social status in terms of respect from the village;

increase in political participation in terms of voting in elections; and some increase in the confidence to speak to anyone.

The second category was change that is specific to a particular NGO mobilization strategy. These changes were seen as reflections of differences in the goals and strategies that shape the interactions of organizations and their members. By comparing the survey data for Samata and ASA, we found strong support for the hypothesis that the goals and strategies pursued by NGOs matter with regard to the kinds of changes they are able to bring about in the lives of their members.

While there seems to have been a growth among members of both organizations in their various health and economic capabilities (whether taken together or differentiated by sex), Samata members appear to have become better equipped in terms of their political capabilities – using negotiating skills, working in the legal system and making themselves heard.

In every scenario of community participation, older Samata members had taken significant strides in making their presence felt and meaningful, within both formal and informal spaces in the community. They had taken an active part in the informal justice proceedings of their village, been active in those local committees responsible for the informal governance of the village community, knew the names of key political figures and organizations, had voted and encouraged others to vote, had interacted with local administration and locally elected officials and had participated in collective protests and campaigns to uphold their rights and to challenge injustice. ASA members were less likely to report any of these impacts. The extensive presence of ASA members in informal spaces possibly had little to do with their membership of ASA.

ASA and Samata members share many of the same attitudes. However, there was greater acceptance among ASA members that violence against women by their husbands may be justified. On a related theme, relatively few ASA members felt that there had been a reduction in violence against women in their community over the past ten to fifteen years. This indicates a greater sense of insecurity among ASA members than among the female members of Samata. Again, whether it is violence against women or other types of injustice, ASA members have been unable to effect an entry into any space where they can make a difference (note their lack of participation in *shalish* and local government). The data reveal that, when they speak of gaining a greater voice since joining, it is mainly in terms of speaking to people from all strata of the community (which is a positive thing), rather than in terms of protesting against any injustice; nor has there been a change in their ability to voice their opinions freely and fearlessly. Therefore, it is not surprising that membership of ASA is less able to instil a sense of improvement in the justice system than is membership of Samata. Although both ASA and Samata members believe that they get more respect from their fellow villagers, Samata members are more likely to believe that they are also respected by elected and government officials.

The contrast in impacts reported by Samata (on the one hand) and by ASA (on the other) supports the basic hypothesis of this study. While the NGO sector appears to have certain generic effects on people's lives, those organizations that had invested substantial time and effort in building up the capacity of their membership to participate in the life of the community, to stand up for their rights and to fight injustice reported impacts that were very different from those reported by organizations that had confined themselves to a narrow microfinance agenda, in the belief that 'economic empowerment' would provide the route to empowerment in other domains. It is therefore among the membership of Samata that we find evidence of changing attitudes and practices which, if generalized across Bangladesh, would lead to the kind of active and engaged citizenship that is capable of holding the state accountable – even among its poorest citizens. Similar findings were also reported in a separate study of Nijera Kori, an organization which also engages in social mobilization (Kabeer with Haq Kabir and Huq, 2009).

It is in the membership of ASA, a microfinance organization that takes an extremely minimalist approach to service provision, that we are least likely to find such change. The question that later research will attempt to answer is to what extent some of the other organizations in our study – organizations that attempt to combine financial services with a degree of awareness-raising – are able to come closer to the kinds of democratic outcomes reported by Samata.

Notes

1 We would like to acknowledge the excellent assistance provided by Lopita Huq, Kabita Chowdhury and Saiful Islam.

2 Alexis de Tocqueville (1805–59), a French political thinker and historian who explored the relationship between the state and the individual in western societies.

3 However, it is worth noting at this stage that the general findings of our bivariate analysis for the two organizations are supported by the multivariate analysis.

4 The Union is the lowest administrative unit in rural Bangladesh and the Union Parishad is its elected council.

5 Government administrators at the Upazila level, which is the lowest tier of administration.

4 · Building democracy and citizenship at the local level: the Núcleo Representativo das Associações do Dombe Grande

IDACI FERREIRA AND SANDRA ROQUE

Introduction

Over the past ten years, the discussion about democratization processes in Africa have seen several political observers and scholars (van de Walle, 2001; Ake, 2005; Olukoshi, 2006) asking whether liberal democracy has been able to bring about effective political transformation and social and economic development. Although in many African countries a system of formal democracy has been established and elections have been held regularly, these authors point to strong control and centralization of political power, and to control of national resources by political elites that restrict the space for citizen participation, redistribute few resources and demonstrate little accountability.

In Angola, however, although the 'macro' political structure has been sending out signals that it is centralizing power and control, over the past few years there have been debates and initiatives towards greater participation in public and political space. A new participatory dynamic has emerged at the local level that has the potential to contribute to the construction of democracy in the country. To examine this dynamic, we will look at the Núcleo Representativo das Associações do Dombe Grande (NRA – Federation of Representative Associations of Dombe Grande), a federation of fifteen local associations that emerged in the 1990s in the comuna[1] of Dombe Grande, a small town some 63km from the provincial capital, Benguela. We ask if the political and social dynamic of the NRA's experience of mobilization has empowered ordinary citizens, and whether this can be seen as the beginning of deepening democracy. We seek to understand the local dynamics of this associative movement, to see whether it provides an opportunity for those social groups that have long been excluded from meaningful political participation to have an impact on the country's democratization process.

The chapter begins with a brief overview of the role of civic associations in African democratization and development, before moving on to discuss the history and politics of democratization in Angola. We then turn to examine the trajectory of the NRA and its member associations. Finally, we focus on the evolving relationship between the NRA and local government, discussing what it shows about the opportunities and limitations of civil society participation in processes of democratic deepening.

Civic associations in the democratization processes

Although democracy has spread around the world in recent decades,[2] several scholars and political activists have pointed to the limitations of the 'liberal democratic model' that is generally proposed. The liberal model of democracy, critics say, puts an emphasis on electoral processes and on a set of procedures and institutional designs, neglecting citizen participation in public affairs and generally disregarding the specific historical features and trajectories of each country (Santos and Avritzer, 2002; Olukoshi, 2006; Gaventa, 2006b).

In Africa, electoral democracy was widely adopted in the 1990s – an era that has been pinpointed as a very important time of political change, and one of great optimism. However, the limitations of African democratization have also been widely noted. Critics point to the way in which democratization processes have focused mainly on changes to the political system, without paying much attention to economic and social rights (Ake, 2005). Critics also point out that electoral democracy has allowed powerful elites to become legitimized, has favoured the growth of patrimonial political regimes, and has achieved little in terms of empowering ordinary citizens (Ake, 1996; Chabal, 2006; van de Walle, 2001; Messiant, 2006; Vidal and Andrade, 2006). Deepening democracy in Africa, critics say, should also mean improving the social and economic lot of ordinary African citizens – that is, it needs to pay attention not only to citizens' political rights but also to their economic and social rights (Ake, 1996; 2005).

In recent years, civil society has been seen in developing countries as a vehicle for deepening democracy. Civil society organizations (CSOs) provide an independent space for structuring the common goals of citizens, for articulating their demands for rights, for influencing public policies and for providing additional checks and balances on government behaviour (Edwards, 2004; Gaventa, 2006b). However, the concept of civil society itself has also generated debate in academic and development aid circles. The dominant view in the 1980s, which presented civil society as providing the ideal path to solving all the problems of developing countries, has been challenged. One of the important dimensions in the debate on developing countries, especially in Africa, is how the conflation of 'civil society' with 'non-governmental organizations' (NGOs) – usually understood as providing services funded by government and international development agencies (Howell and Pearce, 2001) – has reduced the social and political role that these organizations could have. Olukoshi (2006), for example, notes that NGO-supported processes are often driven by international development agencies and may not always be based on local social dynamics. While there is broad agreement on the positive role that civil society may play in democratization and development, any analysis of it needs to be based on the specific histories and contexts of each society (Edwards, 2004; Gaventa, 2006b).

Several authors stress the plural impact that civic associations in particular have on democracy (Putnam, 2003; Avritzer, 2002; Warren, 2000). As collective actors, these organizations have contributed to democratization by representing and fighting for the interests of particular social groups. Some authors argue that the role of associations in the construction of citizenship and democracy is related to their objectives and their attitude to collective action (Chen et al., 2007). For instance, there are associations whose field of interest is economic and whose scope is restricted to their membership; they have no commitment to a larger collective. Other associations are more concerned with the common good and act to promote transformation in society.

Moreover, associations can also contribute to the construction of political subjects and can enhance citizens' political participation and their power over public policy. Associations may function as 'schools of democracy', as they socialize individuals into practising core civic and democratic values, such as tolerance, dialogue and deliberation, trust, solidarity and reciprocity. In a recent study on citizenship in São Paulo and Mexico City, Houtzager et al. (2007) confirmed the value of associations in what they call the exercise of 'active citizenship'. Associations, these authors say, enhance levels of 'active citizenship'; that is, they make citizens more active – for example, in seeking collective solutions for the self-provision of goods, in engaging with public institutions for the provision of public goods, or in holding state bureaucracy accountable for the provision of those goods. However, these authors note, although associations contribute to making 'active citizens', and consequently to increasing levels of political participation, they do not significantly affect the quality of the relationship between the government and citizens in general, or levels of government accountability, and may make only a limited contribution to the overall democratic processes (ibid.).

As other authors argue, associations are more capable of intervening in a broader public arena when they are able to interact and link with other organizations, and with political and social actors, to struggle for collective demands and defend common interests (Edwards, 2004; Chen et al., 2007). So the transformative power of associations may sometimes be perceived over-optimistically, as associations in isolation may have little impact on wider political participation and democratization.

The case of the NRA in the small town of Dombe Grande will show that in the context of a very new democracy with a limited democratic political culture, such as Angola, civic associations, even at a very local level, can contribute positively to democratization, as they support citizens' empowerment, help spread democratic values and promote the emergence of 'active citizens'. We argue that, in the context of a country with a long history of authoritarian, controlling and centralizing governance, the empowerment of citizens, increasing interaction between the state and its citizens and greater (even if only marginally) state accountability are results that are not to be dismissed lightly. However, we will also point to the limitations of local action by associations, in terms of making any significant impact on broader political processes or influencing policy. In countries where the state has historically been strong and centralized, meaningful policy decisions may be kept at a state administration level that these associations cannot reach.

Angola's democratization process

Angola has had a long history of political and social control. Its colonial history was marked by a long Portuguese dictatorship and by a colonial system that was based on strong direct rule and, until 1961, on an oppressive 'native policy' that denied a large majority of the population political and social rights (Messiant, 1983; Pélissier, 1978; Chabal and Vidal, 2007).

Angola became independent from Portugal in 1975, after a war of liberation that lasted fourteen years. The majority of Angolan citizens felt that independence contained the potential for their participation in the country's political and public arenas. However, the one-party socialist government that was established after independence was soon identified with the efforts of the ruling party, the Movimento Popular de Libertação de Angola (MPLA – Popular Movement for the Liberation of Angola), to control and centralize power (Vidal and Andrade, 2006). Deep political divisions between the three liberation movements – the MPLA, União Nacional para a Independência Total de Angola (UNITA – National Union for the Total Independence of Angola) and the Frente Nacional de Libertação de Angola (FNLA – National Front for the Liberation of Angola) led to a civil war that became bound up with the politics of the Cold War and the geopolitics of southern Africa.[3]

The government and UNITA signed the Bicesse Peace Accords in 1991, ending sixteen years of war, and the country adopted a democratic constitution that allowed for freedom of association and multiparty elections, the first of which were held in 1992. However, UNITA refused to accept the result of these elections and returned to fighting a war, which ended only in 2002 with the death of Jonas Savimbi, UNITA's president. During this decade, formal democracy barely functioned, as the war crippled the democratic process. Angolan citizens continued to live under a strongly centralized regime, with limited freedom of expression and association. Vidal and Andrade (2006) note that, during the long civil war, not only did Angola become a more centralized country, but power increasingly became focused on the president. A small political elite also came to control Angola's rich natural resources, especially its oil and diamonds, through a patrimonial and clientelistic system that encouraged inequalities among the population (Chabal 2006; Vidal and Andrade, 2008).

It was during this period of hesitant democracy and war that independent civic organizations started to emerge. According to Chabal (2008), these have included the 'classic NGO' (generally supported by external donors to provide services), professional associations (which bring together people who have common professional interests) and community associations (such as water groups and farmers' associations). While it is true that many of these organizations are mainly service providers working with humanitarian aid programmes, it is no less true that several of them have introduced and worked with concepts like participation, participatory governance, citizenship and human rights – concepts that had not been part of Angolan political discourse and action for a long time.

In many dimensions of social and economic life, change has been rapid since the war ended. Vast programmes of reconstruction and economic development have been carried through, and Angola's economy grew by 16–20 per cent a year between 2005 and 2007 (Centro de Estudos e Investigação Científica, 2007). However, these high economic growth rates still have not led to a decline in the poverty headcount, which in 2005 was 68.2 per cent (UNDP, 2006).[4] Meanwhile, inequality has increased: the Gini coefficient[5] rose from 0.54 in 1995 to 0.64 in 2005 (Centro de Estudos e Investigação Científica, 2007).

Change is occurring in the political arena, albeit slowly. Angola's second parliamentary elections since 1992 were held in September 2008, and the MPLA won a spectacular victory with more than 80 per cent of the votes cast. Political observers have been asking whether this new political scenario will leave any room for democratization or for a broader distribution of the country's wealth. Certain processes to decentralize local governance – widely presented as a new framework to improve democratization and development in Africa – have been adopted in Angola. In some areas of the country, these should lead to the creation of *autarquias*, elected local government bodies with political and administrative autonomy and resources with which to operate. However, questions have been raised about the extent to which Angola's government, given its long history of control and centralization, will be willing to concede political power to local participatory governance processes.

NRA: characteristics and trajectory

Founded in 2001, the NRA is a federation of fifteen local associations that had been formed since 1997 by people coming together voluntarily at the village or neighbourhood level. The majority of these associations represent small-scale farmers, who also constitute the highest proportion of their members (most were formed by war-displaced peasants). A minority of the NRA's member organizations are civic associations, offering civic education services to citizens and members of the police force. The characteristics of all the NRA's member associations are shown in Table 4.1.

The NRA has several main functions. It brings together and represents the demands of its member associations to the local government and donors. It provides services for its member associations, such as training, advice on their constitution, mediation with potential donors, technical agricultural assistance and monitoring of the associations' credit activity.

The associations of small farmers in the NRA are all membership based: that is, their activities are directed at the needs and interests of their members (Chen et al., 2007). These activities revolve around providing agricultural services to the members – microcredit for agricultural inputs, common facilities for crop storage, management of water pumps for irrigation. Most of these activities are supported through credit schemes funded by external donors – NGOs, international development agencies or banks.

By contrast, two of the three civic associations in the NRA (ODSC and ADSAC – see Table 4.1 for details) were founded by people from the

TABLE 4.1 Summary of the associations

Name	Created	History and membership
1. Associação para a Promoção das Comunidades Rurais (APROCOR – Association for the Promotion of Rural Communities)	1997	First association in Dombe Grande, created by cattle owners under the name ACTG; became APROCOR in 1999. Five members.
2. Organização para o Desenvolvimento Social (ODSC – Organization for Social Development)	1997	Created as a community commission by people from Forno neighbourhood. Twenty members.
3. Associação para o Desenvolvimento Social e Ambiente Comunitário (ADSAC – Association for Social Development and the Community Environment)	1998	Created by teachers, public officials and residents of Dombe Grande. Thirty members.
4. Associação para o Desenvolvimento da Cultura Mudombe (ADCM – Association for Mudombe Cultural Development)	1999	Created by a group of Mundombe people. Seven members.
5. Associação dos Camponeses para o Desenvolvimento Social (ACDS – Association of Small Farmers for Social Development)	1997	Began as ACDSD, a community commission of people displaced by the war, led by a government official. Divided into three in 1999, forming ACDS, ADPC and AMCDS (see below). Fifty members.
6. Associação para o Desenvolvimento Social das Comunidades Rurais (ADSCOR – Association for Social Development of Rural Communities)	1999	Created by former public officials and others from Dombe Grande who want to work for themselves. Membership fallen from twenty-four to seven.
7. Associação para o Desenvolvimento das Comunidades do Luaxo (ADCL – Association for Development of Luaxo Communities)	1999	Created by displaced people living in Luaxo village, originally named ACDD and involving 250 families. After the war ended, and many returned to their areas of origin, ADCL emerged from those remaining in Luaxo and some residents. Thirty-five families.
8. Associação dos Camponeses Organizados do Luaxo (ACOL – Association of Luaxo Organized Small Farmers)	2004	Created by small farmers from Luaxo. Twenty-five families.

Activities	Support
As ACTG: advocacy for cattle owners; as APROCOR: agricultural and livestock production; small businesses	ADRA; Afrikagrupperna (Swedish NGO)
Microcredit; civic education; health and sanitation; promotion of local associations	ADRA; Angolan government; Ic-Net Jika (Japanese NGO); Fundación CEAR (Spanish NGO)
Civic education for citizens, public officials and police; training on associative issues for small farmers; sanitation; microcredit for members	ADRA; World Learning (American NGO); Afrikagrupperna; Sol Bank (private sector)
Cultural activities in schools; support for local cultural groups	ADRA, through its Onjila educational programme; Afrikagrupperna
Agricultural production; access to credit and markets; water-pump; management civic education	ADRA; Afrikagrupperna; Fundación CEAR; Sol Bank
Technical assistance to small charcoal producers; civic education; infrastructure for cattle vaccination	ADRA; NRA
Agricultural support; microcredit; water-pump management	ADRA; Fundación CEAR
Microcredit; water-pump management; health and education mobilization	NRA; ADRA

TABLE 4.1 Summary of the associations (cont.)

Name	Created	History and membership
9. Associação para o Desenvolvimento dos Pequenos Camponeses (ADPC – Association for Development of Small Farmers)	2001	Emerged from ACDSD; currently led by people of the community. Twelve families.
10. Associação para o Desenvolvimento do Canto (ADC – Association for Canto Development)	2003	Created by micro-business oriented groups. Four members.
11. Associação para o Desenvolvimento dos Camponeses de Bandeira e Chingombo (ADCBC – Association for Development of Bandeira and Chingombo Small Farmers)	2004	Created by small farmers from Bandeira and Chingombo, displaced by war. Seventeen families.
12. Associação de Camponeses de Vilyambwill (ACV – Association of Vilyambwill Small Farmers)	2007	Created by people from Vilyambwill neighbourhood, influenced by ODSC and NRA. Twenty-five members.
13. Comissão de Professores do Luaxo (APD – Commission of Teachers of Luaxo)	2004	Created through the educational programme of ADRA to promote cultural activities in schools. Not active at the time of the research.
14. Associação das Mulheres Camponesas para o Desenvolvimento Social (AMCDS – Association of Women Small Farmers for Social Development)	2001	Women's group that emerged from the ACDSD. Not active at the time of the research.
15. Associação para o Desenvolvimento das Comunidades do Kuyu (ADCC – Association for Development of Kuyu Communities)	1998	Began as a Fishery Committee in Kuyu village, but was affected by conflict between government officials and associations and disappeared. It re-emerged in 2007 with new leadership and support from the NRA. Fourteen members.

Note: The Mundombe are the ethnic group that originally lived on the coast of Benguela province, who are now outnumbered by the Ovimbundu people who migrated in from the central highlands of Angola.

Activities	Support
Agricultural development; access to microcredit; water-pump management	ADRA; Afrikagrupperna; Fundación CEAR
Management of a maize mill	NRA, ODSC
Agricultural development; access to microcredit; water-pump management	NRA, Fundación CEAR
Agricultural development	NRA, IC-Net Jika
Exchange of experiences between teachers; improvement of extracurricular activities	ADRA, through Onjila educational programme
Agricultural development; access to microcredit	ADRA, NRA, Afrikagrupperna
Development of fishery activities in Kuyu	ADRA, NRA, IC-Net Jika

town of Dombe Grande. Their leaders have secondary education, and either worked (or continue to work) as civil servants or in the public sector. Their civic education activities, funded by a range of external donors, include work on human rights, elections, health and sanitation. The three civic organizations (the two mentioned above plus APROCOR – see Table 4.1) are founding members of the NRA, and one in particular (ODSC) has played a big role in encouraging the emergence and consolidation of new associations.

The membership of farmers' associations is increasing (unlike civic associations). Farmers' associations have shown an ability to improve the material well-being of their members through their production-related activities. This has had a visible impact on the lives of local communities and has boosted affiliation to these associations by other individuals and groups. For example, the membership of a group that provides credit to local farmers increased from twenty-five to forty-five members in three years; meanwhile, the membership of another group that provides supporting cultural activities in school services fell from thirty to just seven over the same period. Many rural communities operate in the context of great material vulnerability, and so improving their agricultural production capacity and their material well-being is one of their main objectives in coming together and forming associations. Associations operate as intermediates to help these communities gain access to technical expertise and credit to fund different agricultural inputs, tools and services that increase production.

The membership of most civic associations has been declining as they have been confronted with increasing difficulties in funding their activities. During the war, some of these small local associations were given funding to distribute food aid or to implement peace-building programmes. Today's development programmes in Angola require specific technical expertise, and these associations cannot offer that. As a result, they have less work, are less well funded and are unable to provide small subsidies to their members; declining membership is, therefore, linked to the inability of these associations to support the livelihood of their members.

There is evidence that both farmer and civic associations have contributed to an increase in the awareness of rights and self-esteem among their members. For example, a female member of a civic association that had supported her in claiming her house back from a powerful figure in Dombe Grande observed:

> One of the biggest achievements of my experience with the association

is to have become aware that I am somebody like any other person; that I am seen as a person as much as a police officer is; that I am considered as a person as much as a prominent person is. This means that I have the same status as somebody who holds a prominent position [in society]. My rights are similar to those of this other person. If there is something that goes against my dignity, I can place the complaint with an official entity that will respond to my concern.

What lies behind these and the other positive effects of associations? In the remainder of this section we trace the roots of the NRA, describing three distinct foundation phases against the background of Angola's turbulent recent history.

The emergence of an associative movement The emergence of many of the associations that constitute the NRA in Dombe Grande should be seen in the context of Angola's situation at the start of the 1990s, and the burgeoning number of associations that formed after the establishment of the 1992 Constitution. However, a major local factor in the origin of the Dombe Grande associations was the presence of Acção para o Desenvolvimento Rural e Ambiente (ADRA – Action for Rural Development and the Environment) in the area since 1993. Founded in 1991, soon after the end of Angola's one-party regime, ADRA began as a 'development NGO',[6] focusing its activities on rural areas and implementing programmes dealing with agriculture, credit, formal education and civic education. In 1993, it was called upon by the government to participate in the humanitarian effort in an area of Dombe Grande that had received, from the interior of the country, thousands of people who had been displaced or otherwise seriously affected by the war.

The work of ADRA in Dombe Grande can be divided into two significant periods. The first period began in 1993, when the organization embarked on food distribution in the village of Luaxo, some 10km from Dombe Grande town. The second period commenced in 1997, when the organization extended its activities to other villages of the *comuna*, including Dombe Grande town, and started working not only on humanitarian aid, but also on institutional development and on strengthening the capacity of local groups. It is during this second period that many other associations emerged and that the NRA was formed.

Between 1993 and 1997, even though ADRA was engaged in distributing food aid in Luaxo and its activity was founded upon humanitarian assistance, its intervention also brought in elements of community development and participation, based upon notions of community organization. One of the methods ADRA used to increase community participation was the creation of 'community commissions'. Made up of elected local leaders, one of the main purposes of these commissions was to establish a link between ADRA and the community receiving humanitarian aid. Some of these community commissions became the associations that later formed the NRA; others stopped functioning and never became associations. The quality of leadership was fundamental to the transformation of some of these commissions into associations.

Other associations that are part of the federation today and that were also very active in the creation of the NRA were founded independently of ADRA. They emerged at the end of the 1990s from initiatives by citizens of the town of Dombe Grande. Their leaders were better educated than the leaders of other groups, with some being teachers, activists from evangelical churches and civil servants. One was formed by a group of cattle owners seeking some protection against cattle stealing, which was rife in the *comuna* during the war.

So when ADRA started operating in the town of Dombe Grande in 1997, there were already groups of citizens who were willing to organize collective action and who had been engaged in public life, tackling common problems faced by the population of Dombe Grande – for example, improving the town's sanitation, better organizing sellers in the local market or talking about civic education in the *comuna*.

While ADRA strongly supported these community commissions and existing small civic groups, the organization's practice during its early years was described by one NRA leader, Antonio Cachilingo (in a 2007 interview), as 'quite controlling'. It issued many directives, but seldom shared responsibilities or decision-making power with communities. In addition, most of the community commissions it created were composed of powerful local figures. Although ADRA decided to start an institutional capacity-building project in Dombe Grande in 1997, its way of operating did not change much. Local leadership was not fully involved. This did nothing to encourage autonomy of the groups, and indeed led to conflicts between the leadership of the small associations and ADRA staff. It was only in 1999 that ADRA's way of operating really changed and it started to encourage the emergence of autonomous associations and, eventually, the NRA.

The foundation of the NRA ADRA's work was fundamental to the founding of the NRA in 2001. After 1999, ADRA directed its action towards institutional development and capacity building in Dombe Grande, placing the emphasis on, for example, training in project design and civic education. The organization was particularly successful in setting up evening discussions on such themes as associative issues, rights and the new political context in Angola. The discussions would bring members of the associations and ADRA staff together with ordinary citizens of Dombe Grande. In these spaces, participants shared experiences and discussed difficulties and ways forward. Furthermore, ADRA started funding small activities carried out by the groups, such as credit schemes for agricultural activities or small civic education interventions. ADRA also worked in an advisory capacity, supporting local groups in the formulation of their legal statutes, providing back-up on discussions with the state about its relationship with civil society and about legislation, and encouraging exchanges between local community commissions and other community groups outside the *comuna* of Dombe Grande.

In fact, this change in approach, the training sessions and the debates strongly encouraged the empowerment and autonomy of the groups. Initially, ADRA's main dialogue partner was the Associação para o Desenvolvimento Social e Ambiente Comunitário (ADSAC – Association for Social Development and the Community Environment), but later the dialogue was expanded to the collective of associations formed by ODSC, ACDS, APROCOR and ADCM.[7]

As we describe later, the new approach also helped to reduce the tension that existed between community groups and the local government officials who were also involved in training and debates. Some of these community groups became associations and developed strong relationships among themselves. It was then that the idea for the creation of the NRA emerged.

Two related factors seem to have driven the founding of the NRA by associations in 2001. One was the strong political tension experienced by local associations in the face of the controlling attitudes of government officials; the other was the withdrawal of ADRA from Dombe Grande in 2001 in the wake of the military insecurity that had been increasing in the *comuna* of Dombe Grande since the end of the 1990s.

Although the 1992 Constitution gave citizens the right to form associations, independent associations were still viewed with great suspicion by the government, where the legacy of the one-party system still lingered on. Even when they were not suspected of supporting UNITA, these associations were still perceived as a potential threat to the government, since, at a time of great political and military instability, they could point to the government's social failings and undermine its image both internally and externally. As a result, the government tried to control and put pressure on independent groups. Under this growing pressure from the state, local associations realized that they had to come together to resist the government's tendency to seek to control their activities.

Although ADRA did liaise with the groups to coordinate its withdrawal and the transfer of responsibilities, and although it continued to support them from its office in Benguela, the local associations in Dombe Grande felt they had been left high and dry – 'orphaned' – at a time of particularly strong political pressure and military instability. The NRA, then, came into being when its founders realized that they had to be united in order to gain more power and to survive; that by standing together they could boost their power to negotiate their demands and represent their interests with local government and external agents. After its formation in 2001, and stimulated by the end of the civil war in 2002, the NRA became the main player in working with the citizens of Dombe Grande, pushing discussion on associative issues and rights further, and expanding these debates into other areas. ADRA has continued to support the NRA, involving it in training activities, promoting exchanges with groups from other provinces, lobbying donors on the NRA's behalf and funding small activities.

We should make two observations about the process that led to the formation of the NRA. First, the associations were able to come together in order both to increase their power and to deal with the tensions arising from the local state institutions' threatening attitude – that is, these associations had understood the point of coming together in a larger network to fight for and defend their interests. Second, the reaction to the withdrawal of ADRA was primarily a feeling of loss and insecurity. While this could have discouraged these recently created associations, in point of fact ADRA's withdrawal from Dombe Grande prompted them to take control of the process.

Consolidation of the associative movement There are few CSOs in Dombe Grande: apart from the NRA and its member associations, there are a few church-based groups working on civic education and health education. The NRA and its most active members have been instrumental in the emergence of several new associations and, therefore, in the expansion of the associative movement. The local and municipal governments and leaders of churches recognize the relevance of the NRA and its associations in promoting better social and economic conditions for poor people and in disseminating the idea of citizens' rights.

Some of these associations emerged with the direct or indirect support of ADRA. Others, created after 2001, were the result of the direct action of the NRA. Two of these – a teachers' association and a women's association – failed to survive.[8] Table 4.1 shows that, after 2003, the number of local associations in the *comuna* of Dombe Grande doubled – including in areas where ADRA had been working since the early days of its intervention in the area, such as Luaxo.

As the number of associations grew and the NRA became stronger, it developed its capacity to establish contacts and relationships outside the limits of Dombe Grande and to expand its network. For example, the NRA currently serves as the intermediary for its member associations in contacting and establishing relationships with international NGOs and development agencies to mobilize financial resources and fund specific activities. The NRA has been able to mobilize the support of several donors,[9] and to negotiate loans with banks. Most of these institutions support the credit schemes of farmers' associations, which constitute an important support to members' livelihoods and have a significant impact in terms of citizenship, since they allow for increased self-esteem and capacity to intervene in public life.

Recently, the NRA has also been able to develop relationships with civic organizations from other municipalities in the province – in particular in Benguela, the provincial capital. At present, the NRA is the representative of community associations in the provincial coordination group of CSOs that is responsible for organizing an annual CSO conference, the first time that community associations have engaged in this space. The federation has also participated in provincial and national meetings of communities that have been organized annually by ADRA. These meetings aim to bring the communities of different provinces together to discuss their interests with decision-makers and partners.

The NRA's relationship with the local administration

As was mentioned above, one of the NRA's main functions is to draw together the demands of its member associations and set them before the local administration for discussion. The possibility of dialogue between the local government and representatives of local associations is particularly significant, given Angola's long history of authoritarian governance and the great distance between state institutions and citizens. In the particular case of Dombe Grande, the NRA's presence at meetings with the local government represents a major achievement, as the relationship between the local administration and local associations was very tense between 1997 and 2000.

Associations and local government: an evolving relationship The relationship between associations and local government has evolved gradually, from tension and conflict between government officials and some associations at the end of the 1990s, towards current greater dialogue and cooperation. This is a result of several factors. First, at the end of the 1990s, the Angolan state started a decentralization process that effectively reached the lower levels of state administration only a few years later. Second, political changes in Angola at the beginning of the 1990s allowed for the emergence of discourses on greater participation and engagement with the state by citizens, and this influenced not only certain sectors of society but the state administration as well. Third, the end of the civil war in 2002 contributed to a reduction in government suspicion of independent social groups. Finally, whereas ADRA worked exclusively with local groups outside the state administration for some years, in 1997 the organization developed a new approach to its intervention in Dombe Grande. This greater focus on institutional development involved both associations and government officials.

As members of the government in Dombe Grande began to be involved in debates and training related to new legislation, rights and civic education, their attitude towards local associations started to change. Direct support from ADRA to local government had a meaningful impact on the administration, both in its work and in its own perceptions of its role, as was pointed out by Francisco Nicodemos, the vice-administrator of Dombe Grande, in a 2007 interview:

> Currently, the work of the Administration is much better. There is another dynamic, more interaction with others. In that time [the socialist period] everything was centralized. The party gave the rules for everything, the laws, the destiny of the country – I was also part of this system, but I can make this analysis now.

He continued by discussing the local administration's perception of local associations and their public role in Dombe Grande:

> In the past there was no clarity in relation to the work of the associations. The relationship was not good. Currently, the Administration recognizes the importance of the associations to the communities. They are involved in actions against poverty and this is a goal of the government. We have the common task of improving the lives of communities.

However, if the vice-administrator's statement acknowledges the importance of local associations in Dombe Grande, it also seems to indicate that this particular state official might view local associations as being limited to 'fighting against poverty', and that they could not possibly have any political impact. One of the results of an improved relationship between the local administration and the NRA was that in 2005 the NRA was invited to participate in the Administration Council,[10] and, in 2007, to be part of a more participatory space – the Conselho de Auscultação e Concertação Social (CACS – Council for Social Consultation and Dialogue),[11] in which both the local administration and representatives of civil society participate.

The growing participation of the NRA in the discussion of issues related to the social and economic life of Dombe Grande has been noted and welcomed by the organization, as Cristiano Luís, the NRA's president, observed in a 2007 interview:

> We [the NRA associations] take the issues to the [Administration] Council and discuss possible solutions. We have some examples that show that we are having influence in some ways, such as in moving the town's slaughterhouse, criminality in town, illegal selling of medicines in Canto's health centre, the attitude of one local leader who was against the community.

While the participation of non-government members in the consultative councils of the local administration in Dombe Grande used to require an official invitation, this changed in 2007 with the creation of CACS, which, for the first time, provides an institutionalized space and a set of regulations for the participation of CSOs in the government's decision-making processes at the provincial, municipal and communal levels. According to the law, CACS aims to provide support to different levels of the administration in discussions and decision-making processes concerned with political, social and economic measures. The law clearly states that representatives of civil society are to be part of those forums, and that CACS should be consulted before the approval of local development programmes, action plans or reports related to these plans.

In November 2007, representatives of the NRA, churches, peasant associations and traditional authorities formally started to participate in CACS in Dombe Grande. As in other places in the country, the representatives were still 'invited' to participate by the local government, as the criteria for, and mechanisms of, representation in CACS had not yet been clearly defined.[12]

So far, what CACS in Dombe Grande has shown is that it can function at the local level in a more open way than at higher levels of state administration. In Dombe Grande, as a result of the *plano de desenvolvimento local* (PDL – local development plan) process described below, as well as of the greater proximity achieved between local associations and the local administration, discussions that take place in local councils result in debate, dialogue and negotiation between these different entities. At the municipal and provincial levels, however, although members of civil society do participate in CACS, government officials tend to regard these forums merely as places for sharing information with civil society. There is much less room for debate and negotiation. Given the processes that both associations and the local administration have gone through in Dombe Grande since the mid-1990s, participatory governance is not a novelty for them.

However, while the participation of local associations in the processes of local government may have increased, the Dombe Grande administration is lacking the financial, human and material capacity to provide any real response to the citizen demands that the NRA brings before the local councils. The centralization of state administration still presents a significant obstacle to achieving effective participation in local governance. Although, at the local level, government and local associations are interacting, discussing and thinking together how to improve local social and economic conditions, at present local governments have neither any real power to take decisions nor the financial capacity to implement any decision that is taken as a result of citizens' requests. As a study of the Angolan decentralization process has noted, while considerable success has been achieved in promoting dialogue between active citizens and local government structures – which, in the context of Angola, is already an achievement – progress on providing services tends to be slower, as decision-making is still centralized and financial decentralization has yet to be completed (JMJ International, 2006). In Dombe Grande, this decision-making process was linked to the formulation of a PDL. The PDL process is a good example of increased state–citizen engagement at the local level, but it also illustrates how this increased participation in public life may not result in effective improvements to public services or to the material well-being of citizens.

The local development plan: greater participation but no implementation ADRA began to discuss a PDL for Dombe Grande with the local administration and associations in 2001. However, the initiative was postponed until 2003 because of the ongoing military conflict. Similar processes were happening in other parts of Angola, where NGOs, supported by donor agencies, were attempting to foster participatory governance – encouraging engagement between state institutions and citizens, and improving the capacity (material, information and knowledge) of local governments.

The PDL in Dombe Grande mobilized the local government, the NRA and its member associations, church-based organizations, the private sector and other local actors. The process took nearly three months; it was based on participatory methodologies and involved several collective sessions. The first step was to carry out a social and economic diagnostic analysis of the situation in Dombe Grande; only then could the planning process start. This process was never finalized, however, since there was no follow-up at the municipal and provincial level to settle the budget. In fact, neither the municipality of Baía Farta, to which the *comuna* of Dombe Grande reports, nor the provincial government participated in the process. This was a strategic mistake by ADRA and probably one of the reasons for the material failure of the overall attempt. ADRA's mistake was partly the result of an illusion (shared by many development organizations at the time) that it could be engaged in development planning and implementation processes at the local level without involving higher levels of state administration. Many NGOs thought they would be able to mobilize the resources they needed to design and implement these local development plans from other NGOs or from international development agencies.

Opinions as to what the PDL was and what it achieved vary across different levels of state administration and among local actors. Although the process was stimulated by ADRA, it apparently responded to local demands for, and expectations of, participation in public life by members of local associations; moreover, it met the expectations of local government that it would assume a more active and meaningful role. Indeed, the PDL process allowed the local administration to feel empowered, and enabled it to imagine how much more effective and meaningful its role could be if it had more resources and greater administrative autonomy. For the administration of Dombe Grande, the PDL was the best experience of planning carried out in the *comuna*. There is considerable regret that the process could not be pursued. As Vice-Administrator Nicodemos said in his 2007 interview:

> The PDL had great importance for the *comuna*, and some actions that are currently being implemented stemmed from that plan, such as the extension of the school network and the works on the Coporolo River. We did not have the capacity here in the Administration to do the budget for the plan ... there are people in the provincial government who still think that the budget is a 'state secret'. There is still a backward

> mentality in many of our attitudes, but I agree that this is a stage we are going through, and that we will overcome this phase. And I agree that the PDL will be a central point of our action here at the *comuna* level.

As a planning official working in the provincial government pointed out, the PDL should be perceived as a good experience. But in 2003, it was 'ahead of its time', as there was not yet a legal framework to support it: the Decentralization Act that created the CACS was promulgated only in 2007. Four years earlier, the very different political context – still tense after the recent end of the war – was not conducive to supporting and developing this kind of experience.

As a result, if the PDL constituted a learning experience for civil society groups on the one hand, and for local government on the other, it also revealed the difficulty of providing local governance without effective coordination with – and buy-in by – higher levels of government. Given the difficulties inherent in moving from decision-making to implementation at the local level, the success of such processes as the PDL necessitates serious engagement by higher levels of government.

Concluding remarks

This chapter describes the emergence and consolidation of local associations in Dombe Grande, a small town in Angola. It shows that the role of ADRA, an Angolan NGO working on rural development and on strengthening local associations and the autonomy of small farmers, was fundamental to the process. ADRA directly supported the formation of the first farmers' associations in Dombe Grande, as well as the foundation of the NRA. It also provided considerable support to most of the civic associations in the federation, in the form of information, training, access to wider networks and access to funding. Although the emergence of the NRA was supported by ADRA, the federation nowadays is quite autonomous and is expanding its capacity and influence. The NRA is providing direct support for the creation of other associations, in particular farmers' associations. It has also been able to reach out, expand its contacts and access wider social and political networks, including some outside Dombe Grande. It has established direct contacts with international organizations and banks, and has secured funding for the activities of its member associations.

Some authors challenge the role of CSOs in the democratization processes in Africa (Olukoshi, 2006). It is true that these questions arise, in many instances, from a conflation of CSOs and NGOs providing services. Our case study shows, however, that the political and social processes, and the role played by NGOs like ADRA and associations like the NRA, are complex and may have mixed (but still interesting) results in terms of democratization.

The social and political impact of the NRA in Dombe Grande is manifold. First, the mobilization of the NRA and its associations, especially the membership-based farmers' associations, has contributed to an improvement in their members' material well-being. More than the civic associations, the farmers' associations have been able to provide solutions to the economic and social problems faced by their members. However, we also describe how the action of the NRA and its civic associations has helped to improve citizens' awareness of their rights, increase their self-esteem and develop their notions of citizenship.

We have also shown how local associations and the NRA have contributed to a significant change in relations with the local state administration – from confrontation and open conflict at the end of the 1990s to a more collaborative relationship, culminating in the NRA being invited to participate in local councils in 2005.

However, while today there are spaces in Dombe Grande for debate and dialogue between the local administration and representatives of the town's citizens, the opportunities for implementing decisions and improving public service delivery are still limited. Decisions on how to use financial resources are still centralized at the provincial level, and the real capacity for local administration to provide public social and economic goods is small. Support from the higher levels of state administration, which may have the resources to boost service delivery, is not common.

Furthermore, even if more participatory processes of governance are under way in such places as Dombe Grande, and even if stronger citizen participation is having an impact at the lower levels of state administration, centralization of governance is still strong at the higher levels, and control over major decisions still rests with the provincial government. So, although the state administration of Angola has embarked upon a decentralization process that should lead to increased levels of participation in local governance and to local state administrations having a greater capacity to deliver public services, the results of the process are yet to be seen at those levels of administration where such results would have the greatest impact, in terms of both participatory governance and public service delivery.

Going back to our earlier discussion of the impact of associations on democracy, it would seem that the NRA and its associations have played the empowering and educative role highlighted by participatory democracy theorists (Pateman, 2003) and to have had a significant impact on the exercise of a more active citizenship in Dombe Grande (Houtzager et al., 2007). However, the capacity of these local associations to influence the broader democratization process and public policies, and to improve public service delivery effectively, may be limited.

Although the relationship between the administration and local associations has certainly improved, it is possible that the state may wish to circumscribe local associations' activities, restricting them to just the provision of social and economic services. While local associations may be acclaimed when they support the state in providing social services, their demands for rights and state accountability might not be quite so welcome.

Moreover, the broader political context is one etched by a long history of state centralization, a major power imbalance between state and society, a great fragility on the part of state institutions and a total absence of society in decision-making processes. Consequently, although the achievements of the NRA and its associations should by no means be disregarded, more sweeping changes in policy and democratization in Angola will require a combination of citizen mobilization, democratic reforms and a firm commitment by the Angolan state across the whole range of administrative levels.

Notes

1 Angola is divided into provinces, municipalities, communes and villages. Dombe Grande is a commune in Baía Farta municipality of Benguela province. It has a population of 85,000, mostly made up of people from the Ovimbundu ethnic group.

2 According to Freedom House (www.freedomhouse.org), by 2003 some 121 of the 192 states of the world were considered formal democracies.

3 During the 1980s, Angola was invaded several times by the apartheid regime ruling South Africa.

4 Other social indicators have also remained unchanged since the end of the war: the infant mortality rate has been 154 per 1,000 since 2004; average life expectancy at birth is 41.7 years, compared to 40.7 in 2004; the rate of schooling is 25.6 per cent, compared to 26 per cent in 2004 (Centro de Estudos e Investigação Científica, 2007).

5 The Gini coefficient is a parameter used to measure inequality of income distribution. The coefficient varies from 0 to 1. The closer the Gini coefficient is to 0, the lower the income inequality in a country, i.e. the better the income distribution. By contrast, the closer the coefficient is to 1, the higher the concentration of income in a country.

6 By saying that ADRA is a 'development NGO', we wish to differentiate the organization from the category of 'classic NGO' proposed by Chabal (2008). Although

ADRA is mostly funded by external donors, the organization has clearly developed a particular social and political project.

7 See Table 4.1 for more information about these groups, including their full names.

8 Table 4.1 also shows that, during the years 2000 and 2001, when military and political turmoil was at its height, no associations were created.

9 In particular a Japanese NGO, Ic-Net Jika, and a Spanish NGO, Fundación CEAR.

10 Since 1999, the Law 17/99 has allowed for 'invited' participation by independent associations in local consultative councils.

11 Created by the Decentralization Act 02/07 of 3 January 2007.

12 There is no clear indication of how these groups should be chosen or elected, which has led to debate within civil society about representation in these spaces.

PART TWO

Social movements: contesting political authority and building state responsiveness

5 • The Indigenous Peoples' Movement, 'forest citizenship' and struggles over health services in Acre, Brazil

ALEX SHANKLAND[1]

Introduction

For marginalized minorities, democracy brings dilemmas. In particular, it brings dilemmas of engagement with the democratic state, which is expected both to uphold the rights of minorities and to implement the will of the majority. Engagement through elections – the standard arena of democratic politics – is hampered by the small share of the total vote that minorities can muster, so that, if they are to have any success, alliances will be needed. Such alliances may depend on minorities framing their demands and identities in ways that dilute or contradict the cohesion of their own mobilizations (Ramos, 2002).

Other engagements with the state bring their own dilemmas. Participation as self-provision or co-production of outsourced state services – the mode of engagement favoured by neoliberal approaches – may divert the energy mobilized by rights-claiming strategies into management, and muddy once-clear accountability relations (Dagnino, 2008). Participation as the exercise of voice in shaping public policy – the mode of engagement favoured by deliberative approaches to democracy – may require minorities to frame their arguments in ways that devalue their own discursive logics and to acquiesce in notions of citizenship that tend to reject their rights claims as special pleading (Williams, 1998; Young, 2000). Given these tensions, it is unsurprising that minorities often choose to avoid engagement with state-sponsored participatory arenas, preferring a path of strategic non-participation (von Lieres, 2006; Robins et al., 2008).

This chapter draws on the experience of the indigenous peoples of Acre State in the Brazilian Amazon in dealing with these tensions over the two decades since Brazil's return to full democracy, symbolized by the promulgation of the 1988 Constitution. This has been heralded as inaugurating a new era of unparalleled democratic deepening and as giving constitutional as well as moral legitimacy to the rights struggles of social movements. Of these, one of the most prominent during the 1987–88 Constituent Assembly was the Movimento Indígena, or

Indigenous Peoples' Movement, which emerged from modest beginnings in a series of local assemblies sponsored by the Catholic Church to promote some of the most visible and effective mobilizations for constitutional rights recognition (Athias, 2007).

Other successful mobilizations in this period, such as that of the Movimento pela Reforma Sanitária (Movement for Health Reform), evoked an inclusionary notion of democratization by seeking the recognition of universal rights – such as the right to health – on the basis of equal treatment for all Brazilian citizens (Cornwall and Shankland, 2008). The Movimento Indígena, by contrast, campaigned for the right to difference, securing constitutional recognition of indigenous peoples' 'social organization, customs, languages, beliefs and traditions' (Brazil, 1988: 136, my translation). In the process, it evoked a transformative notion of democratization – one whose underlying logic implied a transformation in the identity of Brazil itself, from a unitary society where homogeneity was to be pursued by state policies of forced 'acculturation' and absorption of ethnic minorities, to a pluriethnic polity where the state's task was to mediate between the claims of multiple Brazilian cultures (Duprat, 2002).

In the period after the promulgation of the 1988 Constitution, the underlying tension between universality and difference was complicated further by the rise of neoliberal approaches that sought to turn civil society organizations from vehicles for rights-claiming into implementation partners for targeted delivery of outsourced public services. These tensions contributed to the fragmentation of the national Movimento Indígena. Across Brazil, regional branches of the Movimento Indígena established different organizational forms and followed different pathways of engagement, as new alliances, enmities and opportunities emerged from democratic struggles at the federal, state and municipal levels.

This chapter seeks to explore these issues by focusing on movement dynamics in Acre State over a period of some eight years after 1999, when a new state government took office with a pro-indigenous agenda and when changes in federal government policy led to widespread outsourcing of indigenous health services. This period saw the focus of the Acre Movimento Indígena shift from an emphasis on rights-claiming mobilization outside the state to direct participation in the management of outsourced government health services – and then back again. The chapter explores the complex and sometimes contradictory strategies and tactics that representatives of Acre's Indigenous Peoples' Movement have deployed in response to the dilemmas of engagement with the state.

This exploration draws on the findings of an action-research project undertaken between 2005 and 2008 with the health rights non-governmental organization (NGO) Associação Saúde Sem Limites (SSL – Brazilian Health Unlimited Association), which began when the SSL was approached by several indigenous leaders who were seeking help in dealing with the apparently disastrous consequences of their foray into health service management. The project aimed to facilitate a process of critical reflection among representatives of Acre's Indigenous Peoples' Movement on their experiences of engaging with the state on health policy and services, with a view to mapping out strategies for future action.[2]

In keeping with the broader purposes of this book, this chapter asks what democratic outcomes flowed from the different forms of engagement pursued by the Movimento Indígena in Acre. In particular, it explores the possible trade-offs between different types of democratic outcome: between recognition and redistribution, and between inclusion and transformation (Habermas et al., 1998; Young, 2000; Fraser and Honneth, 2003).

Finally, it interrogates these trade-offs to see whether they can yield more broadly relevant insights into the dilemmas that minorities must confront as they engage with the state in mobilizing for democracy.

Indigenous peoples, the state and 'forest citizenship' in Acre

Acre lies in the far west of Brazil, and the indigenous population of the state, currently numbering approximately 12,000, accounts for less than 3 per cent of its inhabitants (Ricardo and Ricardo, 2006: 570).[3] Acre's indigenous citizens belong to fourteen different ethnic groups. While these groups have different levels of contact and familiarity with non-indigenous society, all were directly affected by the occupation of Acre during the rubber boom of the late nineteenth and early twentieth centuries – a time of intense conflict between the incoming *seringueiros* (rubber tappers) and the existing indigenous population. To this day, inter-ethnic relations in Acre are marked by the legacy of the rubber boom, as some indigenous groups allied themselves to the 'rubber barons', while others fled or resisted violently and suffered extensive processes of massacre, displacement and enslavement (Hemming, 1987).

Despite this legacy of conflict, in the late 1980s *seringueiro* leaders fighting for the preservation of the rubber-rich rainforest declared a 'Forest Peoples' Alliance' with Acre's indigenous peoples. The threat posed by the aggressive expansion of cattle-ranching into Acre, along new roads built by the federal government with funding from the World Bank and the Inter-American Development Bank, helped to create the sense of a forest-dwellers' common cause. This was articulated by the *seringueiro* leader Chico Mendes, who became an internationally revered 'green martyr' when he was murdered by ranchers in December 1988. However, while several indigenous leaders publicly supported the Alliance, its foundation in a forest-dweller identity shared by *seringueiros* and indigenous people alike was far from unproblematic. A key issue was the fact that there was no unanimity among the indigenous leaders as to where their 'ethnic interests' (Ramos, 2002) lay with regard to the Alliance. Before long, disputes over the benefits and risks of associating the indigenous cause with that of the *seringueiros* had become one of the main axes of tension within the Acre Movimento Indígena. This reflected both the movement's internal cleavages and the ideological differences among its non-indigenous allies.

In the Juruá Valley region of Western Acre, which lies furthest from the state capital Rio Branco, indigenous groups had a history of joint grassroots mobilization with non-indigenous *seringueiros* against a common oppressor, the 'rubber barons'. As these groups began to form their own movement organizations in the 1980s and early 1990s, they were supported by Brazilian NGOs and academics who also worked with the *seringueiro* movement, and by international groups whose green agenda was particularly receptive to the framing of a 'forest peoples' identity. In Eastern Acre, by contrast, the indigenous groups had become disengaged from their non-indigenous *seringueiro* neighbours as the rubber estates declined, and never formed grassroots alliances with them. Here, indigenous groups came into regular contact with urban society earlier than in the Juruá, and began to send their young people to school in Rio Branco. This produced a generation of young, educated leaders who were able to establish links with pro-indigenous NGOs and the national Movimento Indígena, culminating in the creation of the União das Nações Indígenas do Acre e Sul do Amazonas (UNI – Union of Indigenous Nations of Acre and Southern Amazonas), established in 1986 as the first regional branch of Brazil's national indigenous movement organization (Iglesias and Valle de Aquino, 2005a: 152).

Although the UNI was initially supported by the same activists who had been helping the indigenous communities of the Juruá to link up with the *seringueiro* movement, its leadership swiftly moved into the orbit of the Catholic Church's Conselho Indigenista Missionário (CIMI – Indigenous Missionary Council), which was ideologically opposed to alliances that diluted the distinctiveness of rights claims based on an exclusive indigenous identity. Under its influence, the UNI moved away from both the Acre-based Forest Peoples' Alliance and the national Movimento Indígena leadership, which it accused of lacking legitimacy and of leading the indigenous cause astray through ill-chosen alliances. Eschewing the green global networks of the pro-Forest Peoples' Alliance groups in the Juruá Valley, the UNI instead developed links with international NGOs espousing rights and poverty agendas. The UNI's leaders also used their strategic base in the state capital to capture significant amounts of Brazilian government and multilateral funding.

For a decade after the promulgation of the 1988 Constitution, Acre was ruled by a succession of state governments whose attitudes to indigenous peoples ranged from indifference to outright hostility. In this context, both the *seringueiros* and the Movimento Indígena gave priority to engaging with the federal government (where allies had taken up senior positions) and with the NGO networks and global development actors who had become increasingly interested in Acre in the wake of the international outcry over the murder of Chico Mendes. Then, in 1998, the state elections were won by a coalition led by Jorge Viana of the Partido dos Trabalhadores (PT – Workers' Party). Though he came from one of Acre's most traditional political clans, as a forester in the early 1980s Viana had worked with Chico Mendes, and had subsequently helped *seringueiro* union leaders to establish the PT in Acre. One of his key advisers, Antônio Alves, devised a campaign strategy based on reaffirming Acre's identity as a 'forest society', and went on to develop a concept that became the rallying cry for a decade of PT-led administrations in the state: *florestania*.

The notion of *florestania* – derived from combining *floresta* (forest) and *cidadania* (citizenship) – was conceived as an explicit challenge to the universalizing version of citizenship that had come to dominate social policy debate and progressive political discourse in Brazil since 1988. As Alves himself pointed out, the undeniably urban origins of *cidadania* are indicated by the fact that it is cognate with *cidade*, meaning town or city (Alves, 2007: 1). *Florestania* was intended to represent citizenship as imagined by the peoples of the forest, rather than by the peoples of the city.

The term was enthusiastically adopted by Viana's two administrations. By the time of his second period in office, it had become the key signifier of Viana's claims to be implementing a radical new policy agenda centred on the rights and interests of the 'forest peoples' – despite increasing concern that his re-elected government was, in fact, giving greater priority to road building than to forest preservation. It was maintained by Viana's successor, Binho Marques, who took office in 2007 at the head of Acre's third successive PT-led administration.

These claims of a new agenda were not aimed solely at the 'forest peoples': they were as important for the external funders that the state government was wooing, as it sought to finance its ambitious infrastructure development plans. The state government's claim to be promoting *florestania* was likewise important to the sizeable number of urban voters who sympathized politically with the forest-dwellers' cause and the distinctive Acrean identity that it evoked. The earlier campaign of non-violent resistance to deforestation had also been seen as a manifestation of this same spirit – part of a common struggle to defend the state against cattle-ranching incomers, whose advance threatened to destroy Acre's traditional way of life.

For these claims to remain convincing, the ideas that had inspired the creation of the Forest Peoples' Alliance needed to be kept alive, and Acre's indigenous groups needed to be seen to be 'on board'. This imperative gave the Acre Movimento Indígena a strategic political importance that was out of all proportion to the small number of voters that its leaders could claim to represent. During the three PT-led administrations, the Acre State government has made strenuous efforts to demonstrate its recognition of indigenous peoples' distinctive identity and its commitment to their rights by courting Movimento Indígena leaders. This has served as a useful legitimator of government claims to be promoting a distinctive and innovative agenda – one that came both as a break with Acre's own anti-indigenous, environmentally irresponsible past and as a fresh contribution to political debate at the national level in Brazil, where several members of the Acre PT became prominent after the election of Luiz Inácio Lula da Silva to the presidency in 2002.

These efforts were reflected in several government initiatives, and Inter-American Development Bank and Brazilian National Development Bank loans to the Acre State government for road building were made available for micro-projects proposed by indigenous and *seringueiro* community associations, under schemes labelled 'support for traditional peoples' and 'promotion of *florestania*' (Iglesias and Valle de Aquino, 2005b: 126). Following criticism that dialogue with the Movimento Indígena had been too sporadic during Viana's first term in office, at the start of his second term in 2003 he established the Secretaria de Estado dos Povos Indígenas (SEPI – State Secretariat for Indigenous Peoples), which was subsequently transformed into a special advisory department of the Governor's Office. This combination of initiatives represented a more sustained and extensive effort to demonstrate the inclusion of indigenous peoples than any previous state government had mustered, and for external and internal audiences alike it seemed to give substance to the claims of the Viana and Marques administrations in Acre that theirs were truly 'governments of the forest'.

The creation of posts for indigenous leaders inside the state government and the growing availability of state funding led the Acre Movimento Indígena to become increasingly enmeshed with the Viana and Marques administrations – and thereby with their internal party politics. The two largest parties in the ruling coalition were the PT and the Partido Comunista do Brasil (PCdoB – Communist Party of Brazil), whose tactical cooperation on the government benches of the Acre State Legislative Assembly belied an intense strategic rivalry. With an eye to bolstering their credentials as authentic 'friends of the forest peoples', both parties had been recruiting indigenous leaders since before Viana's first election. As a result, the existing ethnic, historical, regional and ideological cleavages within the Movimento Indígena were overlaid by a further layer of inter-party tension.

Broadly speaking (with some exceptions), leaders from the Juruá Valley with a history of backing the Forest Peoples' Alliance tended to support the PT, while leaders from Eastern Acre with a history of supporting the UNI leadership were more likely to belong to the PCdoB. The PT supporters tended to occupy the more senior posts made available to indigenous leaders within the state government apparatus. This was perceived as a threat by their rivals among the PCdoB supporters, who saw the growing hegemony of *florestania* as a trend that weakened the distinctively indigenous identity of the movement and risked reducing it to total dependence on the state government. They sought to respond by consolidating their hold on the key positions within the UNI, leading the state-level Movimento Indígena organization to develop what Iglesias and Valle de Aquino describe as a 'symbiotic relationship' with the PCdoB (2005a: 164). In order to guarantee some autonomy in relation to the state government, they strengthened their relationships with the Acre offices of those federal government agencies over which the national-level PCdoB had some influence. One of the most important of these was Fundação Nacional de Saúde (FUNASA – National Health Foundation), the agency responsible for health services for indigenous peoples. The intersection of conflicting party interests and divergent views on whether it was the pursuit of inclusion or of autonomy that best served the strategic interests of the state's indigenous peoples turned out to be critically important in the health sector, which was to become a key political battleground and ultimately the site of the disintegration of the Acre Movimento Indígena.

UNI, FUNASA and the outsourcing of indigenous health services

In 1999, an alliance of Movimento Indígena activists and health reformers succeeded in pushing through a law mandating the creation of an 'indigenous health sub-system' of the national Sistema Único de Saúde (SUS – Unified Health System) that had been created nine years earlier to implement the constitutional vision of universal health rights. Their argument was that this universal system did not respond adequately to indigenous peoples' right to difference, since it recognized neither their territories (which often extended across the state and municipal boundaries used to organize the SUS) nor their specific cultural practices and understandings of health and disease. The law ordained that the 'sub-system' should be organized around *distritos sanitários especiais indígenas* (DSEIs – special indigenous health districts) and should respect the cultural differences of indigenous peoples. When FUNASA, an executive agency of the Ministry of Health with a deeply bureaucratic culture, was given responsibility for managing the DSEIs, it found it lacked both the skills and the staff to deliver services directly. Instead, it tried to outsource management of the DSEIs to an assortment of civil society organizations and other groups. These included not only NGOs, university departments and missionary groups, but also indigenous peoples' organizations themselves. One of the first Movimento Indígena organizations to sign an outsourcing contract with FUNASA was the UNI in Acre. During the 1990s, the UNI had acquired a reputation as a pioneer among regional indigenous organizations in Brazil for its engagement in health policy, both through institutionalized participation and through direct provision of primary care services, delivered by village health workers trained by the group of health professionals who would later set up the SSL. This experience of substituting for the provision of state services was not without its problems, but it was broadly successful and bolstered the UNI's legitimacy with grassroots constituencies in regions – such as the Juruá Valley – where its Rio Branco-based and PCdoB-affiliated leadership had limited support. It also gave the UNI the credentials to be included by FUNASA on the list of possible partners for the federal indigenous health service outsourcing programme.

In October 1999, the UNI signed management contracts with FUNASA for the two DSEIs covering Acre and its neighbouring region of Southern Amazonas. However, under UNI management, the two DSEIs performed poorly, having widespread staff-retention problems and difficulty in maintaining immunization schedules and community health worker training programmes. Significantly, there were widespread indigenous complaints of insensitive and even racist behaviour among health staff hired by the DSEIs in Acre, despite the fact that their services were under the nominal responsibility of a Movimento Indígena organization and guided by a national policy that emphasized the importance of differentiated care, indigenous participation and intercultural working practices (FUNASA, 2002). This undermined the validity of claims by the UNI leadership that its assertive approach to management of the DSEIs –which frequently included overruling service delivery plans developed by the non-indigenous health staff and reallocating funds according to political rather than technical criteria – was necessary to maintain the organization's autonomy, safeguard the health and cultural rights of its indigenous constituents and prevent the service from being run along lines arbitrarily established by non-indigenous people.

As a social movement organization geared to mobilization and small-scale project management, the UNI lacked the systems and skills needed to deliver large-scale service provision effectively, and its leaders were reluctant to take advice from any 'white people' other than their political advisers in the CIMI and the PCdoB, few of whom had any significant management experience. It was clear by 2002 that management capacity was overstretched and that UNI leaders had no clear strategy for improving performance. Instead, they set out to shore up their position by buying political support with funds diverted from the health services. As well as strengthening their links with the PCdoB, which gave rise to subsequent accusations that DSEI funds had been used to support the party's election campaigns (Machado, 2005), they sought to secure the loyalty of grassroots leaders through clientelistic bargains and lavish displays of generosity. However, despite increasingly insistent rumours that the DSEIs' management problems were being exacerbated by corrupt practices, FUNASA was initially complacent, and transfers to the UNI continued until the last quarter of 2003.

In 2004, changes in the political control of FUNASA and a rising chorus of protest at the poor performance of the indigenous health sub-system as a whole led to a series of recentralization measures. Movimento Indígena organizations became the prime targets in a scapegoating process, and a wave of audits and interventions in outsourced providers led to most services being either reassumed by FUNASA or transferred to other NGOs or municipalities. During this process, the UNI's DSEI management contracts were suspended.

Crisis and rebirth in the Acre Movimento Indígena

The UNI's leaders reacted to the suspension by protesting that they were the victims of politically motivated persecution by FUNASA managers eager to divert attention from their own involvement in 'irregularities', and released a public statement insisting that:

> the indigenous communities see the UNI as their legitimate representative, which has unceasingly spoken out against the acts of violence and abuses of their rights to which indigenous peoples have been subjected, while at the same time struggling to transform these communities' demands into public policy. (UNI, 2004: 1; my translation)

Nonetheless, the DSEI management disaster led to a crisis of legitimacy for the UNI leadership. In July 2004, the UNI *conselho fiscal* (scrutiny committee) convened a special assembly of indigenous leaders to discuss responses to the crisis. This approved the suspension of the UNI coordinators and the appointment of a 'provisional coordinating body'. Its concluding statement ended with a ringing declaration that:

> the Movimento Indígena is not dead ... it is being reborn stronger than ever, learning from the mistakes of the past and preparing the way for us to achieve self-determination as indigenous peoples who are aware of the duties and obligations we carry to our people and to the State. (quoted in Iglesias and Valle de Aquino, 2005a: 166; my translation)

In early 2005, the provisional coordinating body conducted a series of community visits, meetings and seminars to discuss a radical reshaping of the structure of indigenous representation in Acre, aimed at promoting greater decentralization of power and at increasing the accountability of the indigenous leadership in Rio Branco. After a series of unfavourable civil and labour court judgments left the UNI facing a bill that could potentially have run to several hundred thousand dollars, the organization was formally declared bankrupt and was wound up. In May 2005, a general assembly of indigenous leaders created a successor organization, the Organização dos Povos Indígenas do Acre, Sul do Amazonas e Noroeste de Rondônia (OPIN – Organization of Indigenous Peoples of Acre, Southern Amazonas and North-western Rondônia) and elected new coordinators.

These events were funded by Acre's Governor Viana, who had become alarmed at the meltdown in the UNI and the subsequent acrimonious dispute between the PT-aligned provisional leadership of the organization and its PCdoB-affiliated predecessors, which was drawing in non-indigenous politicians from both sides and threatening to fracture the governing coalition's unity. The collapse of the UNI also risked leaving a vacuum that could disrupt Viana's strategy of establishing a range of reliable indigenous movement interlocutors, at a time when he was gradually extending state government influence into indigenous territories through SEPI. Viana was clearly hoping that the indigenous representatives who came to Rio Branco to choose the leaders of the UNI's successor organization would elect his allies.

In the event, however, the OPIN elections were won by candidates linked to the PCdoB and the former UNI leadership. As well as calling in all the favours they could to secure election, the victorious candidates argued forcefully for the need for the Movimento Indígena to maintain its autonomy in relation to the state government. Once elected, they positioned OPIN in opposition to the PT-led 'government of the forest', despite the fact that the flight of the international donors who had supported the UNI had left OPIN dependent on handouts from SEPI. Since 2005, most of the OPIN leadership group's energy has gone into strident attacks on the state government in general and on its favoured indigenous leaders in particular.

At the project's reflection workshops in 2006 and 2007, we encountered a paradoxical sense that the UNI's collapse had been both a shocking blow and an important stimulus for indigenous mobilization in Acre. Some groups – minorities within the minority – had found the regional Movimento Indígena organization unable or unwilling to act as a channel for their interests, but now began to emerge as social movement actors in their own right. The result was a shift away from regional-level representation of a generic indigenous identity towards mobilization around a wide variety of often overlapping local, ethnic, professional, age-related and gendered identities. Many workshop participants cited their own activities in these diverse mobilizations as evidence that 'the leaders in Rio Branco are not the Movimento Indígena – we are the Movimento Indígena'.

One of the most striking cases was that of Acre's indigenous women leaders, some of whom set up their own regional organization in 2005. So successful were they at raising funds for their women's health, craft marketing and grassroots organization projects that by July 2007, when I visited their new headquarters, I found OPIN's leaders occupying a small corner of it on sufferance. (They had been evicted from their own headquarters after failing to account for state funds received through SEPI, and had begged the use of a room from the women, who, just a few years before, had been a largely disregarded presence in a UNI office dominated by men.) Reflections emerging from indigenous women's group discussion sessions held during the workshops suggested that at the local level, too, they were speaking out – and being heard – much more than before in internal movement spaces.

Other forms of representation were also growing in importance. Since 1998, there had been a striking growth in the number of local and sub-regional associations, encouraged by the availability of state government funding for community development projects that required an officially registered association as a vehicle. After the UNI's collapse, many of these began to take on a more overtly political role, which included a growing involvement in debates and struggles over the future of indigenous health services in Acre.

Indigenous engagements with the state over health services since the collapse of the UNI

Following FUNASA's break with the UNI, responsibility for local-level indigenous health services was increasingly passed to municipalities. This raised accountability issues: indigenous participants in the reflection workshops complained that municipal mayors were diverting funds to other uses and allocating jobs according to clientelistic calculations, while FUNASA was unable or unwilling to control these practices. The indigenous health sub-system included guaranteed indigenous representation in statutory *conselhos* (councils), modelled on the structures designed to provide for *controle social* or citizen oversight in the national SUS (see Chapter 9, this volume). However, the UNI had failed to invest in strengthening these institutions, preferring to centralize control in the hands of its own leadership. As a result, the under-resourced DSEI *controle social* structures initially proved incapable of holding to account either FUNASA or the municipal power brokers.

Insensitive behaviour and racism among non-indigenous health staff, already a problem when the UNI was running the DSEIs, were described as endemic, with humiliation by 'white' professionals (particularly of indigenous women) and disrespect for traditional medical knowledge described as widespread. OPIN's coordinator, Manoel Gomes Kaxinawá, told the first research workshop that:

> for a doctor to care for our people he must respect them; if he calls an indigenous woman a 'greasy Indian', that is where poor health starts ... if we are to have good-quality health care, then at the very least we must be treated with respect by the technical staff.

Gomes also emphasized that the movement had abandoned its discredited agenda of becoming directly involved in service provision. Instead, he called for a strategy based on demands for respect, on the training of indigenous people to replace 'white' professionals, and on strengthening *controle social.* When he addressed the project's concluding workshop a year later, he was even more explicit about the need to move away from direct involvement in service provision, stating that the UNI's mistakes had stemmed from the fact that 'we got it into our heads that we should do the job of the state'.[4]

It could be argued that OPIN's focus on *controle social* was opportunistic, since its leaders had failed to strengthen accountability to indigenous health service users when they were directly involved in DSEI management through the UNI. Now that they had no possibility of occupying their former roles as service managers, a return to a rights-claiming position outside and against the state was logical enough. However, Gomes reflected a wider trend among Movimento Indígena leaders in supporting efforts to strengthen controle social. Workshop participants stated that, despite the limitations of the *conselhos*, they were valued as potential spaces for securing recognition and engaging the state, and described how some were being reclaimed by grassroots leaders seeking a channel to express the discontent of their communities.

One example of the revitalization of *controle social* was provided by the local indigenous health council in the remote municipality of Marechal Thaumaturgo in the Juruá Valley, whose chair, Davi Waine Ashaninka, emerged as a rising star of the Movimento Indígena after confronting the local mayor and demanding that federal indigenous health funding transfers be properly accounted for. He took his case to a national radio station based in Brasília after he was met first with stonewalling and then with threats. While I was visiting Marechal Thaumaturgo in July 2007, a number of other indigenous leaders from the municipality arrived with an offer to back him up with direct action, bringing warriors to occupy the building that housed the municipal health secretariat. He dissuaded them, stating that he preferred to stick to more conventional advocacy channels, which included bringing a court action against the mayor. This eventually led to an agreement that the municipality would invest some of the diverted funds in restoring the infrastructure used by the local indigenous health service.

In other parts of Acre, indigenous groups demonstrated an increasing willingness to take the kind of direct action proposed by the Marechal Thaumaturgo leaders, as discontent with the 'municipalization' of health services spread in the post-UNI period. In the first half of 2007, a DSEI health team was held hostage in a Yawanawá village and a group of Kaxinawá leaders from the River Jordão community occupied the *pólo-base* (health team field station) in Jordão municipality. Significantly, both these cases of direct action were accompanied by other political strategies: in the case of the Yawanawá, a demand for a meeting with senior state government and FUNASA representatives; and in the case of the Kaxinawá, an online campaign to denounce municipal mismanagement and to demand transfer of the *pólo-base* to indigenous control (Machado, 2007).

The River Jordão Kaxinawá used e-mail and blog postings, following a trend set by others, including the River Amônia Ashaninka and the River Gregório Yawanawá.[5] The Pianko 'royal family' of the River Amônia Ashaninka, which has produced several important indigenous leaders (including Francisco Pianko, appointed by Governor Viana to head SEPI and now the indigenous affairs adviser to Governor Marques), runs a much-visited community association website that combines blog entries on indigenous culture and politics with advertising for the traditional handicrafts marketed by the association. Yawanawá leader Joaquim Tashka is a prolific blogger, who has used his command of English and green discourse to attract foreign visitors to the annual 'Yawá' festival hosted by the River Gregório community, which is also assiduously attended by Acre politicians keen to burnish their credentials as supporters of *florestania*. It was after attending the 2008 Yawá festival that Acre Senator Tião Viana was persuaded to help mobilize the state government and FUNASA to implement an emergency health programme for the River Gregório Yawanawá, whose international celebrity sat uneasily with extremely high rates of morbidity and mortality from water-borne and sexually transmitted diseases.

The fact that this programme was led by the Secretaria Estadual de Saúde do Acre (SESACRE – Acre State Health Secretariat), with FUNASA reduced to a supporting role, reflected a broader emerging trend in the post-UNI period. During the course of our project, sometimes with direct support from the project team, indigenous leaders began to make increasingly active efforts to involve the state government in mediating relations with FUNASA and the municipalities. SESACRE had not hitherto played a significant part in the indigenous health system, since formal responsibility for regulating the system lay with the federal government, and those health units under direct state government management tended to be large hospitals located in urban areas, rather than clinics close to indigenous territories. Attempts to draw the state government into more direct involvement had been blocked by the UNI and continued to be opposed by OPIN, but with the UNI's collapse and OPIN's weakness the shift towards engagement with the state government gathered momentum.

Sensing this opportunity, Juruá Valley indigenous leader Anchieta Arara presented a package of proposals for restructuring and democratizing the management of the system, for which he secured the support of a number of local indigenous associations. SESACRE staff made it clear that they were interested in taking action – but they pointed out that, if they were to take on FUNASA and the municipalities, they needed to be legitimated by both the Movimento Indígena and the SUS *controle social* structure. This led to SESACRE inviting the project team to support the participation of indigenous delegates at the September 2007 State Health Conference, which duly approved a resolution calling for state government intervention in the indigenous health system. Since then, SESACRE has moved cautiously towards a more sustained and strategic engagement with indigenous health in the state – though it remains to be seen how far it will be willing and able to adapt the standard SUS approaches that have been its hallmark, in order to deal with the specific challenges of working with indigenous peoples and to achieve its stated aim of delivering health with *florestania*.

Outcomes, tensions and trade-offs

I suggested at the start of this chapter that assessing democratic outcomes requires us to distinguish between inclusion and transformation, and between recognition and redistribution. The story of indigenous peoples' mobilizations in Acre over the last two decades is undoubtedly one of remarkable progress towards greater inclusion. Yet the evidence remains mixed on whether there has indeed been a transformation in the material conditions under which Acre's indigenous peoples are living,[6] or in the level of fulfilment of their constitutional rights of access to health services that are both medically effective and respectful of cultural difference.[7]

There has certainly been a very significant growth in investment in indigenous health services by government institutions at all levels. However, though advances have undoubtedly been made, improvements in health indicators fall well short of what might have been expected, given the overall rise in spending (Coimbra et al., 2006; Verdum, 2009). At the same time, the quality of service provision shows little sign of reflecting in practice the progressive tenets of the national indigenous health policy. In Acre in mid-2009 – a decade after the formal creation of the indigenous health sub-system and the election of the first 'government of the forest' – indigenous communities could still go for months without receiving a single visit from a health team; indigenous leaders seeking to exercise their constitutional rights to demand accountability from health service managers could still be met with threats and racist abuse; indigenous women could still suffer humiliating experiences at the hands of government doctors and nurses; and indigenous children were still two to three times more likely than non-indigenous children to die before they reached their first birthday.

If the impacts of resource redistribution on indigenous health and well-being have fallen short of what might have been expected, this is especially surprising given that indigenous people are arguably more politically visible in Acre now than at any time since it was first conquered during the rubber boom. Formal spaces for indigenous participation have continued to proliferate, and in recent years an indigenous leader has sat (metaphorically) at the right hand of the governor, as a special adviser. This extremely high level of 'symbolic inclusion' of its indigenous minority by the Acre State government would seem, on the face of it, to be a recognition gain for the indigenous population as a whole. However, it could be argued that it has actually detracted from redistribution in two important ways.

First, it has allowed the state government to signal that indigenous peoples are fully 'on board' with the *florestania* agenda, when in fact the policy space for shaping the actual content of this agenda is severely constrained by what Young (2000: 55) calls 'internal exclusion', whereby formal inclusion coexists with an inability to influence key decision-making processes. Similar processes of 'internal exclusion' are also apparent in policy areas where the federal government plays a significant role, such as the indigenous health sub-system (Shankland and Athias, 2007). Thus, attention has been deflected from the fact that the redistribution of financial resources has had far less impact on both the distribution of well-being and the distribution of power than might have been the case had different policy choices been made.

Second, it has favoured perverse processes of redistribution within the indigenous minority that have increased internal inequality – both because recognition itself has been unevenly distributed and because this has reinforced unequal patterns of material redistribution. When state officials cite specific examples of indigenous communities with whom they are working, or seek out indigenous representatives for policy dialogue, they almost invariably look to the hyper-visible groups, such as the River Amônia Ashaninka and the River Gregório Yawanawá. This skewed recognition can all too easily be reflected in skewed redistribution: although there has undoubtedly been an overall redistribution of health system resources towards providing infrastructure for indigenous health service delivery, the participatory mapping exercises at our project workshops highlighted glaring inequalities in the allocation of those resources that closely matched the unequal pattern of representation in formal participation spaces. The significance of access to representation in influencing resource allocation is also evident when we look at distribution among different areas of health care: as long as the exclusively male leadership of the UNI dominated regional representation, spending on specific women's health programmes was limited to minimal provision mandated by national policy, but when indigenous women's interests were better represented after the UNI's collapse, additional funding was rapidly secured for an extension of reproductive health services and for work with indigenous midwives.

Inter-ethnic and inter-regional inequalities certainly existed in the heyday of the UNI, but they worsened after its collapse. The disintegration of the UNI replaced a highly centralized system of political representation with a more fragmented one. While this has allowed some formerly under-represented groups to stake greater claims to specific resources and programmes, the absence of a dominant representative structure capable of mediating between different claims means that ultimately the extent of redistribution depends on the effectiveness of each group's representation strategies. The UNI failed to ensure full equity in access to resources among Acre's indigenous groups, but at least its 'pan-indigenous' ideology maintained a discursive space in which this could be struggled for, while its regional base provided a framework within which redistribution could take place. Without it, what remains is a quasi-market situation, in which a shift towards greater equity can only be assured by an explicit state focus on establishing socially just criteria for redistribution. However, there are few political incentives for the state to adopt such a focus and to tackle the invisibility and exclusion of some groups, so long as the hyper-visibility and demonstrable inclusion of others continues to be accepted as evidence that *florestania* is becoming a reality for the original 'forest peoples'.

This reflects the broader strategic dilemma that has faced the Movimento Indígena over the last two decades: the tension between democratization as inclusion and democratization as transformation. Ramos attributes this tension to 'the cracks in the very constitution of modern Western ideology', which mean that:

> if, on the one hand, the humanist quest for universalism has come to be the hegemonic idiom in which human rights are expressed everywhere regardless of cultural differences, on the other hand, universalism co-exists with an equally humanist quest for relativism, according to which values are not universal but culture-bound and as such should not be submitted to universal principles. (2002: 256)

In the specific setting of Acre, this is played out in the internal Movimento Indígena debate over whether indigenous peoples should ally themselves to other groups, or whether they should insist on the distinctiveness of an indigenous identity. The complexity of the challenges posed by these dilemmas is clear from the variety of responses that they have produced among indigenous groups in Acre – as well as from the irony that the ideology of *florestania*, which many indigenous leaders reject as diluting their right to difference, was itself formulated to argue for the recognition of difference (Alves, 2007).

One lesson that emerges from the Acre case is that, while these dilemmas can generate painful tensions within minority groups, they in no way deprive them of agency. Political action by movement organizations – often brilliantly successful, at other times contradictory or counterproductive – can represent an intense learning process, whose evolutionary leaps and dramatic setbacks are an integral part of the ongoing renegotiation of authority and identity between minority groups and democratizing states. The dynamism and creativity of the Movimento Indígena in Acre has thrown up a multiplicity of strategies for engagement with the state – from formal participation in *controle social* institutions, to use of the media and the courts, to clientelistic bargaining and party-political manoeuvring, to online activism and 'unruly' direct action. These have been shaped by the nature of the prevailing opportunity structure at different times, and by shifting political trends and alliances at local, state, federal and international levels. The movement's leaders have had to operate within what has sometimes been a very narrow space for manoeuvre – but their choices have not simply been determined by structural constraints, and throughout they have consistently demonstrated an overriding determination to preserve their own agency.

These choices, of course, included those that led to the downfall of the UNI. The roles of neoliberal state-shrinking dogma and incompetent or ill-intentioned FUNASA management cannot be ignored; but the large-scale diversion of health service funds to other uses was, in the end, a political choice. Some sense of political purpose can be glimpsed amid the stories of petty corruption and individual greed. For example, if funds really were diverted to PCdoB election campaigns, that may have been an attempt to buy the formal political representation denied to indigenous people by demography and the concentration of economic power in 'white' hands. Nevertheless, this choice had terrible consequences: it represented a missed opportunity to alleviate the suffering of indigenous communities that had long been denied access to decent health care, and while the fall-out from it may, in many ways, have re-energized the Movimento Indígena, it also gave copious ammunition to the anti-indigenous propagandists who trade in racist stereotypes of 'lazy thieving Indians'.

In the end, it was hard for us, as outsiders who are at the same time politically engaged with the Movimento Indígena, to interpret these choices in any conclusive way. As Warren and Jackson note:

> engaged researchers studying indigenous movements not only face complex ethical challenges but can also find that activists' behaviour can elicit impressions of savvy strategizing, innocence, contempt, resistance, complicity, or genuine perplexity that rapidly appear and disappear – all behaviour difficult to characterize in categorical terms. (2002: 21)

However, one attempt to 'characterize in categorical terms' the behaviour of the UNI's leadership did emerge from a discussion with one of my SSL colleagues, in which she described them as '*revolucionários e golpistas*' – revolutionaries and con-artists.

The 'revolutionary' component of their behaviour was reflected in their rhetoric of indigenous distinctiveness and the importance of political autonomy, and in the barrage of public denunciations of the state government that they kept up even when it was paying their bills. This oppositionist stance can also be seen as an attempt to shift the terms of engagement with the 'white state' by refusing to sign up for a 'bit part' in *florestania*. Arguably, the mismanagement of the DSEIs also had a 'revolutionary' component, in that UNI leaders regularly overruled the 'technical' decisions made by non-indigenous professionals on 'political' grounds – interpreting indigenous *controle social* not as the power to demand accountability, but as the power to give direct orders. This was part of a pattern of constantly interrogating the legitimacy of universalist SUS ideology and the technical, political and bureaucratic apparatus that was trying to consolidate its hold over the indigenous territories of Acre via the provision of 'western' health services, even while the UNI's leaders were benefiting politically and financially from it. Although other groups in Acre engaged with the state in very different ways, there were many signs of the same 'revolutionary' spirit even among those who had formally aligned themselves with *florestania*.

The 'con-artist' aspect refers not to the strategic 'revolutionary' aims of the movement leaders, but to the way in which they were pursued: by emphasizing theatrical displays, bombastic rhetoric and sudden short-cuts, rather than the long slog of building a solid and inclusive movement base for conventional democratic engagement. Again, the self-serving elements of this behaviour are undeniable; but there may also have been a strategic value to actions that preserved an element of unpredictability and danger in the public persona of the Movimento Indígena. If a group lacks the demographic and economic weight to pursue its interests under the normal rules of the democratic game, it may achieve more by pursuing a guerrilla politics of unruliness in the face of 'neoliberal governmentality' (Ferguson and Gupta, 2002). Arguably, by incorporating groups and factions who both supported and opposed *florestania*, and by pursuing strategies of 'unruly' direct action alongside 'orderly' institutional participation, the Acre Movimento Indígena as a whole has achieved more than it could have done by sticking to a single path. This reflects a strategic insight that is valid for other marginalized minorities in contemporary processes of democratization: being invited to play on a field from which you were previously excluded is important, but it may not get you very far unless you are simultaneously challenging the rules of the game.

Notes

1 I gratefully acknowledge the research support provided by the Institute of Development Studies at the University of Sussex, the UK Department for International Development and the Economic and Social Research Council.

2 The project evolved through an ongoing process of dialogue between the leaders, my SSL co-researchers (Maria Elvira Toledo, Maria Ferreira Bittencourt and Hélio Barbin Júnior) and me to include a series of reflection, planning and training workshops, as well as individual interviews and micro-level case studies, and has been a truly collective effort. Nevertheless, this paper represents my interpretation of these reflections, and any errors or biases are my own.

3 These figures refer only to the population of officially recognized indigenous territories; they exclude the estimated 3,700 indigenous people living in Acre's urban areas, and the unknown number of uncontacted indigenous people living in the remote headwaters of the Acre–Peru border zone (Virtanen, 2007).

4 Quotes from SSL video *Fala Txai: Os Índios e a Saúde no Acre* (Damasceno, 2008) and workshop transcripts; my translation.

5 See http://apiwtxa.blogspot.com/ and http://awavena.blog.uol.com.br/.

6 One example is Jordão, which has the largest number of indigenous people among its population of any municipality in Acre and a well-known indigenous leader as its vice-mayor. Jordão has the lowest municipal Human Development Index (HDI) in the state, and in 2008 was highlighted by the UNDP Human Development Report office for Brazil as having one of the ten lowest HDI ratings of all the country's 5,500 municipalities. See www.pnud.org.br/administracao/ reportagens/index.php?id01=3121&lay=apu (accessed 11 May 2009).

7 A few months after the last of

the project workshops, SSL team member Maria Ferreira Bittencourt visited the indigenous territories of the Upper Envira and reported that some health indicators among the Kulina communities there were actually worse than when she had worked with them over a decade earlier, before the DSEIs were established (Bittencourt, 2007).

6 · Citizen action and the consolidation of democracy in Nigeria: a study of the 2007 movement

JIBRIN IBRAHIM AND SAMUEL EGWU

Introduction

This chapter is about the struggle to consolidate democratic gains in Nigeria through citizen mobilization, following President Olusegun Obasanjo's attempt to change the constitution in order to prolong his tenure in office for a third term. It examines the mobilization of an anti-third term camp, which was drawn from Nigeria's parliament, civil society, opposition parties and the popular masses. In particular, we will focus closely on the role played by the 2007 Movement, a coalition of parliamentarians who formed the nucleus of the opposition to the tenure extension bid. This fierce battle for the soul of Nigeria's democracy, which was openly fought by pro- and anti-third term groups between January 2005 and May 2006, was resolved when the National Assembly moved to throw out the Constitutional Amendment Bill, which (if passed) would have made Obasanjo's tenure extension a reality.[1]

This chapter is also about disagreements over the meaning of democracy. President Obasanjo had one definition of what constitutes democracy, which can be seen from the way members of his entourage normally introduced him on public occasions – as the 'founder of modern Nigeria', with a 'divine'[2] will to combat corruption, streamline state institutions, introduce due process into economic governance, and send the country along the path of rapid economic development. So important was this mission to the president and his team that they believed themselves justified in using all possible mediating powers of the state to change the rules, so that they could continue in office. To them, democracy meant 'good governance', in the narrow sense of promoting accountability and due process. As such, they did not hesitate to participate in massive vote rigging in the 2003 and 2007 elections, so that the 'good governance' team could continue its 'good work' (Transition Monitoring Group, 2007; Ibrahim, 2007).

Running counter to this notion of democracy was the version upheld by Obasanjo's opponents: it was linked to the preservation of institutions and populist economic policies. By this understanding of democracy, respecting constitutional limits to terms of office was a necessary part of the democratic process in a country where crises of political succession have remained endemic. Consequently, contesting the extension of the presidential term of office became part of the larger struggle against Obasanjo's policies of public expenditure cuts (especially in health and education); massive retrenchment in the public services; constant increases in the price of petroleum products; and privatization of public enterprises. Throughout the eight years of Obasanjo's presidency, civil society and labour groups organized strikes and public demonstrations against the steady rise in petroleum prices and the economic hardship. In short, many Nigerians had a concept of democracy that was diametrically opposed to that of Obasanjo and his team. Our study shows that, for many, the removal of the Obasanjo regime became a sine qua non for the possibility of deepening democracy.

Nigeria's political economy and the political context

Nigeria has an estimated population of 140 million, and is a federal democracy consisting of thirty-six states and a federal capital territory, further subdivided into 774 local governments. Prolonged military rule (for thirty out of the fifty years since independence) has had a considerable effect on party democracy and elections, eroding constitutional federalism through massive centralization of power and resources, violating the rights of citizens, rubbing away at the rule of law, and enshrining a culture of arbitrariness and impunity that has resulted in high levels of corruption. Military rule ended in 1999, and the return to democracy under the Fourth Republic was heralded by a new constitution. Obasanjo was the first president of this new era.

Nigeria's population comprises over 375 ethnic groups (Otite, 1990), almost equally split between Muslims and Christians; it has a literacy rate of less than 60 per cent. Although not constitutionally entrenched, the existing six geopolitical zones are well recognized as the basis for sharing power and promoting equity among the component parts of the federation.[3] Nigeria's plural and diverse ethnic, regional and religious character provides a key defining context for its electoral democracy. The ethnic groups that live in Nigeria vary in size, history and influence, and the tendency for the political elite to politicize and exploit these identities has led to an intense competition for state power and publicly controlled resources.

The politicization of ethnic and sectional identity has responded dynamically to the changing character of federal politics and the shifting context of the struggle for power and resources. For instance, from the late colonial period to the end of the First Republic in 1966, 'politics of difference' played the three regions of the day – east, north and west – off against each other (each region coinciding with the interests of one of the three largest Nigerian ethnic groups). However, the feeling of oppression expressed by the ethnic minorities within these regions generated considerable social tension towards the end of colonial rule, and this survived into the post-independence era as demands for the creation of new states and local governments in the new Nigeria.

A dominant feature of contemporary Nigerian politics remains the major role played by ethno-regional political organizations. Key expressions of ethnic and regional platforms today include the Arewa Consultative Forum (ACF) (representing the core north, which is, rather simplistically, identified as Hausa-Fulani), the Afenifere (the platform of the Yoruba-speaking population of the south-west) and the Ohaneze N'digbo (advancing the interests of the Ibo-speaking population in the south-east). There are other ethno-regional organizations that represent the various ethnic minorities, and these are useful in the mobilization of communal identity for electoral purposes. Against this background, and despite an increased liberalization of the political space, Nigerian political parties have remained fragile; their institutional weakness is a central challenge in establishing a healthy electoral democracy.[4] The main reason for this weakness is the predominance of a core of practitioners within the political class: they came to the fore under successive military regimes, when there was an absence of internal democracy within party organizations and during a long period of decline in ideology- and issues-based politics in parties and campaigns. The political parties are also weak in terms of democratic accountability, being answerable neither to their members nor to the Nigerian populace (despite the fact that they are publicly funded).

The postcolonial path to economic development – and the role of the state within it – was heavily influenced by the colonial model. It was essentially defined by the following: a state-led approach to capitalist modernization; a dependent strategy, which emphasized a significant role for foreign capital; an import-substitution industrialization strategy; and a philosophy of development that excluded most ordinary people from meaningful participation in the development process.

The emergence of the petroleum economy in the 1970s, however, is what has had the most significant impact on the Nigerian political economy. Between 1960 and 1964, agriculture accounted for 79 per cent of GDP on average. By the end of the 1980s, oil revenue had displaced agriculture, and made up over 80 per cent of the Nigerian state's foreign earnings. This change had a number of consequences for Nigerian society: in particular, the pre-eminence of oil encouraged the emergence of a 'rentier' state and eroded the basis of the Nigerian state's social contract, as rent extracted by the state from oil companies replaced tax as the basis of public expenditure (Guyer, 1994). Today, oil and gas continue to account for over 80 per cent of Nigeria's foreign exchange earnings and about 70 per cent of government revenues. More importantly, the new oil wealth has strengthened a system of rent-seeking capitalism, where wealth is placed at the disposal of a few. This system is characterized by clientelistic arrangements and by the establishment of patron–client networks that are sometimes based on ethnic groups (Joseph, 1987). This model of politics, with bargains struck between members of the elite, benefits few, perpetuating as it does informal channels of influence instead of state structures, and effectively breaking the state down into personal fiefdoms. In the context of electoral democracy, the state is perceived as a coveted prize to be won by the coalition of elites that bind together in political parties.

Despite the boom in oil wealth, an economic crisis hit the country in the early 1980s. This led to a series of market-based adjustment policies, beginning with the Structural Adjustment Programme and followed by the National Economic Empowerment and Development Strategy (NEEDS). Both programmes sought to effect broad economic and politico-administrative reform, in order to ensure sustainable economic growth and efficiency and to improve the accountability of the state and its institutions. The policy framework of NEEDS provided the basis for indiscriminate privatization of state-owned ventures and the enrichment (through corrupt means) of party supporters and the technocratic elites. Both groups were drawn into the vast existing network of patron–client relationships.

The result of this history of military rule, ethnic politics and endemic rent-seeking and patronage is that contemporary Nigeria has a distorted federal system, in which enormous political and economic power is concentrated in the presidency. The president dispenses patronage across the country, runs the ruling party, subordinates the legislature and stifles the judiciary. The funding and control of other 'executive' bodies, including election management bodies, security agencies and anti-corruption bodies, have affected the democratic integrity of the electoral process. Against this background, it is hardly surprising that an attempt to further extend presidential power provided a catalyst for the mobilization of a movement to defend and consolidate existing democratic institutions and processes.

A note on methodology

The data generated and analysed in this study come from primary and secondary sources. The primary sources include in-depth interviews and focus group discussions. Twelve members of the 2007 Movement were interviewed, as were several individuals in government and civil society who played important roles in connection with the tenure extension issue. Two focus group discussions were held with between six and ten members of the 2007 Movement. The first was at a retreat organized for members of the movement at the Obudu Cattle Ranch in Cross River State; the second took place in Abuja, where a significant number of the members of the 2007 Movement resided. The research also made use of documentary sources, especially press statements and interviews, supplemented with extensive examination of newspapers and magazines of the time.

The emergence of the tenure extension campaign

The campaign to prolong the tenure of the president drew upon a wide range of support, including the technocratic group that had articulated and implemented President Obasanjo's reform agenda; those who would benefit from having Obasanjo continue in office (especially through the stripping of national assets);[5] and the machinery of the ruling party, including political 'godfathers'. The campaign equally enjoyed the support of many legislators in the National Assembly, who (according to several of the 2007 Movement members interviewed) were allegedly paid between US $400,000 and $500,000 each for their support.

Early warnings that President Obasanjo might have a hidden agenda to extend his tenure in office could be found in the brazen manner in which – conniving with the Independent National Electoral Commission (INEC), 'political fixers' and security agencies – he rigged the 2003 elections. The election rigging was aimed at securing Obasanjo a second term, allowing him to consolidate his hold on power and to manoeuvre himself into position for a third term. Evidence of electoral malfeasance can be found in the documented reports of observers and monitors at the 2003 elections (Justice Peace and Development Commission, 2003; EU Election Observation Mission, 2003) and the alleged confessions of individuals involved.[6] Evidence can also be found in the judgment delivered by the Federal Court of Appeal on the presidential election petition filed by General Muhammed Buhari, the main opposition candidate, who had run on the All Nigeria People's Party (ANPP) platform.[7] In its ruling, the court nullified the votes President Obasanjo obtained from his home state of Ogun, while still upholding his victory.

No sooner had Obasanjo settled down to his second term in office than the media were awash with speculation that a move was afoot to amend the constitution in order to extend the length of time a president could stay in office. That speculation was fuelled, first, by the appointment of the Constitutional Reform Committee in 2004, which subsequently proposed a six-year tenure for the president that would take effect (retroactively) from 2003.

Simultaneously, the National Assembly Constitutional Review Committee, which had been dormant, suddenly became interested in the constitutional review process. In 2004, it initiated public hearings that focused narrowly on the issue of the length of executive terms of office. However, this initiative stalled and the battle for tenure extension shifted from the National Assembly to the National Political Reform Conference (NPRC). The NPRC was an ad hoc assembly of members appointed by the president, state governors and corporate bodies to discuss the country's political problems. It was convened in place of either the popularly demanded Sovereign National Conference (SNC) or an alternative national conference, and was to assist with the president's personal political ambition of staying in power beyond 2007. It seems clear that this was Obasanjo's intention: having consistently ignored calls for a platform for political dialogue of any kind, and after rejecting the proposal to convene the SNC, he quite suddenly became interested in the NPRC, to the point of expressing a willingness to fund it outside the National Assembly's appropriations mechanism (and without its approval).

Origins of the 2007 Movement

Participants in the 2007 Movement began to come together around June 2005. The movement did not emerge through the conscious construction of a political platform for the purpose of fighting tenure extension, but was a child of circumstances. It coalesced spontaneously in response to the suspicion that the president and his supporters were planning to extend his time in office. One 2007 Movement member, Haruna Yerima, explained that the movement had emerged from informal discussions and consultations among a few opposition party legislators, who had become increasingly concerned that, given the vast arsenal of resources available to the president, it could become a fait accompli for him to secure a third term in office (interview, 18 July 2007).[8]

The nucleus of legislators that started the 2007 Movement included Yerima, Uche Onyeaguocha, Aminu Tambwal and Victor Lar, all of whom were members of opposition parties in the House of Representatives; key members from the Senate included Senators Uche Chukwumerije, Saidu Dansadau, Udo Udoma and the late Idris Kuta and Sule Yari Gari.[9]

Their essential motivation was to defend democracy in Nigeria. Some were members of the Good Governance and Democracy Group, which was formed soon after the president's inauguration in June 2003, under the leadership of Dr Usman Bugaje. Members of the 2007 Movement understood democracy as a system of governance that rests on strong institutions of political parties, a legislature and a judiciary. One member, Datti Baba-Ahmed, explained that a key requirement of democracy is that public officials in the executive and the legislature must be truly elected. Consequently, he argued, so-called 'elected leaders' who come to power through organized private armies that rig them into power are worse than trained military officers who seize power by force (interview, 18 July 2007).

In another interview, Bugaje observed that Nigeria has experienced regression rather than consolidation in its politics because democratic deficits have been omnipresent since the country returned to civilian administration. He pointed to a number of issues to validate this view: the weakness of the party system, characterized by a lack of internal democracy and open and transparent primaries within the parties; the weak culture of opposition politics and the tendency for members perceived to be part of the opposition actually to be working for the ruling party; executive interference and a lack of independent funding, leading to an absence of institutional legislative autonomy; and the subversion of the judiciary (interview,18 July 2007). These flaws fed the perception of those forces opposed to his tenure extension that the Obasanjo years were regressive.

Many of the legislators who started the 2007 Movement did not think they could successfully challenge the president's bid for a third term, largely because they considered the forces behind it to be awesome in nature: the vast resources of the state, the machinery of the ruling PDP, and the wealth of the beneficiaries of the Obasanjo government's reform agenda. This awareness partly informed the decision of the 2007 Movement to mobilize Nigerians around the issue of the need to hold the 2007 general elections, rather than around tenure extension as a specific issue. At the same time as canvassing opposition to tenure extension, they also wished to deal with other reform issues, such as electoral reform, the timely release of money appropriated for INEC, close monitoring of the Ministry of Finance to ensure the release of money, and the revalidation of voter registers (interview with Onyeaguocha, 18 July 2007).

The parliamentarians who created the 2007 Movement as a platform to defend democracy were fully aware of the political risks involved. Several of its members came under intense pressure from friends and relations who were close to the presidency or who had some vested interest in the success of tenure extension. Onyeaguocha told us that some of the president's key appointees, with whom he had personal ties and relationships, offered him financial inducements to back the third-term cause – inducements which (though he did not succumb to them) he described as 'irresistible' (interview, 18 July 2007). Nevertheless, however daunting the task appeared to the parliamentarians, the motivating factor for launching their campaign (and the reason behind the subsequent recruitment of more voices from within the National Assembly) was a desire to make a point by registering their opposition and drawing attention to the danger presented by the tenure extension proposal. The 2007 Movement, which in the middle of February 2006 had only eight legislators as members, had increased its membership to twenty-eight by the end of that month. The decision of the Alliance for Democracy (AD) leaders to join the movement and a declaration of support by four legislators from Lagos State encouraged the nucleus of the movement to announce the existence of the group publicly, through newspaper advertorials entitled 'Concerned Legislators against a Third Term'. At this early stage, each willing member was required to sign their name as a symbol of open defiance to the president's ambition. Once the existence of the Movement was announced through the public media, legislators began to clamour for membership and the 2007 Movement blossomed into an actual movement, sustained and nurtured by the voluntary contributions and sacrifices of its members.

The continuation of the tenure extension campaign

Obasanjo's team had constructed its justification for tenure extension around ideological themes. First, they argued that it was essential to increase the number of possible presidential terms in office in order to consolidate the gains of economic reform. They suggested that opposition to the reform programme was tantamount to an undermining of the national interest, and that the western world and international financial institutions would withdraw their support for Nigeria's economic reform process if Obasanjo was no longer available to provide strong leadership. A second justification openly appealed to ethnic and regional sentiment, through a subtle campaign insinuating that tenure extension for Obasanjo was the only way to ensure that his region – the south – could redress the historic imbalance (with the north) in terms of the length of presidential control.

Despite the fact that it was full of nominees appointed by the president and state governors, the NPRC began to take its job of constitutional reform seriously, by examining and questioning presidential tenure extension, rather than simply advocating it. Alarmed at the possibility of failure, the president's men 'smuggled' into the NPRC a 'draft constitution', which contained a provision for tenure extension. The surreptitious manner in which the 'draft constitution' was introduced generated controversy, because it was not part of the original working documents distributed to the members. The NPRC threw it out and refused to endorse any extension of the number of possible presidential terms of office. The debates were shown on television, and the whole country witnessed speaker after speaker condemning the third term. Political fixers recruited to drive the project were forced to beat a hasty retreat and shifted their attention to the National Assembly, where the constitutional review process ultimately had to be approved.

The National Assembly came up with a list of 110 items to amend in the 1999 Constitution, but it was Section 135(2) – the proposal to allow a presidential 'third term' – that overshadowed all the other proposed amendments. The presidency prepared a memorandum on the constitutional amendment, which was forwarded to the Joint Committee of the National Assembly for Review of the Constitution (JCNARC), led by the pro-Obasanjo Senator Ibrahim Mantu. It was at this point that forces including party chieftains, cronies of the president and the 'new bourgeoisie' that had benefited from Obasanjo's reform agenda, began to coalesce into a force for promoting the tenure extension agenda. More importantly, it provided the much-needed opportunity for individuals such as Mantu and other key functionaries of the PDP and the National Assembly to manipulate the entire constitutional amendment process to suit the political ambitions of the president.

Although the JCNARC was forced to organize zonal consultations on the proposed amendments, the process was heavily manipulated, as notable friends of the president, including state governors,[10] were widely reported to have distributed money to cajole and twist people's arms into supporting tenure extension and to treat it as the most important of the amendment issues. It was, of course, difficult to find documentary evidence of money actually having changed hands, but the rumours were widespread and persistent.

At the end of the half-hearted zonal consultations, the committee chose Port Harcourt as the venue for collating the reports – a city under the 'protective custody' of Rivers State Governor Peter Odili, the most vociferous of the third-term campaigners and a close friend of the president. Despite the orchestrated attempt to drum up support for tenure extension, the proposal failed to enjoy easy passage in committee, as it was challenged externally by the strong media campaigns of the 2007 Movement and its allies, and internally by the relentless voices of the few members of the 2007 Movement who were also on the committee.[11] In order to stand a better chance of manipulating the outcome, the president's henchmen and the leadership of the JCNARC were forced to change the voting procedure from a secret ballot to a voice vote. Despite this, the plot to change the constitution was ultimately defeated on the floor of the National Assembly. We now turn to an examination of the alliances and coalitions that made this defeat possible.

The 2007 Movement and citizen mobilization: alliances and coalitions

The depth of hostility to the extension of presidential tenure was such that – even if the proposal had not been defeated in parliament – opposition would have shifted to the streets. The formidable nature of popular opposition to the amendment largely originated with the leadership provided by the 2007 Movement and alliances forged between civil society, the political opposition, trade unions, religious leaders and citizens – especially street kids – at the margins of society. The popular movements were also aided, perhaps critically, both by an internal division in the PDP, which saw Vice-President Atiku Abubakar oppose Obasanjo, and by the broad support of the international community.[12]

A key strategy of the 2007 Movement was to forge alliances with individuals and groups outside the legislative assembly, including civil society groups, opposition parties and individual politicians who were opposed to the third-term agenda. The 2007 Movement also operated powerful propaganda machinery, by means of which it mobilized citizens and countered the strategies of the 'third termites'. They established a joint platform of the Senate and the National Assembly under Chukwumerije, and it was on this platform that the group addressed media houses, granted interviews, addressed press conferences and placed advertorials in the newspapers.

It is within the context of this convergence of different interests that the support given to the 2007 Movement by eight state governors can be understood.[13] It is instructive that, though there was support for a third term from individual governors and parliamentarians, both the Northern Governors' Forum and the Northern Senators' Forum openly campaigned against the constitutional change.

A number of retired generals also emerged to openly join the campaign. They even organized a forum that brought them together with former heads of state and inspectors-general of police in Abuja, in May 2006. Individuals like retired Generals Danjuma and Haruna were there and publicly warned Obasanjo that he was treading a path to anarchy by attempting to extend his tenure beyond May 2007.[14]

Despite the fact that the president had succeeded in creating a public image as a born-again Christian, many Christian leaders spoke out vehemently against the third-term agenda. The president of the United Church of Christ in Nigeria, Rev. Jesse Adamu, for example, not only warned against tenure extension, which he said could result in chaos and anarchy, but criticized what he saw as a reckless political agenda being promoted in the midst of poverty and hardship imposed on the people by poor governance.[15]

Nor did Muslim leaders and organizations remain on the sidelines: the Conference of Islamic Organizations[16] issued a public statement warning of the presidency's deliberate attempt to stifle INEC by denying it funding; it also accused the presidency of orchestrating ethnic insurrection in the Niger Delta, and of planning the imposition of an interim government. At the level of civil society, an organization known as the National Civil Society Coalition against the Third Term (NACATT) emerged. NACATT members were used to reach out to the general public through press releases.[17] Well before the ill-fated third-term proposal became a matter of public discourse, civil society groups had alluded to the Obasanjo government's hidden agenda to stay in power beyond May 2007. Their suspicion derived partly from the generally slow pace of political reform relative to economic reform, despite a government commitment to both economic and political reform. In particular, the reluctance of the Obasanjo government to provide the necessary impetus to the constitutional review process for much of its first term raised NACATT suspicions that the sudden decision to convene the NPRC was driven by personal considerations.

Other civil society groups mounted vigorous campaigns against tenure extension.[18] They reached out to citizens through press releases and advertorials in newspapers and, most importantly, through grassroots mobilization. The League for Human Rights, in particular, urged elected representatives in the National Assembly to consult their constituents before taking a position on constitutional amendment.

The opposition of civil society to tenure extension was not limited to the traditional pro-democracy and human rights groups. Ethnic and regional groups took part in the campaigns and mobilization against the third-term project. Both the ACF from the north and the Yoruba group Afenifere maintained a dogged opposition to tenure extension. The ACF, whose opposition was founded on the implications the amendment held for northern political ambitions to assume the presidency in 2007, not only saluted the courage of the legislators who crashed the amendment proposal, but strongly condemned the harassment of individuals and groups opposed to the president's ambition.[19] The ethno-regional implications of a potential third term for President Obasanjo provided a number of people with a reason to join the coalition. Obasanjo's personal political ambition was perceived as an affront to the northern political elite, which felt marginalized by the 'power shift' that had made a south-western candidate president in 1999. This strong feeling of marginalization was reinforced by an allusion made by some northern political elites to a pact they had reached with Obasanjo, in which the presidency was expected to return to the north in 2007. Crucially, however, the campaign brought together regional groups from different parts of the country, not just the north. For example, Afenifere condemned Obasanjo's vaulting ambition and demanded a probe into the 17.5 million Nigerian Naira allegedly given to the Yoruba Council of Elders to support tenure extension during the JCNARC zonal public hearings.

The involvement of the trade unions in the campaign against tenure extension is not surprising, given their long history of struggle against authoritarian rule in the country. Although (because of the partisan interest of its president, Adams Oshionmole) the leadership of the Nigeria Labour Congress (NLC) took a rather ambivalent position on the issue, affiliates of the NLC, such as the Amalgamated Textile Workers Union of Nigeria, mobilized support against tenure extension. Professional groups, including the Academic Staff Union of Universities, the Nigerian Bar Association and the Nigerian Medical Association, also joined the broad alliance of civil society and parliamentarians against the third-term bid.

The campaign clearly revealed to the Nigerian media the role they could potentially play in the consolidation of democracy. The media were in the vanguard of the mobilization of public opinion and in building the critical mass needed to defeat the Constitutional Amendment Bill in the National Assembly. However, the salutary role played by the media brought to the fore the importance of the structure of media ownership. For instance, while the government-dominated electronic media showed bias in favour of tenure extension, the print media played an active role in defeating the amendment bill, and the few privately owned electronic media outlets also provided a platform for opponents of tenure extension, reaching out to important constituencies.

Media coverage of the entire third-term debate made it possible for citizens to take a clear and unmistakable position regarding the immediate and long-term implications of tenure extension for consolidation of democracy in Nigeria. The media rallied public opinion in support of democracy by giving coverage to the opposition activity. The live coverage by African Independent Television (AIT) of the proceedings of the National Assembly deliberations on the Constitutional Amendment Bill, in particular, made it more difficult for the presidency to manipulate the process successfully.

While the live coverage made manipulating the debate difficult, AIT also aired a documentary on tenure extension in Nigeria's political history and the boomerang effect of the 'sit-tight' mentality of previous Nigerian leaders. In the lead-up to the programme's screening, the channel ran a series of trails that captured the interest of many Nigerians. These included particularly damning footage and sound bites of Obasanjo (while in opposition) speaking out against tenure elongation when President Ibrahim Babangida's dictatorship embarked on 'transition without end'. Security operatives swooped on AIT and seized the tape in an unsuccessful attempt to prevent its broadcast.[20] This show of desperation by the Obasanjo regime further discredited its tenure extension project.

Another novel ally in the coalition was found in the banking sector. For the first time in Nigerian history, bank staff steadily leaked information to the media on the movement of money to bribe legislators. Just before the vote on the constitutional reform, numerous legislators went to cash their bribes, and many bankers phoned journalists, who rushed to the banks to witness legislators in the act of collecting their bribes. Bankers were also able, quietly, to indicate the sources of the bribes as being withdrawals from excess crude funds, where gains from the rise in petroleum revenues were to have been saved for future use. This was a further demonstration of the extent of citizen mobilization against the anti-democratic tendencies of the Obasanjo regime.

Even street kids joined the ranks of democratic forces: during the debates, they (and young people generally) were energetic in holding members of the National Assembly to account for their poverty. Evidence from across the country showed that elected representatives were not only disconnected from their people, but generally took their constituents for granted on crucial national issues. The consequence was that many legislators incurred the wrath of their voters, who embarked on popular action, including violence, to call them to order. For example, in the south-south zone, young folk attacked Senators Lee Maeba (PDP, Rivers-East) and Bob Ekarika (PDP, Akwa Ibom) because of their support for the third-term agenda. Shortly after the defeat of the Constitutional Amendment Bill, Senator Lee Maeba came under attack in Port Harcourt, in the course of which one of his aides was (allegedly) killed.[21]

The campaign against tenure extension brought together an extremely diverse coalition – perhaps unprecedented in Nigerian history – to defeat a constitutional amendment. In the next section, we move on to discuss what this implied for democracy.

What democratic outcomes?

Opinions among members of the 2007 Movement are divided over the outcome of the struggle it represented. For Yerima and Bugaje, although the group successfully opposed tenure extension, it lost the battle for the soul of Nigeria's democracy. The outcome of the April 2007 elections is one reason for this conclusion: they argue that the political party primaries were rigged and that the general elections were the worst in Nigeria's electoral history. In this sense, since the results favoured his allies, the elections were a personal victory for Obasanjo, even though he had to leave office at the end of May (interviews, 18 July 2007).

Other members, like Wale Okediran, believe that, while the charade of the 2007 elections ensured that legislators with critical voices did not return, the defeat of the tenure extension proposal helped to avert what would have become a major catastrophe. As he put it in an interview on 18 July 2007, 'the struggle waged by the 2007 Movement has made it possible for Nigerians to avoid the path already taken by African countries such as Kenya and, to some extent, Zimbabwe'.

One undeniable outcome of the struggle was the discovery of new pro-democracy forces that had not previously been noticed on the political scene. For example, the anti-third term movement created the conditions whereby religious leaders and institutions could become more actively engaged in the struggle to entrench democratic practices in Nigeria.

The struggle also strengthened the political opposition: leading political figures, including Vice-President Abubakar, former minister General T. Y. Danjuma and Muhammed Buhari, the 2007 ANPP presidential candidate, became important voices in the campaign. Their motives were personal as well as ideological. While Abubakar perceived a constitutional third term to be a threat to his own ambition, Danjuma joined the opposition because he had been threatened by Obasanjo with a withdrawal of his oil block allocation. Other opposition members had fallen out with the president over political differences.

Within the broad alliance that defeated the third term, the role of the political opposition, especially the organizational platform offered by the Conference of Nigerian Political Parties (CNPP), was critical. The CNPP was formed in the aftermath of the 2003 elections to provide opposition political parties with a platform. It sought to mobilize against the electoral antics of the ruling party and other trends that pointed to the potential emergence of a one-party state. Although the CNPP agreed that there were imperfections in the 1999 Constitution, it opposed the proposal for amendments on the grounds that they would provide a vehicle for the president's pursuit of tenure extension. It mounted a trenchant criticism of the agenda and called on Nigerians to engage in mass protest against Obasanjo's ambition.[22]

In many cases, there were violent consequences for those who were vocal on both sides of the campaign, and this may be regarded as having negative implications for democratic deepening. Members of the 2007 Movement interviewed provided graphic accounts of how legislators who supported tenure extension had been humiliated and threatened across the country. Senator Isah Mohammed of Niger State was declared persona non grata in Niger State after he openly cast his lot with President Obasanjo. In Lagos State, the Hon. Ajata, who was said to have taken a bribe to vote pro-third term, had to run for his life when he was threatened with a machete on a visit to his constituency to distribute money. National Assembly members Bako Sare and Ahmed Salik, the latter a former member of the Good Governance and Democracy Group, were disowned by their constituents in Kano State and could only visit their constituencies under police protection.

The case of Senator Umar Hambagda, who represented the Borno South senatorial district and was a known supporter of the third-term project, is particularly striking. Various media reports had exposed his role in the tenure extension plot and revealed that he had collected large bribes. In the wake of these reports, while he was on a visit to Girau, in the Biu local government area, angry constituents confronted him at a project site he was inspecting. Young people there forced him to pay some 60,000 Nigerian Naira from his ill-gotten gains as a 'settlement'. From the project site, Senator Hambagda headed for the emir's palace in Biu, despite security reports that suggested he could be targeted there by youths who had got wind of his presence in the neighbourhood. On the approach to the emir's palace, people stoned his entourage and two of his cars were vandalized. The senator himself was lucky to enter the emir's palace with only a shattered windscreen. Despite the intervention of soldiers and the police, more and more angry young folk turned up at the palace, attracted by the initial skirmish. The emir of Biu, reluctant to have his palace attacked, insisted that Senator Hambagda leave. The senator's jeep, which was driven out of the palace without him, came under attack. Meanwhile, he was smuggled out of the palace in an armoured vehicle, through a gate meant for horses.

Some members of the 2007 Movement were themselves subjected to physical and psychological attack during the struggle. In May 2006, National Assembly member Francis Amadiegwu was physically attacked in Abuja, where a meeting of an anti-third term group, including two former heads of state, two former inspectors-general of police and the then Vice-President Atiku Abubakar, was being held (interview, 18 July 2007). Bugaje, too, could quote several instances of death threats.

Legislators who openly campaigned against tenure extension, and who may be described as the true heroes of democracy, were also targeted for punishment, albeit of a different kind. Some in the PDP were denied registration to the party during an exercise to revalidate membership that targeted Obasanjo's perceived enemies. Others were denied party nominations at the primaries by various means, including use of money to sponsor alternative candidates, the bribing of party officials to mislead candidates about the dates and venues of nomination congresses, and the use of thugs to stop candidates participating in congresses. Consequently, as we discuss in more detail in the next section, many 2007 Movement members were unable to return to the National Assembly after the 2007 general elections.

Defeat of the 'third-term' amendment and aftermath

Despite the defeat of the tenure extension bill on the floor of the National Assembly, there was widespread fear and distrust among the citizenry that the plot was not dead. One widely held fear was that Obasanjo was desperate enough to instigate a political crisis and declare a state of emergency. In that way, he could invoke Section 135 of the constitution to extend his tenure – a move that required only a simple majority in parliament. A series of political events that unfolded rapidly in the aftermath of the bill's defeat certainly seemed to indicate a determination on the part of the presidency to pursue tenure extension by other means. These included the intense ethno-regional competition for the presidency, the wave of impeachments that swept through state governors, and INEC's inert attitude to the elections of April 2007.

The most profound impact of the political crisis generated by the tenure extension bid was the contrived failure of the elections. INEC was at the centre of the flawed electoral process. First, it had failed to follow up on reform of the country's legal and constitutional electoral framework, despite a series of stakeholder consultations in the wake of the corrupt 2003 elections. Second, it lost much valuable time in preparing for the 2007 elections, and its involvement in determining the eligibility of candidates raised fears that the elections were programmed to fail.

Those individuals who were targeted for disqualification and exclusion were known opponents of tenure extension: most of the members of the 2007 Movement who had been elected to parliament on the ruling PDP platform were either denied that platform for the 2007 elections or were expelled from the party. Bugaje, Chukwumerije and Temi Harriman, to mention but a few, were among them. Bugaje and Harriman changed their party platform in response, but Bugaje failed in his bid for the governorship of Katsina State, and Harriman failed to secure a seat in the Senate.

Similarly, parliamentarians from other parties who had opposed tenure extension were prevented from returning to parliament. Yerima, the ANPP governor of Borno State – a staunch opponent of tenure extension – likewise failed to secure re-election.

The open knowledge that this was being done selectively to punish individuals opposed to the third-term agenda undermined the whole credibility of the electoral process.

While INEC sought to disqualify avowed opponents of tenure extension by accusing them of corruption, it rewarded known supporters of the third-term bid by putting them on to party tickets for parliamentary elections and elections to executive positions. For example, Sylvester Ugwu, former president of the Manufacturers Association of Nigeria and someone who campaigned openly for tenure extension, was put forward as the PDP's governorship candidate in Ebonyi State, even though he had come a distant fourteenth in the party primaries.

The final outcome of the elections, comprehensively documented by domestic and international observers, bears the clear imprint of pro-third term politics (Transition Monitoring Group, 2007).

Most of the legislators who took part in the 2007 Movement, especially those who were interviewed and took part in focus group discussions, did not think that tenure extension was dead or that Obasanjo had abandoned his personal quest to continue exercising political influence (despite leaving the presidency at the end of his second term). Many pointed to a number of indicators – not least the way in which the former governor of Katsina State, Umaru Yar'Adua, was anointed presidential candidate of the ruling PDP, despite the fact that he had not been among the frontline campaigners in the build-up to the party convention.

Obasanjo has remained active in Nigerian politics: the constitution of the PDP was changed to make him the only eligible candidate for the chair of the board of trustees of the party. However, as President Yar'Adua consolidated his hold on power he started to clip the wings of his benefactor.

Contrary to the general expectation that President Yar'Adua's emergence would provide a continuation of Obasanjo's rule, Yar'Adua's courage in standing up to him over a number of policy issues rekindled hope that Obasanjo's influence would not loom too large. Despite the new president's demonstration that he is willing to assert his powers, however, the challenge of nurturing and deepening democracy in Nigeria remains a daunting one in the post-Obasanjo era.

The most important point made by those parliamentarians who fought tenure extension is that, beyond the role played by individuals, the real challenge of deepening democracy lies in strengthening democratic institutions, especially the legislature and the judiciary. Interestingly, members of the 2007 Movement, who are leaders in their own right, have continued to provide critical support to legislators in the National Assembly, despite losing their seats in the 2007 general elections. They have been consulted by key committees of the National Assembly that have important oversight functions (including the appropriations and finance committees) (Focus group discussion, 18 July 2007). Moreover, they are regarded as allies of civil society in the struggle to entrench democratic values. All of this provides evidence that they have continued to wield influence both within and outside the Nigerian parliament.

Members of the 2007 Movement have been active in the process of deepening democracy. In particular, they have continued to provide an active voice on civil society platforms that advocate genuine electoral reform. Among other things, they seek to make the INEC structurally independent, in terms of both how the chair and the members of the board are appointed and the funding it receives from the Consolidated Revenue Fund of the Federation. Furthermore, they encourage citizens and their organizations to ensure that every vote counts, and they promote internal democracy in political parties. In addition, they have advised National Assembly committees on constitutional and electoral reform.

On both levels, then, they have made a vital contribution to the electoral reform agenda that seeks to make the 2011 general elections more transparent and credible. In short, they have been active in the struggle to entrench democratic practices on three key fronts, namely: the development of more effective political parties that can play a role in democratic consolidation; the reform of the electoral process; and advocacy aimed at reforming INEC.

Concluding remarks

Significant threats to Nigeria's democracy remain. At the same time, however, there is genuine hope that citizen action can create the conditions necessary for the consolidation of democracy.

The threats exist on two levels. On one level, the constant subversion of the rules could undermine democracy as a rules-based game: the most basic rule – that people must be allowed to vote and their votes made to count – must be obeyed. On another level, it is vital that citizenship be strengthened and connections established between the electorate and its leaders. The idea of the 'people's mandate' is of utmost importance in this regard. The notion of the accountability of leaders to citizens makes sense only if it is understood that leaders rule because they enjoy a mandate from the people, and not because they have rigged the elections.

The tenure extension debate dramatized the ongoing struggles within Nigerian society between, on the one hand, vested interests and forces that seek to undermine democracy, and, on the other, institutions, groups and individuals that seek to safeguard and deepen democracy. But, even more fundamentally, the debate on (and the defeat of) the tenure extension agenda draws attention to the role and importance of citizen action in the project of deepening democracy. These roles continue to be played in combating other ploys to achieve tenure extension in the aftermath of the defeat of the Constitutional Amendment Bill.

One issue that has arisen from this study is the great capacity of incumbents to use state power to mediate and change the agenda set in motion by democratic actors. In this case, the struggle was to kill Obasanjo's third-term agenda and send him back to his farm once his two presidential terms were over. In response, Obasanjo employed state power in a bid either to force Nigerians to accept his choice of president or to create such conditions as would necessitate the declaration of a state of emergency, which would have enabled him to stay on in power. He sought to use the 2007 elections to throw the process of mobilization off course.

The processes we have reviewed in this study are responses by democratic forces to actions on the part of a regime bent on reversing democratic gains. The gains – hard won after decades of struggle against military authoritarianism – were being dismantled by a cabal that was betraying both the spirit and the letter of a new constitution that defined the norms of a democratic state. In a sense, what we have reviewed was a state crisis in Nigeria. It was a crisis during which people in the corridors of power substituted personal interest for the interests of the state. President Obasanjo did not express the interests of the Nigerian state: he acted on behalf of himself and the cabal surrounding him.

Following the 2007 elections, the new president admitted, during his inaugural address on 29 May 2007, that the elections had lacked integrity and that he would reform the process. In August of that year he established the Electoral Reform Committee (ERC), which submitted its report in December 2008. We, the authors, took part in the ERC – Jibrin Ibrahim as a member and Sam Egwu as a consultant. The committee included important personalities who had been involved in running a state that was struggling to democratize, among them a retired chief justice of Nigeria, an inspector-general of police and an army general who had served in the Obasanjo regime. We were often astonished that, in debates, those who ran the state apparatus were conscious of the fact that incumbents frequently did not act to promote the general good or even the interests of the state, and that (more often than not) they were self-serving. There is a notion of 'hybrid governance', which might well here be taken to mean the imposition of the personal interests of a ruling cabal on the state, with the aim of weakening (and indeed subverting) the state and its norms.

On the critical issue of democratic outcomes and democratic gains, the question is whether some kinds of mobilization are more likely than others to lead to forms of governance that permit more democratic outcomes. In seeking an answer to this, it is important to bear in mind that state power gives the people who control it an enormous disruptive capacity, enabling them to use it with the express purpose of derailing political mobilization for democracy. However, precisely because of the dialectics of struggle, they are often not able to achieve their objectives. The conclusion reached by this study of Nigeria is eloquent in this respect:

1 President Obasanjo wanted to change the constitution to extend his tenure, and used state power to try to enforce his wishes.
2 A popular movement, under the leadership of the opposition political elite, successfully mobilized to stop and defeat him.

3 He punished the political opposition by using state power to ensure that the majority of those who opposed him were prevented from winning their seats in the next election.
4 He also changed the terms of the debate by imposing another president on the people, on the assumption that the new president would do his bidding.
5 Today, however, the president and those parliamentarians that former President Obasanjo foisted on the country have deconstructed his policies and interests. They are showing the population how excessively high his level of corruption was and, as it were, demonstrating to Nigerians that they were correct to mobilize against Obasanjo in order to deepen democracy.

Democracy does not get deepened in linear progression. However, we can still discern a trajectory along which democratic forces can return the country to a democratic agenda, albeit in a rather staccato way. One lesson that emerges from this study is that we should be wary of leaping to the conclusion that 'the state' is in the opposing camp. Obasanjo failed because, within the state apparatus, people knew he was pursuing a personal agenda; people working for the state leaked information at critical times; many of them pretended to support his plan, while in fact subverting it behind his back; some state governors who funded the third-term agenda in public also secretly funded the opposition in secret.

A second lesson to be drawn from the study is that democracy is too important a human value for us to justify its existence by its putative usefulness in boosting the economy or improving livelihoods. Obasanjo's strategy for self-succession was based on the argument that his economic policies were good for the people. Even those who believed this, however, felt that it provided insufficient grounds to justify prolonging his mandate.

At the same time, when democracy has no positive impact on people's lives, it renders itself irrelevant. Many Nigerians knew that Obasanjo's claims of economic advancement were false, for the simple reason that they were suffering from the effects of economic deprivation. People organized against Obasanjo because they saw none of the economic dividends of democracy.

These lessons reassure us in our conviction that the mobilization and mediation practices that confronted the tenure extension plot provide useful insights into how the struggle to deepen democracy works. These lessons include the importance of forging alliances between pro-democracy elements in the political classes, parliament and civil society to demand the minimum conditions required for the rule of law and constitutionalism to flourish. They also include the need to build a critical mass of people to support democratic processes and values by stressing the organic connection between democracy, development and welfare.

Notes

1 This happened in the Senate on 16 May 2006 and in the House of Representatives on 17 May, killing the bid for a presidential third term.

2 The term 'divine' is not excessive. President Obasanjo started each day with a prayer meeting at 6 a.m., in which God's guidance for good governance was sought, and he built a chapel in the presidential villa. Every Sunday, Nigerians were bombarded on national television by prayers for Obasanjo's vision of Nigeria, which was guided by Christian doctrine and declared to be an expression of God's will for Nigeria.

3 These geopolitical zones are north-east, north-west, north-central, south-east, south-south and south-west.

4 There are about fifty political parties, four of which are major. The ruling People's Democratic Party (PDP) remains dominant, holding power at the national level and controlling twenty-six of the thirty-six states.

5 This group, popularly referred to as the 'Transcorp Gang', was a private company that the government supported with national assets. It became an organ used by the president's business friends (who called themselves 'Corporate Nigeria') and a platform that was used to raise substantial money for President Obasanjo's re-election bid in 2003.

6 President Obasanjo himself admitted on national television that a PDP chieftain from Anambra State, Chris Uba, claimed to have masterminded a rigged governorship election in that state in 2003.

7 The court confirmed that in Ogun State (President Obasanjo's home state) more votes had been cast in the presidential election than there were registered voters.

8 Many of the legislators mentioned between 50 million and 100 million Nigerian Naira as the amount the president was willing to give any legislator willing to support the 'third-term' bid.

9 It was Senator Sule Yari Gari's call on the floor of the Senate, at the bill's second reading, for an 'aye' or 'nay' vote on the Constitutional Amendment Bill that produced the overwhelming 'nay' response that finally killed it.

10 Notable among the governors were Alhaji Abudullahi Adamu (Nasarawa), Alhaji Makarfi (Kaduna), Gbenga Daniel (Ogun State) and Peter Odili (Rivers).

11 Chukwumerije was one of the members who fought tenure extension from within the Joint Committee of the National Assembly, reaching out to the media at critical stages in the deliberations.

12 Statements issued at the height of the tenure extension plot by US and British officials, as well as by the UN secretary-general,

deplored the disrespect being shown to the idea of terms of office, the manipulation of the constitutional review process and the notion that a particular leader was indispensable. These statements show that significant sections of the international community were not carried away by the reform argument.

13 Not only did eight serving governors oppose tenure extension, but they funded the campaigns in one way or another. They were Orji Uzor Kalu (Abia), Attahiru Bafarawa (Sokoto), Bola Ahmed Tinubu (Lagos), Joshua Dariye (Plateau), Ibrahim Shekarau (Kano), Abdulkadir Kure (Niger), Boni Haruna (Adamawa) and George Akume (Benue).

14 *Daily Trust*, 11 May 2006.

15 *Daily Trust*, 3 April 2006.

16 Comprising the National Council of Muslim Youth Organizations, Muslim Students Society of Nigeria, Abuja Muslim Forum, Muslim Corpers Association, The Muslim Congress, Joint Islamic Organizations, Jama'atul Tajididil Islamy and the National Council for the Defence and Propagation of Sharia.

17 NACATT issued a strong statement against the third term, entitled 'Don't Destroy Our Unity with Third Term', *Tell*, 29 May 2006: 1–12.

18 These include the Transition Monitoring Group , United Action for Democracy, the League for Human Rights, the Centre for Democracy and Development, the Civil Liberties Organization, the Electoral Reform Network, the Youth Alliance for Good Governance and several women's groups.

19 *Daily Trust*, 17 May 2006.

20 *Guardian* (Nigeria), 15 June 2006.

21 *Vanguard*, 26 May 2006.

22 *Daily Trust*, 11 May 2006.

7 · How deep is 'deep democracy'? Grassroots globalization from Mumbai to Cape Town[1]

STEVEN ROBINS

> [Deep democracy] constitutes an effort to institute what we may call 'democracy without borders', after the analogy of international class solidarity as conceived by the visionaries of world socialism in its heyday. This effort is what I seek to theorize in terms of deep democracy. (Appadurai, 2002: 45)

> As the tasks of the state have become more complex and the size of polities larger and more heterogeneous, the institutional forms of liberal democracy developed in the nineteenth century – representative democracy plus techno-bureaucratic administration – seem increasingly ill-suited to the novel problems we face in the twenty-first century... Increasingly, this mechanism of political representation seems ineffective in accomplishing the central ideals of democratic politics: facilitating active political involvement of the citizenry, forging political consensus through dialogue, devising and implementing public policies that ground a productive economy and healthy society, and, in more radical egalitarian versions of the democratic ideal, assuring that all citizens benefit from the nation's wealth. (Fung and Wright, 2001: 1)

Introduction: the limits of liberal democracy

Notwithstanding the triumphal post-Cold War celebration of the world-wide spread of liberal democracy, pervasive voter apathy and citizen cynicism continue to be identified as symptoms of the fundamental flaws in the representative and procedural democracies of the West and beyond. In response to this bleak prognosis, governments and donors have shown considerable interest, over the last two decades, in programmes aimed at strengthening 'civil society' and at creating 'active citizenship', especially as they facilitate transitions to democracy. In the context of the collapse of the Soviet Union and the fall of the Berlin Wall, as well as of various popular struggles against apartheid, dictatorships and military regimes in Africa, Asia and Latin America, the idea of 'civil society' has taken on a particularly potent significance in the popular imagination, as well as in donor-driven democracy programmes (Comaroff and Comaroff, 1999). However, celebrations of 'civil society' and transitions to democracy have, in recent years, given way to cynical assessments and to the circulation of new terms, such as 'low intensity democracy' (Gills et al., 1992) and 'democracy lite' (Paley, 2002). Notwithstanding this widespread disenchantment with these thin versions of democracy, the idea of civil society continues to be equated with democratic renewal. This, in turn, has spurred the proliferation of non-governmental organizations (NGOs).[2]

Most studies of democratic renewal have been interested in questions of procedural democracy and issues relating to formal political institutions, regime transitions, elections and party politics. For instance, low voter turnout in the United States and Europe has spurred numerous studies and democracy programmes concerned with the role of social capital (Putnam, 1993a), citizen participation, NGOs and voluntary organizations, all of which were viewed as antidotes to these 'democratic deficits' (Luckham et al., 2003). Among many critics who bemoan the limits of procedural democracy, the existence of civil society organizations is perceived as a panacea, promoting 'active citizenship' in the face of growing voter and civic apathy. For similar reasons, projects aimed at 'deepening democracy' have attracted much attention and debate in academic, donor, activist and NGO circles.

However, the notion of 'deepening democracy' (in the same way as concepts such as empowerment, civil society, participation and citizenship) can mean virtually anything – and yet also, simultaneously, nothing special. In other words, although the polyvalent character of such keywords may be rhetorically productive, they are often analytically weak. It is for this very reason that the purpose of this chapter is to ground the discussion of deep democracy in an analysis of the specific ways in which a South African social movement has attempted to give concrete content to abstract ideas about democratic rights and citizenship. In particular, we will investigate how a globally connected organization that claims to be 'deepening democracy' and working across national borders can end up becoming very parochial and strengthening patron–client relations. In other words, whatever the 'cosmopolitan' orientation of the organization's ideology, its actual practice was fundamentally shaped by local struggles over access to resources.

The discussion here will focus, particularly, on a globally connected social movement – the South African Homeless People's Federation (SAHPF). The SAHPF is a women's organization of the urban poor that is involved in a wide range of activities, including savings clubs, housing and land issues, income-generation projects, community policing and AIDS intervention. In the course of its struggles for access to housing for poor people in South Africa, it has been able to develop both vertical (local/national) and horizontal (transnational/global) networks, alliances and coalitions. Before discussing the actual ideas and practices of the SAHPF, however, it is necessary to provide some background to the political and economic context within which this organization operates.

A brief sketch of the post-apartheid political and economic landscape

South Africa is a relatively wealthy emerging economy, characterized by extreme forms of socio-economic inequality comparable to that found in countries such as Brazil. Following the first democratic elections in 1994, the African National Congress (ANC) government opted for what has been described as a standard package of neoliberal macro-economic policies. Leftist critics (Marais, 1998; Alexander, 2002; Bond, 2000; Terreblanche, 2002) have argued that these neoliberal policies have been responsible for growth in unemployment, major cutbacks in government social expenditure, cost-recovery measures, the privatization of essential services such as water, electricity and transport, and the disconnection of essential services for those in arrears. From this perspective, the ANC government certainly has capitulated to the neoliberal agenda.

Despite divergent explanations for why and how this has happened, there is consensus among these critics that the policies and privatization initiatives under the ANC's Growth, Equity and Reconstruction programme have failed to redress (in any significant way) the forms of racialized poverty and inequality inherited from the apartheid era. In fact, current macro-economic policies have been perceived as exacerbating inequalities that have their roots in colonial and apartheid history. This failure to improve the conditions of the bottom 50 per cent of the population has occurred despite the government's claims to have achieved moderate rates of inflation, a growing economy, and state provision of housing, clean water, electricity and thousands of new classrooms and clinics. This is by no means a 'conventional' neoliberal state: the government has also established massive social grant programmes, has a well-funded and reasonably well-functioning public health system, and has provided over 1.5 million housing subsidies to its poorest citizens. Despite the benefits of a progressive constitution and some improvements in the delivery of services to the poor, South Africa continues to have massive unemployment and one of the most unequal income distribution curves in the world.

It is also the case that a significant number of South Africa's citizens consider some of the liberal rights entrenched in the South African constitution to be western imports that do not reflect African values and provide few material benefits to the poor. These rights are widely believed to entrench 'un-African ideas', such as gay and lesbian rights, same-sex marriages and abortion. Given the growing levels of inequality and unemployment in the country, it is perhaps not surprising that the constitution does not carry the same symbolic freight for the impoverished masses as it does for the middle classes and 'true believers' in liberal democracy.

Critics on the left have also claimed that South Africa's neoliberal economic policies have contributed to the dilution of the socio-economic rights expressed in the constitution, and to a narrowing of the scope of those rights in ways that have negative implications for 'deepening democracy' in post-apartheid South Africa. It would seem that these limitations of the post-apartheid liberal state, especially in the sphere of socio-economic transformation, are precisely why NGOs, religious organizations and new social movements have stepped into the breach. The SAHPF, the Treatment Action Campaign, the Anti-Eviction Campaign, the Anti-Privatization Forum, the Soweto Electricity Crisis Committee, the Landless People's Movement and the national housing activist organization Abahlali baseMjondolo (Shack Dwellers' Movement) can be seen as vibrant civil society responses to the perceived failures of the post-apartheid state, liberal democracy and neoliberal economic policies to address issues of housing, AIDS, job creation and poverty. Ongoing service delivery protests, at times resulting in violence and the destruction of state property, as well as high levels of crime, are also symptoms of the limits of the post-apartheid state's macro-economic policies and socio-economic transformation programmes. The discussion below will focus on a social movement that has experimented with methodologies for mobilizing towards Appadurai's 'deep democracy'.

'Deep democracy' at the tip of Africa?

On 17 September 2002, about 200 people from various race, class and ethnic backgrounds gathered at the Centre for the Book in Cape Town's city centre to hear the internationally known housing activist Sheela Patel. She spoke about the work of an alliance of Mumbai-based slum-dweller federations, which is part of the global network of the Slum Dwellers International (SDI) (to which the SAHPF was also affiliated). The audience included a large group of black South African women and youth from the SAHPF, as well as activists, Members of Parliament, judges, academics and ordinary citizens. This was Patel's twentieth visit to Cape Town as part of an exchange programme between housing activists and slum dwellers from India, Thailand, South Africa and eleven other developing countries that had been going on for over a decade. She spoke of her organization's strategies for empowering the urban poor in India – of the 'horizontal exchange' savings schemes, toilet festivals,[3] self-enumeration and self-census exercises, and various other empowerment rituals deployed by a number of Indian women's federations. She concluded by noting that houses, savings, good governance and accountability were not the primary objectives of the slum dwellers' organizations in the federations. Instead, their aim was to create poor people's networks linking southern countries, in order to fight the isolation and disempowerment engendered by conditions of poverty.

SAHPF members, many of whom had visited India, spoke of their own experiences of establishing savings groups and building their own houses in Cape Town's African townships. They spoke of how organizing as a federation – and being members of a partnership between a social movement and an NGO – had assisted them in accessing state housing subsidies. The Indian model of savings and housing federations had also provided these women with the leverage they needed to access state and donor resources. This 'town hall' meeting in the heart of a still hyper-segregated, post-apartheid city seemed to provide a glimpse into what Appadurai (2002) refers to as 'globalization from below' or 'grassroots globalization'. He suggests that:

> one of the many paradoxes of democracy is that it is organized to function within the boundaries of the nation-state [in order] to realize one or another image of the common good or general will. Yet its values make sense only when they are conceived and deployed universally, which is to say, when they are global in reach. (2002: 45)

This contradiction is heightened in the phase of globalization that exists today, as nation states are increasingly rendered susceptible to the influence of global governance, and as their national borders become more porous in relation to global flows of people, capital, ideas and commodities. Appadurai suggests that there are, essentially, two ways of reviving democratic principles in this scenario. The first way is to take advantage of the speed of communications technologies and the sweep of global markets to compel national governments to recognize the universal democratic principles embedded in the politics of human rights. The second way would have social movements and NGOs promote what Appadurai refers to as 'democracy without borders' – a concept that resonates with the international class solidarity envisaged by the project of world socialism. It is this second method that Appadurai theorizes in terms of 'deep democracy':

> In terms of its semantics, deep democracy suggests roots, anchors, intimacy, proximity, and locality. And these are important associations. Much of this essay has been taken up with values and strategies [such] as inclusion, participation, transparency, and accountability, as articulated within an activist formation. But I want to suggest that the lateral reach of such movements – their efforts to build international networks or coalitions of some durability with their counterparts across national boundaries – is also part of their 'depth'. (2002: 45–6)

Appadurai theorized deep democracy in relation to the activities of affiliates of SDI in Mumbai, who, he notes, are concerned with spreading ideas and practices related to housing, citizenship and participation across national borders. These SDI ideas and practices are also spread beyond and outside the direct reach of state and market regimes (2002: 46). The SDI is also concerned with engaging in partnerships with more powerful actors at the urban, regional, national and international levels. In other words, SDI operates vertically and horizontally. Rather than conceptualizing this form of 'deep democracy' as a coherent political programme or project, Appadurai calls for contextually grounded, historically situated ethnographic studies of particular manifestations of these experimental forms of democracy in various parts of the world:

> Like all serious exercises in democratic practice, it is not automatically reproductive. It has particular conditions of possibility and conditions under which it grows weak or corrupt. The study of these conditions – which include such contingencies as leadership, morale, flexibility, and material enablement – requires many more case studies of specific movements and organizations. (2002: 45–6)

Although the connections forged across borders by social movements are obviously not necessarily either democratic or deep, there does seem to be an assumption in much of the literature of social movements that 'grassroots globalization' is both democratic and deep. For instance, Appadurai does not adequately address, in his very optimistic account of the democratic potential of the SDI's experiments in 'grassroots globalization', the widespread tendency of these global social movements to be 'hijacked' by local and national actors who are determined to access and control political, social and material resources. These anti-democratic outcomes, which tend to result in the strengthening of patron–client relations at the local and national levels, are routinely ignored or underplayed in the mainstream literature on grassroots democracy and global social movements. By contrast, the case study in this chapter highlights the relationship between local struggles for access to resources and the strengthening of patron–client relations that challenge the democratizing impulses underpinning social movement initiatives.

The Cape Town case discussed in this chapter offers a cautionary tale for those studies that romanticize or overstate the democratic possibilities of 'globalization from below'. It also demonstrates the need for more case studies of specific movements and organizations.

Deep democracy from Calcutta to Cape Town

A few years ago, I did research on the Victoria Mxenge (VMx) Housing Federation, a low-income housing scheme situated on the outskirts of Cape Town. The VMx Federation is a community-based organization (CBO) that is affiliated to the SAHPF,[4] which at the time was supported by a Cape Town-based NGO called the People's Dialogue (PD). The PD was composed of mainly middle-class, mostly white professionals, who provided technical, planning and financial services to the federations affiliated to the SAHPF. Like the SAHPF, the PD was affiliated to the global social movement SDI. The SAHPF–PD partnership was formed in 1991 and comprised mostly black African members, of whom more than 85,000 (85 per cent) were women (SAHPF, 2005). Through its connection to the SDI, the SAHPF–PD was part of a network of poor people's organizations that had affiliates in fourteen countries, with memberships that ranged from a few hundred people in Zambia to more than 1.5 million in India. The stated objective of the SDI federations is for members to assume 'ownership of problems and the identification of local solutions that are participatory and inclusive [and] by doing so they automatically create new nodal points of governance, in which organised communities of the urban poor assume their rightful place as development actors' (SDI, 2002: 14). The SAHPF slogan – 'We do not collect money, we collect people' – captures the organization's concern with 'social capital'.

Drawing largely on the Indian experience over the past two decades, the SAHPF–PD partnership promoted daily savings as a 'ritual' that seeks to produce high levels of participation and mutual interaction between federation members – these daily encounters are seen as the 'social glue' that binds communities together. In addition, by investing (albeit limited) funds, members have a material stake in their organization and its decision-making.

Not only do daily savings encourage regular interaction, but they also create a space for the central participation of women in informal settlements and townships that tend to be dominated by patriarchal local structures. They are also meant to shift the balance of power and expert knowledge from technocratic and hierarchical state structures to local, decentralized federations. Savings and loans likewise enable federations to develop the capacity to manage and control finance and to display this local competence to the outside world. Members learn housing design, construction and finance, layout design, brick making, toilet construction, crafts and a range of other competencies, including bookkeeping, census enumeration and information gathering. They get to know methods of identifying vacant land through physical mapping and visits to the deeds offices, and they develop their negotiation skills in order to secure land from the state.

These activities are consciously framed as public performances of local competence and innovation. This serves a number of purposes, not least to pose a challenge to existing class cultures and beliefs about where expertise lies. It is an expression of a politics of visibility and a public demonstration of 'autogovernmentality' or 'governance from below' (Appadurai, 2002). Horizontal exchange (also referred to as 'poor people's pedagogy') consists of visits between federations. This is another important SDI ritual that seeks to foster direct, peer-to-peer learning experiences, rather than the usual expert-driven methods of formal training. These visits also facilitate the creation of new transnational solidarities and networks, and are a catalyst for cross-cultural reflection and analysis by federation members.

The following section focuses on the glaring gap between the official ideology and 'praxiology' of the SDI and the PD on the one side, and, on the other, the everyday practices and local political cultures of the VMx Federation in Philippi, Cape Town.

'Mind the gap': the case of the Victoria Mxenge Housing Federation

> We are doing the daily savings not only to collect money but to collect the lives of the people. We do this so that they can know what is happening next door, what is happening today and tomorrow, how can I help, how can we involve each other daily. (VMx member, Philippi, Cape Town, July 2002)

> The language of the Federation is saturated with [social capital] imagery: 'We build houses in order to build people'; 'we don't collect money, we collect people'. That is all over the show. (Joel Bolnick, PD founder and director, Observatory, Cape Town, July 2002)

VMx is a low-income housing scheme situated on the outskirts of Cape Town. With donor, NGO and state support, this predominantly Xhosa-speaking women's organization has been able to build significant numbers of houses. As a result of its successes, it has captured the imagination of tourists, government officials, NGOs, academics, diplomats, politicians and international figures such as Hillary and Bill Clinton. The VMx housing project consists of single- and double-storey brick houses with neat gardens. It can be described as a 'post-apartheid' low-income housing showpiece. These VMx houses are noticeably larger than the million tiny government-subsidized houses built in South Africa's black townships since 1994.

What is particularly interesting about the project is that, for more than a decade, its members have travelled to various parts of Africa, Asia and Latin America to meet other housing and savings organizations. This global network seems to embody what is increasingly seen as the emergence of an international civil society of global citizens. The members of VMx are primarily working-class, black African women who belong to savings schemes that are affiliated to the SAHPF.

While the ideology of both the PD and SDI stressed the importance of horizontal relations of trust and non-hierarchical, decentralized political structures and practices within and between federations, the SAHPF's decision-making structures were different. Largely as a result of the success of the housing scheme at VMx, and the considerable amount of donor and state funding that it generated, a leadership cluster was able to establish itself as the 'nerve centre' of all SAHPF activities in the Western Cape Province. This leadership established some highly centralized decision-making structures, and was unwilling to relinquish its control and authority over 'junior' federations. This resulted in the consolidation of local hierarchies, power cliques and patronage networks that allowed certain individuals to act as gatekeepers and power-brokers. It also resulted in accusations of financial mismanagement and widespread grievances concerning the alleged undemocratic practices of the leadership. These developments culminated in general disillusionment with savings schemes and a large-scale withdrawal of federation members from such schemes. As an urban planning professional from the PD put it: 'The Federation has still been very successful in securing land in the city and initiating housing developments', but once people get these resources, they often see no reason for continuing to belong to the savings schemes and tend to withdraw from federation activities.

The leadership style of the SAHPF contradicted the democratic vision of SDI and the PD. However, altering these hierarchical political styles and power dynamics proved to be extremely difficult. This was especially the case at showpiece federations that were regularly visited by dignitaries, donors and government officials. One strategy adopted by the PD to decentralize and dismantle these concentrations of power was to attempt to 'reinvent' the organizational structure of federations through a system of rotational leadership. It also worked to resuscitate local savings schemes and devolve decision-making powers to them. These initiatives, however, encountered fierce opposition from a powerful SAHPF leadership that was determined to hold on to power and to resist attempts to decentralize the decision-making structures. This contributed to regular clashes between the PD and the SAHPF.

There were numerous other divergences between the desires, agendas and objectives of the NGO and its CBO partners, the SAHPF and its constituent federations. For instance, the PD, like SDI and its Indian affiliates, believed that the long-term processes of creating and 'scaling up' 'social capital' and community building were more important than product-driven concerns such as housing construction. However, the PD's commitment to building 'social capital' through savings was not always shared by SAHPF members. Unlike their counterparts in India, many South African federation members did not seem to buy into daily savings and other federation activities as 'rituals'.

Another key area of difference related to the political culture of the individual housing federations within the SAHPF. While these organizations were meant to be non-party-political, a number of the leadership figures were seasoned ANC Women's League veterans, who were deeply enmeshed in local, regional and national ANC networks. Furthermore, whereas the PD believed in 'critical engagement' with the government, many in the ANC-aligned SAHPF leadership were willing to allow the federations to be used as ANC political resources. Moreover, unlike their Indian partners, South African federation members tended to view the ANC government as a powerful patronage machine that could be accessed through party-political contacts and channels.

This perception of a powerful state was reinforced by the reality of the state housing subsidies. The state was perceived not only as a ready provider of material resources, but also as a repository of technical expertise and know-how. This SAHPF perception of the power of the technocratic state was very different from the anti-technocratic, anti-hierarchical and anti-bureaucratic perspective of the PD and SDI. Whereas the PD and SDI challenged the expert–client relationship, it seemed that rank-and-file federation members, as well as the leadership, were not always as committed to this anti-technocratic development agenda.

PD practitioners and SAHPF members openly acknowledged the gap between SDI's 'global ideology' of building horizontal relations of trust and solidarity, and the complex social realities that federation members experienced on a daily basis. They were also all too aware that the SDI development paradigm was not necessarily shared and embraced by federation members. This was particularly evident when federation members withdrew from regular participation in savings schemes once their houses were complete.

These competing understandings of development and deep democracy permeated many aspects of the PD's involvement with the SAHPF. The website and newsletter publications of the PD and SDI promoted the long-term building of horizontal relations of trust and social capital. By contrast, the SAHPF leadership at the VMx settlement seemed more concerned with housing delivery and the consolidation of vertical relations of patronage and dependency. This political practice challenged the SDI's vision of an anti-elite, anti-hierarchical, anti-technocratic and decentralized development model. PD members acknowledged that federation members, especially the leadership, seemed more interested in land acquisition and in building houses than investing in less tangible outcomes such as 'trust', 'networks', 'social capital' or democratic and accountable governance systems. These competing development visions and agendas were graphically illustrated in the VMx case.

The SAHPF leadership that emerged from (and that was based at) VMx, having established centralized decision-making structures, began to control and dominate other savings federations in the Western Cape. The centralizing processes intensified with VMx's successes in attracting international media attention, donors and visiting dignitaries. Despite the PD's attempts to 'restructure' and 'reinvent' organizational structures to counteract and subvert the centralization and consolidation of local power around certain VMx leaders, these tendencies and processes persisted. Attempts to decentralize and disperse these localized nodes of power were contested by the strong VMx leadership.

Dissatisfaction with this centralized federation leadership contributed to a decline in participation in the federations in the Western Cape, culminating in the collapse of many savings schemes. The PD's strategy for resuscitating savings collectives also sought to decentralize decision-making power and control over financial resources and delegate these to local-level structures. Dependency on relatively large state housing subsidies, however, meant that South African federations were generally less self-sufficient and less committed to long-term investment in building social and financial capital through everyday savings rituals than were their Indian counterparts. Instead, many SAHPF members sought to gain access to housing subsidies through patronage networks and client–patron relationships at the local level.

Conclusion

This case study has drawn attention to the disjuncture between the official ideology of SDI and the everyday ideas and practices of rank-and-file members of the SAHPF in Cape Town. It has shown how the horizontal, non-party-political, non-hierarchical, democratic ideology of SDI came to clash with the ANC patronage networks and leadership cliques that had developed among the grassroots housing activists in some of Cape Town's townships. Whereas SDI was interested in promoting horizontal forms of 'social capital' and 'deep democracy', a small group of veteran housing activist leaders used their connections with the ANC and NGO leadership to entrench hierarchies and amass personal and material power.

The case study focused on the complex forms of mobilization deployed by SAHPF activists to leverage access to donor funding and state housing subsidies. It also interrogated the SDI concept of deep democracy and highlighted tensions between rights-based approaches to development and locally embedded political cultures of patronage, hierarchy and authority. The case study ultimately raises the questions: how deep is 'deep democracy' and how grassroots is 'grassroots globalization'? Although experiments in deep democracy often encounter the kinds of problems identified in the VMx case study, it seems that such concepts nonetheless continue to hold out the prospect of tackling the limitations and failures of liberal democracies.

This chapter has also attempted to show how the PD and SAHPF used sophisticated strategies of 'cross-border activism' and global networking to create horizontal relations of trust and solidarity. The case study investigated what 'deep democracy' actually means in terms of the everyday practices and strategic priorities of organizations of the poor – such as the PD and SAHPF. It would seem that, despite the numerous difficulties identified in the chapter, the forms of social capital developed through SAHPF rituals of daily savings and 'horizontal exchange' can contribute towards the emergence of self-reliant communities.

In spite of the creative and sustained efforts by SDI federations from Cape Town to Calcutta to build social capital and communities with long-term commitments, the urban poor often have to deal with high levels of distrust and conflict that undermine these social ties and solidarities. Dissatisfaction with undemocratic leadership practices was a widely cited reason for the decision to exit federation savings schemes in Cape Town; however, this was not the case in many other parts of South Africa. But clearly social capital, solidarity and trust – like global capital in the conditions of late capitalism – can be fluid and fickle; here today and gone tomorrow. Yet the successes and longevity of many federations in other parts of South Africa and the developing world suggest that these innovative organizations can indeed meet many of the needs of poor people living under the harsh conditions of neoliberalism and the global retreat of the developmental state.

In 2005, three years after Sheela Patel's talk, the Cape Town SAHPF and the PD were in a state of deep crisis, as a result of financial mismanagement and serious conflict between the PD's middle-class professionals and the SAHPF's working-class leadership. Deep divisions had also surfaced between the VMx leadership and rival federations in Western Cape Province. In 2005, as a result of these intractable conflicts, it was decided to disband the PD.

It had become apparent that the VMx leadership had accumulated extraordinary influence and power in ways that undermined the SDI's model for deep democracy, with its emphasis on non-hierarchical, decentralized leadership and grassroots mobilization. Instead of promoting this SDI model, the VMx leadership had established a centralized style of leadership that tightly controlled federation resources in fundamentally anti-democratic ways. Whereas the SDI's model seemed to work well in India and other parts of Asia and Africa, in Cape Town's predominantly Xhosa-speaking township of Philippi it had produced an authoritarian leadership. Rather than viewing this state of affairs simply as a reflection of a political culture specific to the townships of the Western Cape, I argue elsewhere that the VMx case study tells us something more general about the politics of clientelism and patronage in the post-colonial world (Robins, 2008; Robins et al., 2008).

Notwithstanding these disappointing reports 'from the field', for many NGO activists, academics, donors and policymakers the emergence of social movements such as SDI reflects the burgeoning of a global civil society that offers prospects for a renewal and deepening of liberal democracy in the global South. Yet, in many cases, these well-intentioned civil society interventions end up looking like anything but deep democracy. The VMx case study shows how attempts to deepen democracy through the SAHPF network ended up (unwittingly) reinforcing local power asymmetries and patronage networks. It demonstrates that the SDI model of deep democracy, when viewed from Cape Town's African townships, failed to produce horizontal networks and democratic forms of social capital and solidarity. Instead, it reveals the ambiguous, and at times highly contradictory, relationship between SDI's global vision of deep democracy and the everyday local realities and political practices of the community-based leadership of this social movement for the urban poor. However disappointing this example of 'deep authoritarianism', it is quite conceivable that SDI experiments with deep democracy elsewhere could have very different outcomes. In other words, as Appadurai suggests, there is a need for contextually grounded studies of historically situated manifestations of these experimental forms of democracy in different parts of the world.

Notes

1 A longer version of this chapter can be found in Robins (2008).

2 As Sampson (1996: 128) noted in an ethnography of a Danish agency involved in democracy programmes in Albania, 'few NGOs meant less democracy, more NGOs meant more democracy'.

3 See Appadurai's (2002) fascinating account of SAHPF's SDI partners in Bombay, in which he analyses SDI rituals of 'toilet festivals' and what he refers to as 'the politics of shit'. Appadurai describes a carnivalesque spirit of transgression and bawdiness that prevails during toilet inspections in the presence of middle-class government and World Bank officials. This is interpreted by Appadurai as an attempt to redefine the private act of humiliation and suffering – shitting in the open – into a scene of technical innovation and self-dignification. It is seen as an innovative 'politics of recognition from below'.

4 In 2007, as a result of deeply entrenched tensions and conflicts within the SAHPF, a new breakaway organization was formed called the Federation of the Urban Poor (FEDUP).

PART THREE

Citizen involvement in formal governance mechanisms

8 · The infinite agenda of social justice: *dalit* mobilization in Indian institutions of local governance

RANJITA MOHANTY[1]

Introduction

Over the past two decades, states around the world have been promoting participatory local democracy through new institutional forms of local governance. While the new institutions promise to include the poor and the marginalized in decision-making, encouraging them to exercise their option to participate politically, there are caveats, issues and challenges that characterize local governance institutions and the processes that take place within them. These statutory spaces, referred to as 'invited spaces', have opened up possibilities for grassroots participation in decision-making on local development and governance; however, as state-created and regulated spaces, they also suffer from many limitations. Consequently, their actual potential to encourage substantive participation by marginalized populations has often come under searching scrutiny (Cornwall and Coelho, 2007).

In India, following a constitutional amendment in 1992, local governance institutions called *panchayats* were formed in rural areas. *Panchayats* are responsible for ensuring economic development and social justice for rural populations. A third of the seats in *panchayats* are reserved for women, a third for *dalits*[2] (low castes) and a third for tribals (indigenous people) in order to ensure their membership and participation. However, the mere act of making people who were hitherto excluded from political participation and decision-making formal members of a local government has not guaranteed their actual inclusion in these institutions.

Even as their representation is sought, agendas are finalized and, in many instances, actual decisions are taken before their opinions are solicited. Often, there is such disparity in the power and influence of *panchayat* members that it becomes very difficult for less powerful members to influence a decision. Hence, we find women excluded from a predominantly male space; illiterates excluded because the literate can control the documents, records and accounts; and low castes and the poor excluded because the locally dominant caste and economically powerful groups continue to occupy the positions of power in these state-created institutions (Mohanty, 2007).

The rhetoric of participation – or, more accurately, of the touted participation – by the marginalized remains a constant in the state version of participatory democracy. This is promoted through what is proclaimed as participatory local governance, but the state does nothing to equip people for this participation. Government declarations of participation, therefore, have remained full of empty rhetoric, making it necessary for people to mobilize and make their own claims. Civil society often provides spaces where people learn the skills to articulate, represent their interests, organize and lead (ibid.).

This chapter presents the findings of a study conducted in Sabarkantha District Gujarat, where the deep-rooted practice of having certain people marked as 'untouchable' has left the *dalits* on the margins of society and polity. There will be a discussion of *dalit* mobilization in *panchayat* institutions – spearheaded by local civil society organizations (CSOs) – aimed at securing social justice for them. This is one of the critical tasks that local governance institutions must undertake to ensure local democracy. I will critically examine the interaction between *panchayats* which have been promoted by the state as participatory democratic institutions and the mobilization of poor, low-caste people seeking social justice. This will illustrate the democratic deficits that continue to plague institutions despite large-scale mobilization, and will show some of the democratic gains that can be achieved when the most marginalized of groups mobilize.

The central question of this chapter deals with the democratic outcomes that flow from mobilizations for social justice that take place within institutions created by the state to promote democracy. By analysing the democratic outcome of the *dalit* mobilization in *panchayats* in Sabarkantha, I will focus on three critical dimensions that constitute a democratic outcome: democracy within local governance institutions, democracy in social relations and democracy in the distribution of development resources to *dalits*. The research reveals that substantial gains have been made in ensuring the redistribution of developmental goods and services to *dalit* communities, but that the institutions themselves have remained largely closed. Institutions have been resistant to accepting *dalits* as equals, and the occasional *dalit* attempt to equalize social relations has yet to make an impact on the institutions. The study reveals a number of paradoxes in the practice of development and democracy as it exists in local governance institutions and in the social setting where the institutions are located.

The chapter is divided into four sections. The first provides the location, issues and methodology of the study. The second contains an overview of participatory local governance institutions: how social justice is framed within them and the issues surrounding *dalit* participation in them. The third is a discussion of three critical facets of *dalit* mobilization: mobilizing for institutional efficacy, mobilizing for developmental redistribution and mobilizing to widen the social space for equality and dignity. The final section raises some issues concerning the paradoxes of democracy and development as evident from the interaction between *dalit* mobilization and local governance institutions.

Locating the study[3]

Sabarkantha is one of the twenty-five districts that comprise the state of Gujarat, in the western part of India. The 2001 Census recorded 7.1 per cent Scheduled Caste[4] (SC) population in Gujarat and 8.3 per cent SC population in Sabarkantha. The prominent *dalit* sub-caste groups that constitute the SC population in Sabarkantha are *vankars* (weavers), *chamars* (leather workers and tanners), *chenbas* (who make bamboo products), *tirgars* (who, in the past, made bows and arrows), *turis* (barbers; they also beat drums during festivals), *garupandyas* (who perform religious rituals for the *dalits*) and *valmikis* (village garbage cleaners). *Valmikis* are the lowest in the sub-caste hierarchy of the *dalits* and are considered the 'lowest of the low'. *Dalits*, in addition to their caste occupations, also work as wage labourers – many of them in agriculture or construction. Some of them have small landholdings, but the produce from their own fields is not enough on its own to support them.

When local governance institutions were formed following the enactment of the 73rd Constitutional Amendment in 1992, the government of Gujarat also enacted special legislation to create social justice committees (SJCs) to function as *panchayat* subcommittees. SJCs were created by the state to promote the agenda of social justice, which includes the values of equality and participation, and the egalitarian distribution of development resources, so that marginalized populations (particularly the *dalits*) could overcome domination and exclusion. However, the political and administrative will of the state ended with the amendment, and any power the committees have has remained on paper only. In some villages, committees were set up but did not function; in others, they were not established at all. In principle, the *panchayats* are to work on the agenda of social justice by recruiting members from *dalit* communities through election. A third of the seats in each *panchayat* are reserved for *dalit* members, and *dalit* members are to make up the

SJC, with the approval of the head of the *panchayat*. The SJC, in turn, is responsible for extending economic development and social justice, as administered by the *panchayat*, to *dalit* communities.

After the introduction of this constitutional provision, the efforts by the *dalits* to take advantage of it resulted in a serious backlash, with upper castes retaliating – often violently – when *dalits* questioned inequalities and exclusion. With little intervention by higher government institutions and authorities to support *dalit* efforts, the *panchayats* remained the bastion of upper castes until CSOs began addressing the issue. When *panchayat* elections were held in Gujarat in 2002, Unnati,[5] a CSO based in Gujarat's capital, Ahmedabad, took the initiative to mobilize both SJC members and *dalit* communities to work for social justice. Drawing membership from local CSOs, a network named Samajik Nyay Manch (SNM – Association for Social Justice) was created to push the agenda of social justice within the *panchayat* institutions.

In the course of fieldwork for the study (2006–08), five 'reflection workshops'[6] were organized with SJC and *panchayat* members, *dalit* communities and CSOs in Sabarkantha District.[7] Two workshops were organized at the district level and three at the sub-district 'block' level. The workshops were occasions for people to reflect on the issues of social injustice, the role of SJCs, the support they received from the *panchayat* and other governance agencies, reactions and resistance of local dominant groups, and mobilization facilitated by the SNM. When I began fieldwork, the *panchayat* and SJCs had almost completed their five-year term, and it was possible for them to be reflective about overall mobilization, as well as about their own performance. When elections were held again in 2006, reflection workshops brought together new and old SJC members to provide the new members with a review of the past and to link them with former members, so that they could gain both support and benefit from the experience of the former members. Besides the workshops, I conducted ethnographic enquiry in four villages in Idar Block – Deoli, Netramali, Jethipura and Virpur – which are heavily populated by *dalits*. Interviews were conducted with the chairperson and members of the SJC, the *panchayat sarpanch* (chairperson) and leaders of the SNM. I had several opportunities to have extended conversations with colleagues in Unnati. Altogether, I spoke to 200 people in the space of two years.

Participatory local governance institutions and social justice

Social justice is a ubiquitous concept within the state's definition of liberal democracy in India (Mahajan, 1998). In the pan-Indian framing of social justice, fuelled by a liberal democratic ethos, it is expressed in two different forms: as fundamental rights and as directive principles. Fundamental rights are inalienable rights guaranteed by the Indian Constitution; directive principles are expressions of state policy, which are put forward in the form of directives and guidelines that the state uses to form policies and to execute them. If a person's fundamental rights are violated, they can go to court to guarantee the protection of those rights. Directive principles, on the other hand, are not enforceable through court intervention. The right not to be treated as an untouchable and the right to equality in public spaces fall within the domain of fundamental rights, whereas affirmative action, the paying of equal and fair wages and the fair allocation of developmental goods and services are the domain of directive principles. Local governance institutions have been organized and created as mechanisms to enact the realization of directive principles.

In the early 1990s, with the passage of a constitutional amendment, the state entered a decisive phase in its efforts to bring about social justice. These amendments addressed the developmental needs of marginalized communities, including *dalits*, by seeking to reinvigorate local governance institutions in rural areas so as to include marginalized communities in decision-making at the local level. The amendments sought to have *panchayats*, as institutions of self-governance, located in a village or in a cluster of villages, and to have them tied, functionally, to the blocks and districts by a three-tier system of governance. *Panchayats* were to be responsible for assessing local needs and local planning after assessment, and were to be given budgets to implement those plans. Membership of the *panchayat* was to be by election, with seats reserved for *dalits*, tribals and women, so that they could stand in the elections and enter active politics.[8]

The *panchayat*, as an elected body, is accountable to the *gram sabha*, the village assembly constituted by all the residents of a village or cluster of villages. A *panchayat* can have subcommittees to deal with education, infrastructure, women's issues, health and other issues. SJCs, as part of the *panchayat* system, are formalized in the state of Gujarat, and each has a chairperson who is nominated from among its members.

The first recommendation to constitute SJCs as part of the *panchayat* system in Gujarat came in 1972 from the Zinabhai Darzi Committee, which was formed by the then government of Gujarat. The committee envisaged SJCs as a way to promote what it called 'democratic socialism' through democratic decentralization (Government of Gujarat, 1972). SJC members were to be recruited from elected *panchayat* members, and if no appropriate members could be found in this way, they were to be recruited from the *gram sabha*. Two tasks were designed for the SJCs – to promote the agenda of fair distribution of economic goods and opportunities, and to take measures against social discrimination and atrocities committed against the low castes, tribals, women and other marginalized groups. These provisions were incorporated when Gujarat formulated its local governance legislation in the wake of the 1992 constitutional amendments. However, it could not make the SJCs absolutely autonomous, as was recommended by the Zinabhai Darzi Committee, and instead made the SJC a *panchayat* subcommittee. The SJC was given the authority to make decisions, but these were conditional upon ratification by the *panchayat*, which also allocated budgets for the implementation of any such decisions.

Apart from giving the *dalits* entry into the *panchayat* through affirmative action and the formal legitimization of their 'power' within the *panchayat*, the state does little to ensure that *dalits* exercise that power to their advantage. Despite being conceived and formalized as participatory and inclusive institutions, there is, in fact, nothing inherent in the local governance institutions to prevent them from continuing to reinforce social stereotypes of caste. In fact, the exercise of power by powerless groups in the same social setting that tries to keep them forever subservient intensifies and provokes caste violence as a response. Quite frequently, this violence manifests itself within the institutional spaces of local governance.

Situated as they are in the very society from which their members are drawn, local institutions can hardly transcend the structural positioning that conditions social relations around the issue of caste. Who is treated with respect? Whose voice is heard? Who carries authority? Who makes decisions? These matters are decided not so much by the power a person holds within the *panchayat*, as by the already existing network of social power relations, which in turn determines the subjectivity of members. It is a reflection of existing social relations when *dalit* members (particularly *dalit* women) are subjected to verbal abuse at *panchayat* meetings – behaviour that is ignored by the *panchayat* secretary, who is a lower-level administrator from the block administration and whose responsibility it is to attend the meetings and write up the minutes.

The following two quotes from our study area in Gujarat illustrate how the upper castes still retain power within the *panchayat*. Talking about the Bhavnagar *panchayat* in Idar Block (Sabarkantha District), one writer observes:

> The dominant castes invited a *dalit* to be the *sarpanch* only on the condition that he would not sit on the same chair meant for the *sarpanch* and would not drink tea from the same cups used to serve the members of the dominant castes. Simultaneously a person from the dominant caste became the *upsarpanch* (deputy chairperson). Hence the actual powers remained with the dominant castes and the role of the *dalit sarpanch* was limited to signing bills and other papers of the *panchayat* under the direction of the *upsarpanch*. (Satpathy, 2006: 54).

As the *dalit sarpanch* of Deoli village in Idar Block, Manjula has to face a lot of verbal abuse in the *panchayat*. As she puts it:

> Of course the high-caste people have no choice but to vote a *dalit* into power when the rules are set for that. But then they want someone who they can dictate to and keep subservient. Since I am not much educated and I was never visible in public life of the village, they assumed that I would obey them in every respect. Being a *dalit* and being a woman, I was socially vulnerable. But when I got into the position of a *sarpanch* I realized that I could do so much for my people. And the high-caste people never liked it.[9]

In another context, writing about how high castes react to their loss of power (or to the *dalits*' gain of it) and about how high castes misconstrue the local governance arrangements, Sumathi and Sudarsen quote a well-off, upper-caste village man: 'Donate the country to the communists so that everyone drink *kanji* (rice gruel) and equality could be maintained.' The man, reacting adversely to *dalit* entry into *panchayats*, 'equates the principles of a positive discrimination of political participation at the grassroots level to communism' (2005: 3754).

When the political will of the state ceases with the formal declaration of *panchayat* guidelines, it is not unlikely that the agenda of *dalit* political participation in the local institutions will suffer, for the reasons mentioned above. As might be expected, this has happened in the Sabarkantha villages. *Dalit* aspirations to take advantage of the new constitutional provision have resulted in serious backlashes, where the upper castes have retaliated often violently when *dalits* have questioned inequality and exclusion. Without much intervention by higher government institutions and authorities to support *dalit* efforts, the *panchayats* have remained the bastion of upper castes. In the absence of efforts to mobilize *dalits* in the early days of the SJCs, their power was confined to paper in the official files of *panchayat* and block administration.

Dalit mobilization in *panchayat* institutions in Sabarkantha

Dalit mobilization in India has a long and chequered history (Ilaiah, 2001; Shah, 1994; Omvedt, 1994, 2001, 2003; Pai, 2002; Zelliot, 2001). Their mobilization has sought to address a variety of issues, such as caste inequalities and atrocities committed by high castes; low economic status and poverty among *dalits*; their cultural marginalization within Hindu culture; their entitlement to fair wages and decent living conditions; and their right to live in dignity. In addressing these issues, *dalits* have taken to diverse methods, ranging from forced temple entry (to break the caste norms that do not allow them to enter Hindu religious places), through mass conversion to Buddhism (to escape the exploitative Hindu caste and religious system), to cultural mobilization (to establish the distinct identity of *dalit* culture) and the organization of *dalit* political parties (to gain power within the state system).[10] By these methods, *dalits* have been vocal in their criticism of the caste hierarchy and have acted against the inequalities that permeate every aspect of their living and that shape their relations with the powerful – including the state.

Dalit mobilization within *panchayat* institutions, however, is a recent phenomenon that differs from earlier mobilizations. While addressing the old and hitherto unresolved issues of social exclusion and social justice, the mobilization has not only taken place within institutions created by the state, but has been facilitated by state affirmative action directives. This entry into the state institutions of the *panchayat*, however, does not guarantee much unless *dalits* make their own claims to rights and power, bring their own agendas and make their presence visible. Since this mobilization is one taking place in and through state-created institutions, state-given notions of social justice have influenced it. Yet it is not completely governed by what the state offers: alternative ideas, notions and politics, shaped by the mobilization itself, are also being brought into state-created institutions in order to influence and expand them. Nonetheless, the state framework of local governance prevails, and its emphasis on offering development opportunities for *dalits* eclipses more political framings of social justice. This jeopardizes the idea of promoting social justice as a matter of democratic right. And this, as we shall see below, has given rise to paradoxes of development and democracy that have a significant bearing on the outcomes of *dalit* mobilization for social justice in Sabarkantha. The CSO Unnati was the first to work towards reviving the SJCs in Sabarkantha during and after the 2001 elections. Unnati's interactions with *panchayats* began when it initiated a pre-election voter-awareness campaign (PEVAC) in Sabarkantha, aimed at raising awareness of the *panchayat* elections scheduled for 2001. To facilitate the campaign, it opened the Panchayat Resource Centre in Khedbrahma Block of Sabarkantha District. In the course of the PEVAC, Unnati interacted both with the elected members of *panchayats* and with the communities, and worked in partnership with other CSOs in four blocks in Sabarkantha – Idar, Prantij, Himatnagar and Modasa – as well as with a network of SJC members, to address issues of social injustice. The PEVAC made Unnati and its partners realize that social justice was a critical issue that needed focused intervention. And so, with eight CSOs, the SNM collective was formed in 2002 to activate and energize the SJCs and mobilize the *dalits*. The formation of the SNM inspired other CSOs in the district to join the network, and four organizations from three other blocks – Vijay Nagar, Bhiloda and Vadali – joined the SNM. The network has evolved into a vibrant one, which has energized the *dalit* agenda of social justice. It organized the SJC chairpersons in clusters at block, district and provincial levels to galvanize support for *dalit* mobilization through a strategy that moved them to claim membership in the *panchayat*, bring issues of social injustice to the SJCs and the *panchayat*, and improve practices at the local *panchayat* and in higher government institutions. Thus the network helped to bring issues of social justice into public spaces.

Dalit mobilization for social justice in local governance institutions in Sabarkantha, as carried out by the SNM, has three critical goals: the institutional efficacy of *panchayats*; redistribution of developmental provisions; and social equality and dignity.

Mobilizing for institutional efficacy This dimension of the mobilization rests on the premise that *dalit* participation and leadership in *panchayats* will be ensured if the institutions in question function efficiently. Institutional effectiveness is often judged in terms of the effort made to put officially prescribed structures and procedures into place.

After *panchayat* elections were held in 2002, Unnati conducted a study of the status of SJCs in the district. They found that SJCs were not being formed in most villages and, where they were, that members were being selected arbitrarily by the *sarpanch* and *talati* (*panchayat* secretary, a government employee placed at the block headquarters) without consultation with other *panchayat* members. The SJC members selected through these procedures had no information about the roles they were expected to perform within the *panchayat* system. Consequently, the first task the SNM undertook was to organize a meeting with the chairpersons of all the SJCs located in the eight blocks where CSOs from the SNM worked. The first ever meeting discussed the status of the village

SJCs and strategies to activate them. Following this meeting, the SNM decided to seize the initiative and wrote to the block development officer and the *talati*, demanding that they take steps officially to form SJCs. This initiative, which the network members supported and monitored closely, led to the formation of SJCs in all the *panchayats* in the eight blocks of Sabarkantha District.

SJC members were mobilized through various capacity-building efforts that sought to equip them with information about their roles, rights and responsibilities within the *panchayat* system; they were also given training on social and governance-related issues in the region. To ensure that the SJCs functioned effectively, SJC networks were formed at the block, the district, and later on, the state level. Representatives from village SJCs were selected to form the block network and were given responsibility for addressing social justice issues at the block level through interaction with government officials. Representatives from block networks were chosen to form district networks, with a mandate to address issues that arose from villages and blocks and to deal with the government at the district level. Subsequently, a state network of SJCs was formed by taking representatives from the district network. Social awareness campaigns were organized periodically, with rallies and cultural shows that included folk music and theatre. At the very beginning of organizational efforts, in September 2002, a meeting was arranged between SJC members and high-ranking government ministers. A *sammelan* (large conference) was convened at the Himatnagar town hall, where approximately 1,500 people, including members of SJCs and *dalit* communities from different parts of Sabarkantha, came together to tell their stories to a group of ministers, in the presence of academics, the media and non-governmental organizations (NGOs).

Mobilizing for redistribution of developmental provision Economic development is an important feature on the agendas of SJCs, which have a responsibility to take care of the developmental needs of *dalit* communities. Research has revealed that SJCs have actively pursued developmental activities for their communities. Critical development services include connecting water and electricity to *dalit* households, getting them land or houses, constructing cement roads to connect *dalit* living areas with the rest of the village and with the main road to a city, and getting *dalit* names on the list of those below the poverty line, so that they can start to take advantage of government subsidies meant for the poorest of the poor. These developmental services are of critical importance to the well-being of *dalits*. Not only are the SJCs responsible for these services, but their efforts to foster development are also highly appreciated by their communities.

The development resources that the SJCs bring their communities come from the redistribution of benefits from already existing government programmes, rather than from fresh allocations. However, redistribution has been viewed as important, since resourceful people in a village and *panchayat* have always appropriated the benefits intended for the *dalits*, and on many occasions government authorities have either supported this practice or have remained indifferent to the needs of the *dalits*. In addition, special programmes and funds earmarked for *dalits* have often not been utilized, as *dalits* were either unaware of them or could not pursue them on their own. In this context, the SJCs have struggled hard within *panchayats* to get the provisions meant for *dalit* communities to their intended beneficiaries. In fact, the efficiency and success of SJCs in distributing these development resources has come to be seen as an indication of the strength of *dalit* leadership within the *panchayat* and as a manifestation of *dalit* needs, voices and decision-making within it.

Mobilizing for social equality and dignity What began as a movement to activate the political powers of the SJCs and to appropriate developmental schemes, goods and services for the lower castes has gradually begun to address issues of social discrimination, violence and abuse. The emphasis was (and still is) on material needs for *dalit* economic empowerment; but there have also been cases where the committees have sought to, as it were, 'claim social space'. They have, for instance, claimed burial space for low castes on village common land and made cultural space for *dalits* in festivals. Social space has also been claimed through behavioural and attitudinal changes consciously made by the *dalits* themselves: for example, they choose not to sit on the floor when higher-caste individuals appropriate the chairs during a meeting, or not to eat off the plates kept separate for *dalits* during village feasts. Another space-claiming activity has been to have *dalits* celebrate large festivals like Holi (Festival of Colours) or Diwali (Festival of Lights) in the same place as the high castes celebrate them. In a few cases, showing complete disregard for caste rules, *dalits* have entered the temples of high castes.

All these radical acts have added the dimension of 'dignity' to social justice. Dignity is a word that does not have a place in the vocabulary of the state or of democratic discourse, but has emerged from the struggles of *dalits* themselves, as they attempt to define what democracy means, in both its political and its social forms, for the most deprived communities. They are starting to make strong claims to the right to live in a dignified manner and to be treated with dignity. Of all the ways they have chosen to claim equality and inclusion, their seeking of dignity has been the most radical, since it strikes at the heart of a social system that discriminates against a set of human beings described as 'untouchables' and manifests itself as a *dalit* claim for a distinct identity. As *dalits* mobilize to participate more in local governance institutions, this struggle for dignity has manifested itself in the acquisition by *dalits* of such symbolic assets as an office room, a letterhead and a stamp bearing the name of the SJC, all of which help to establish a *dalit* identity and to give *dalits* a feeling of power. *Dalit* members cite this as one of the achievements of their mobilization. Another way in which the *dalit* members of *panchayats* claim identity and dignity is to spell out their caste surnames (which reveal their identity as untouchables) on their nameplates and letterheads, instead of hiding them.

Dalit mobilization in the *panchayats* tells us that the political, material and social aspects of their movement are intertwined and interact with each other in complex ways. *Dalit* groups living in Sabarkantha villages have learned that their struggle is manifold: getting elected to the *panchayat* is only the beginning. What awaits them in office is the need to track developmental schemes and funds for the *dalits*, channel benefits to *dalit* homes in the villages, and demand identity and equality on a practical and symbolic level, while at the same time striving to provide equality for all in the social spaces where the people who control those spaces have always discriminated against them.

Paradoxes of development and democracy

It is evident that the granting of political power to and any consequent participation by *dalits* in *panchayats* is rendered ineffective unless the *dalits* themselves mobilize and assert their power. *Dalit* mobilization – as represented through such activities as claiming political space within the *panchayat*, diverting the state-sponsored development resources to *dalit* communities, forcing entry into the social space barricaded by the high caste, or capturing and animating the public space by widening networks and organizing huge demonstrations – has invoked *dalit* identity and given SJCs visibility in the public sphere. In situations where a *panchayat* is also headed by a *dalit*, considerable cooperation has been extended to the SJCs to pursue social justice agendas, even though *dalit* members themselves still endure hostility from high-caste members in both the *panchayat* and the village.

This framing of social justice is, indeed, an intersection between two sets of notions – one that stems from state-given meanings and another that comes from the current subjective experience of *dalits*, as well as from how they envisage themselves in the future. We find, therefore, that *dalit* communities are striving for political power and the redistribution of development resources (such as water, food, roads or electricity) at the same time as they continue to construct social justice for themselves, using the term 'dignity' to signify their need to live with respect. By framing their search for social justice in terms of 'dignity', they have highlighted the atrocities and prejudices that they encounter within the Hindu caste structure. Striving for dignity is a piece of radical political imagining that does not exist in the vocabulary of the state or of formal democracy, but the *dalits* have articulated this concept in their quest for social justice.

Yet, this claiming of political and social space has not democratized local institutions enough for them to be sufficiently inclusive of the *dalits* and their agenda of social justice. The charisma of individual activists and leaders has pushed the *dalit* agenda forward to a significant extent, but local institutions have remained mostly closed.[11] Hence, we find that, at the time of the *panchayat* elections of December 2006, SJCs had still not been formed in many *panchayats* – even though the revitalized SJCs had already been around for a number of years and *dalit* members had mobilized to make them more visible. Where they had been formed, in some cases this had been done by the *panchayat* secretary, in consultation with a few *panchayat* members, thus repeating the history of 2002. Consequently, many *dalits* were not even aware that they had been nominated as SJC members in their own *panchayats*.[12]

The active members of the SJCs, in most cases, are completely caught up in organizing development resources for the low castes – most critically housing, water, electricity and roads. While the efforts made to redistribute basic material goods and services more evenly have positive implications for those who want to live in dignity, problems arise when SJCs extend their efforts to address social discrimination and atrocity issues: this raises suspicion within the higher echelons of power. In the series of reflection workshops that were organized during the study, we encountered these developmental and democratic paradoxes. When asked to describe what constitutes social injustice, SJC members listed a number of issues for *dalits*: denial of burial grounds; restrictions on their temple entry; cases of violence against *dalit* women; continuation of the traditional occupation of removing dead animals from the village; low wages; and the lack of decent housing, water, electricity and good roads. The same members, when asked about the role of SJCs, enumerated all the developmental activities they had pursued or wanted to pursue. When we probed a little deeper, they said that they also valued the distinct identity of the SJCs, because they gave *dalit* communities a stake in the *panchayats*. They also recalled the efforts – few in number but critical nonetheless – that they had made to address the issues of social discrimination in their villages. Local government restricts the democratic politics of *dalits*, in that the official discourse limits *dalit* imagination to development issues. It supports this narrow discourse by creating development schemes and funds, while shrugging off cases of social atrocity as occasional occurrences or aberrations. As one SJC chairman put it during a reflection workshop in 2006:

> You go to the district collector with a request for a water connection to the *dalit* communities, the fellow will try to help; you go to report a case of social atrocities [*sic*], he will hit the roof, deny that such cases happen in his jurisdiction, and worse, he will not hesitate to say that you are simply fabricating a case against a high-caste person.

These paradoxes of development and democracy originate in the way the state frames institutions of local governance. The pursuit of social justice in these proclaimed participatory spaces has been predicated upon two principles – affirmative action to give *dalits* entry into *panchayats* and social inclusion through engagement with development planning and resourcing. Hence, any *dalit* mobilizations that take place within the state sphere must perform within this state-given framework, which also guides institutions of local governance. As is evident in the *dalit* mobilization in Sabarkantha, mobilizations occasionally stretch the framework, when the members bring in radical discourse and practices of social justice. However, the overarching framework of the state prevails and limits both the institutions and the mobilization that takes place within them.

Mobilization within state-created institutions, therefore, has progressed more in the direction of working with the state than of questioning it. Neoliberalism has substantially reinvented the state–civil society collaboration within the partnership model it popularized, in which the state and civil society are viewed as 'partners' in governance. As the state outsources to civil society not only delivery of services but also the agenda of building democracy which – theoretically at least – was part of the state agenda, state and civil society actors are now willing to sit together to debate and deliberate. Within the partnership framework, civil society is assigned the task of doing whatever the government finds itself unable to do: for instance, disseminating information in popular languages, raising awareness and building capacity through training. In short, civil society is expected to enable social groups to be part of local self-governance programmes. Mobilization involves mediation between the interests of the powerless and those who occupy seats of authority. Therefore, rather than making radical rights claims on the state, we find the SJCs adopting negotiation and persuasion as their strategies to achieve social justice.

In this partnership under neoliberalism, which Chandhoke (2003) calls the pluralization of governance, there is always the danger that the state may control and manipulate civil society, choosing only those civil society actors that it feels comfortable talking to. Hence, while mediation is essential to level the playing field for democratic politics, it has the potential to limit the autonomy of civil society. As the SNM experience suggests, civil society can expand its work within the limited framework of partnership to add momentum to mobilization; but there are limits to how far the framework can be expanded. The SNM, while performing a mediating role, also mobilized the *dalits* to claim rights and entitlements, and yet it had to exercise caution in order to avoid the perception that it was critical of the state (or indeed even acting against it). The SNM also realized that its mobilization could only address those rights that the state felt comfortable with – or, in a sense, 'allowed' to be part of public discourse.

Consequently, talking about the rights of SJCs within *panchayats* was never perceived as problematic; but talking about the right to be protected against social atrocity was. The policy framework of the state that governs local institutions isolates *dalit* experiences of untouchability and brutality, and keeps these away from public discourse. Hence, those CSOs that mobilized *dalit* claims to the right not to be subjected to caste atrocities, or that provided legal services to *dalits*, spoke of social justice from the standpoint of those on the opposite side from the state, with the state (as expected) either ignoring them or mounting counter-attacks against them. Members of the SNM, because of their mediating role, were not merely constrained from addressing caste atrocities, but were hesitant to join with the organizations that were raising such issues, fearing to lose their good relationship with the state.[13]

Final reflections

Reflecting back on the question posed by this study, three broad conclusions about democratic outcomes or their absence follow from our analysis of *dalit* mobilization within institutions of local governance.

First, local institutions have opened up to *dalit* political participation and to their ambitions, but have remained largely closed to any substantive inclusion of *dalits* as equals, despite tremendous pressure and assertion by *dalit* representatives. *Dalit* mobilization has given visibility to SJCs, which help to provide a *dalit* identity within *panchayats*. There are instances of *dalits* asserting their political position within the local institutions and bringing a social justice agenda forward for discussion and action within *panchayats*. However, the institutions themselves have demonstrated their inability and unwillingness to be sufficiently inclusive of the *dalit* presence or of *dalit* voices and interests.

Second, the opening up of social spaces for *dalits* has remained limited, as has their inclusion in those spaces that have been jealously guarded by the upper castes. In consequence, there is little scope for effective *dalit* membership of *panchayats*. The local institutions seem to be operating without much reference to the changes in social space. Consequently, issues of social equality and dignity have yet to be addressed within the institutional practices of *panchayats*.

Third, entry into local governments and mobilization by CSOs has resulted in *dalit* access to development resources for housing, water, electricity and roads. This is the most significant gain that has been made by the *dalit* mobilization. To a large extent, the mobilization has taken care of the redistribution of material resources and the inclusion of *dalits* in 'development'. The fulfilment of material needs is essential to ensure the upward mobility of the *dalits* and to enhance their material well-being. In that sense, material needs add value to the *dalit* quest for equality and dignity, though – given the absence of equality and inclusion in the social spaces of the wider community and in the political spaces of governance institutions – that quest remains only partially fulfilled.

Notes

1 I should like to say many thanks to colleagues from Unnati, particularly Binoy Acharya and Tapas Satpathy for their enthusiastic support for this study in every possible way. They were instrumental in mobilizing SJC members and forming the network of CSOs that are addressing *dalit* issues, and Tapas accompanied me on my numerous visits to the villages in Sabarkantha District and organized (with amazing skill) the reflection workshops we held at the block and then at the district level. This chapter has also benefited from comments provided by Rajesh Tandon, Bettina von Lieres, Vera Coelho, John Gaventa, Lisa Thompson and Arilson Favareto.

2 *Dalits* occupy the lowest rung in the Hindu caste hierarchy, and are known as 'untouchables'. Gandhi called them *harijan*, which literally

means 'children of God', but the lower castes themselves discarded this word, arguing that they were as human as anybody else and did not need to be seen as special children of God. Instead, they adopted the more politically potent word *dalit*, which means 'oppressed' or 'exploited', to raise their claim for equality.

3 The research was conducted in collaboration with Unnati, a CSO based in Ahmedabad (Gujarat), which has played a critical role in *dalit* mobilization.

4 The Indian Constitution refers to *dalits* as 'Scheduled Castes'; they are considered for special treatment and affirmative action.

5 *Unnati* means 'progress' in Hindi.

6 The methodologies for the study were designed within the framework of participatory research, which views research as facilitating mobilization. The dominant method adopted for the study was a series of 'reflection workshops' with the members of SJCs, CSO network members and members of *dalit* communities.

7 For administrative purposes, each state is divided into a number of districts; each district is divided into a number of blocks; and each block contains several villages. The *panchayat* – the name for this three-tier system of governance – begins at the village and ends at the district level. Direct election to membership in the *panchayat* takes place at the village level, and it is at this level that local planning and local participation are provided for by the state.

8 One of the measures the state takes to promote equality is 'protective discrimination' or 'affirmative action'. This describes the system of principles and practices by which the Indian state grants certain privileges to socially and culturally vulnerable groups, so that they can be brought up to par with those who are already privileged. Affirmative action also takes the form of the reservation of seats in education, employment and even political bodies for the lower castes, so that they have an equal opportunity to compete with those who otherwise have the resources on their own to compete.

9 Personal communication, 6 September 2006.

10 The *dalit* movements, particularly in northern and southern India, transformed themselves into political parties and entered mainstream politics at the provincial and national levels.

11 Individual leadership success was visible in almost all the SJCs we visited during our fieldwork. In fact, these individuals were so popular that in the villages people could tell us the name of the chairperson of the SJC, but they could hardly say who the other members were.

12 Personal communication with Tapas Satpathy and members of the SNM, on several occasions during fieldwork 2006–07.

13 Personal communication with members of the SNM, on several occasions during fieldwork 2006–07.

9 • Mobilization and participation: a win-win game?

VERA SCHATTAN P. COELHO, ALEXANDRE FERRAZ, FABIOLA FANTI AND MEIRE RIBEIRO[1]

Governments and social organizations are finding it increasingly difficult to sustain the involvement of citizens in the decision-making processes that surround the development of public policies. There are several risks that are now recognized as potentially harmful to the project of participatory governance. Among them are the absence of lively social forces engaging in participatory processes, and their 'capture' by more organized groups (Avritzer and Navarro, 2003; Coelho and Nobre, 2004; Ansell and Gash, 2008). Two recommendations have been widely suggested to deal with these risks. The first is to redesign participatory bodies (Fung, 2004); the second is to mobilize social actors (Gaventa, 2006a; Mohanty, 2007; Cornwall, 2007). In this chapter, we will argue that these recommendations often lead to a zero-sum game, since mobilization without design increases the risk that more organized groups will 'capture' the processes, while redesign without social mobilization can easily lead to the adoption of formal procedures that contribute to the inhibition of a more spontaneous and vibrant participation. As an alternative, we will suggest that the conjunction of mobilization and design may increase the chances of success of the participatory governance project.

In order to explore the possibilities and limits of mobilization and design in fostering citizen involvement in the decision-making processes of public policies, we have researched the dynamics of *conselhos locais da saúde* (CLS – local health councils) organized in peripheral areas of the city of São Paulo, Brazil. The aim was to understand the relationship between the forms of mobilization that emanate from the citizenry, the architecture of these governance structures and the public-health debates taking place in these areas.

CLSs were introduced by the 1988 Brazilian Constitution, which established the formal transition to democracy after more than twenty years of military regime. The so-called 'Citizen Constitution' defined health councils as mechanisms responsible for bringing civil society organizations (CSOs), service providers and public officials together in health governance. Today, there is a national health council as well as state, municipal and, in large cities, local health councils. Health councils operate in all twenty-six states and nearly all 5,561 municipalities, addressing core issues of priority-setting and accountability. Our research focused on six CLSs located in poor regions of the city of São Paulo, each with a different history of social mobilization. We compared council dynamics in terms of inclusiveness, connections, participation and the debates held. These dimensions are closely related to the three axes which, Dryzek (2000) argues, are essential to democratization: expansion of the number of people effectively included in collective decisions; broadening of the issues and areas of life under democratic control; and extension of the effective participation of autonomous and competent actors.

In the next section, we situate the Brazilian health councils in the international debate about deepening democracy and participatory governance. We then present our research methodology. The fourth section introduces the municipal areas under study. Next, we describe the composition, connections and dynamics of the six CLSs, and present the debates that took place in them. We also discuss the relationship between the local history of social mobilization and the councils' performance. Finally, methodological and analytical aspects of the research are discussed.

The deepening democracy debate

It has increasingly been argued that it is necessary to go beyond implementation of democracy's formal and structural dimensions to release its potential for transformation. In parallel with regular elections, free political parties and freedom of speech and association, the implementation of mechanisms capable of promoting greater citizen involvement in public decisions, greater transparency and a greater and more horizontal flow of information should be encouraged. Throughout the 1980s and 1990s, different theoretical perspectives discussed 'deeper' or improved forms of democracy, and several experiences based on the ideals of participation, deliberation and decentralization were implemented and reported all over the world (Habermas et al., 1998; Fung and Wright, 2003; Dryzek, 2000; Gastil and Levine, 2005; Gaventa, 2006a).

However, many of these experiences exposed the limits and risks present in the processes of 'deepening' democracy. The risks have been set out by a number of authors who are sceptical about the effects of participation. Their warnings echo the concerns previously raised by such authors as Weber (1946) and Schumpeter (1976), who pointed to the possibility of perverse effects. These include the populism and opportunism that permeate leaders who are connected to the masses without the intermediary of parties; fears regarding asymmetries in the ability of different people to mobilize and participate; and warnings that narrow interests will be able to organize more easily, thereby rendering unviable those policies that are aimed at a broader, yet less organized, public. Robinson (2007), in summarizing the findings of comparative research on decentralization and participation, points to five major limitations: a) lack of political commitment or leadership on the part of local elites with regard to the new participatory spaces; b) lack of political mobilization of the poor; c) inadequate financial resources to guarantee the sustainability of participatory experiences; d) lack of institutionalization of participatory spaces and mechanisms; and e) lack of technical and managerial capacity, as well as inequality of information among participants.

On the other hand, a number of authors have shown that, given certain design conditions, the organization of civil society and the involvement of public managers, there are redistributive gains and an increase in participation in the political process by traditionally marginalized groups (Abers, 2001; Wampler and Avritzer, 2004; Coelho and Nobre, 2004). These authors also demonstrate that deliberative processes contribute towards changing the positions and opinions of participants, narrowing the gap between people's opinions on contentious issues (Abelson and Gauvin, 2006).

Recent work that departed from this more optimistic perspective ended up by pointing out that important questions on the democratic potential of participatory processes remain open (Coelho, 2006; Melo and Baiocchi, 2006; Dagnino and Tatagiba, 2007; Bebbington et al., 2008). Given the informality that is a feature of participation in deliberative processes, how can we check whether traditionally marginalized groups with no party-political connections or relationships with public managers have been included in the process or have accessed its distributive benefits? Furthermore, how can we tell if there is greater accountability in the way that the policies are being provided? Are the public policies that are being generated from information provided by civil society representatives innovative?

In sum, these works call attention to the fact that there are currently no specifications about the quality either of the processes (inclusion, involvement and transparency) or of the outcomes that are being attributed to participation (innovation, distribution). What degree of inclusion, or what amount of innovation, needs to be proposed before a process can truly be recognized as representative of deepening democracy? There is also a lack of clarity about when public officials, design or mobilization – factors that appear in a number of studies as obstacles to the processes of deepening democracy – begin actually to facilitate these processes.

In order to tackle these questions, our methodology helps to assess how far participatory processes have come in promoting inclusion, deliberation and innovation. Initially we planned to work with participatory forums located in areas with different stories of social mobilization and different design features, involving public officials with different commitments to the participatory project; however, this strategy proved unviable. We decided instead to concentrate our efforts in areas with different stories of social mobilization, with the aim of identifying the mechanisms that foster a virtuous association between public officials, design features and social mobilization, since all three of these variables have previously been shown to play a role in defining the outcomes of the participatory processes (Coelho, 2006; Wampler and Avritzer, 2004; Heller, 2001).

To investigate the extent to which participatory processes promote inclusion, deliberation and innovation, we followed the approach of a group of researchers (House and Howe, 2000; Rowe and Frewer, 2004; Abelson and Gauvin, 2006; Ansell and Gash, 2008) who have highlighted the need to construct models that enable the analysis and comparison of participatory experiences. Core for these authors is the possibility of identifying procedures and incentives that favour the expression of demands by those with fewer resources. These authors also recognize the importance of investigating the impacts that social participation may have on the realm of policy elaboration and implementation.

To track the types and trajectories of mobilization that characterize civil society actors, we followed another group of authors (whose ideas are published in Cornwall and Coelho, 2007) who suggest that the success of participatory or decentralizing experiences is dependent on the associative contexts in which they are implemented. They highlight the importance of processes of social mobilization in guaranteeing conditions for the participation of actors who have fewer resources. In parallel, authors who deal with the broad notion of social capital maintain that desirable levels of participation and deliberation, along with positive political outcomes, can be achieved only in social environments that have at least some record of civic engagement and political mobilization (Putnam, 1993a; Verba et al., 1995; Costa, 1997).

Both perspectives are recognized as important in the debate over deepening democracy. However, they are generally treated separately in the literature in question. In this study, we bring them together as part of an effort to systematically compare participatory processes in different areas with different histories of social mobilization.

Research methodology and process

The city of São Paulo has a population of over 11 million, spread across thirty-one *sub-prefeituras* (sub-municipalities) that correspond to political-administrative units at a micro, neighbourhood level. The city has a municipal health council, and each *sub-prefeitura* has a CLS. These councils follow the institutional guidelines laid down by the 1988 Constitution, are part of the public health system and are directly linked to the Municipal Health Department.[2]

The case study presented here builds on previous research conducted on the creation and organization of São Paulo's thirty-one CLSs, carried out between 2001 and 2005 (Coelho, 2006). The results of this research

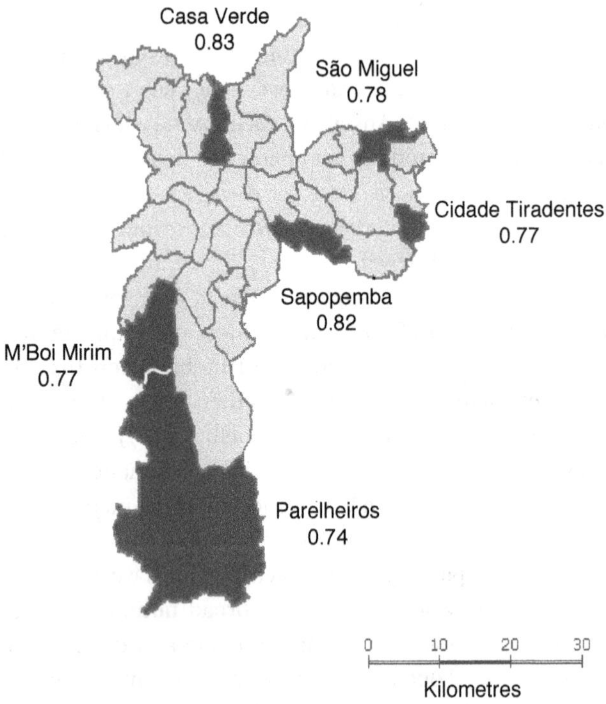

Figure 9.1 Municipality of São Paulo, showing the selected sub-municipalities and their Human Development Index scores

highlighted the fact that there was quite a wide spectrum of participants in São Paulo's CLSs, and that these included a diverse range of interests. However, the research gleaned little new information on the profile of the groups included in the participatory processes, or on the networks that connected them to other groups. There was also a lack of information about the influence of participatory processes on health policy decision-making processes or on the deliberative dynamics of CLSs.

To tackle these issues, we selected CLSs in poor areas of the city. We initially listed eleven possible *sub-prefeituras* with a Human Development Index (HDI) of between 0.74 and 0.83.[3] From these, we went on to select six. Three – São Miguel, Cidade Tiradentes and M'Boi Mirim – had a strong history of social mobilization over health demands; in the other three – Casa Verde, Sapopemba and Parelheiros – there had been fewer of these mobilizations.[4] The CLS in each of these *sub-prefeituras* has a different associational trajectory. The map shown in Figure 9.1 opposite shows the municipality of São Paulo divided into its thirty-one sub-prefeituras, and indicates those selected for the study, also showing their respective HDIs. The next section presents a brief description of the particular features of the social movements in each area.

Four methods were used to describe and compare the six CLSs selected. First, we analysed eighty-three sets of CLS minutes, covering meetings from January 2006 to August 2007.[5] Second, we conducted a questionnaire among eighty-five councillors – a mixture of service users and health managers;[6] of the sixty-one who were service users, twenty-seven represented an association, while thirty-four did not. Third, we carried out participant observation of meetings. Finally, we carried out a review of secondary sources and reconstituted the history of mobilization in each *sub-prefeitura*.

The four assumptions being assessed were that, in the CLSs located in areas with stronger histories of social mobilization on health issues, we would find: a) broader inclusion; b) broader connections; c) broader participation; and d) a higher percentage of proposals aimed at addressing policy problems.

These assumptions will be assessed in four steps, presented below. In the first three steps, we worked with a model that differentiates between inclusion, connections and participation.[7] A list of indicators related to each of these dimensions was defined, and each CLS was assigned a value of 0 or 1 for each indicator (with 1 pointing to more inclusion, participation and connections).

To compare the debates that took place in CLSs, we selected two themes: health issues (which included discussion about health policies and problems with service delivery) and participation (which tackled procedures for elections and meetings). Once the debates were grouped according to these themes, they were coded for nine indicators that covered the way in which they addressed policy problems, managed political influence and defined procedures. Again, each CLS was assigned a value of 0 or 1 for each indicator (with 1 being related to more interventions in a given category).

Introducing the six *sub-prefeituras*: trajectories and profile

In the mid-1970s, the municipality of São Paulo saw a large increase in its population, which contributed to the disorganized territorial occupation of the more peripheral areas of the city. As a result, there was a sharp increase in demand for basic services such as drinking water, housing, education and sewerage. The residents of these newly occupied areas organized themselves to demand access to services, and in many cases this resulted in the formation of popular movements (Jacobi, 1993).

Over the course of these mobilizations, a battle for health services emerged. In 1977, a group of women from various neighbourhoods in the eastern zone of the city began to organize public events and protests to pressure the state's health department into having a health centre constructed in the region (Neder, 2001). The health centre they demanded was inaugurated in 1979, and a health council for the centre was created that same year. The council, which would act as a monitoring group, had its members elected by 8,146 citizens living in the region (Bógus, 1998). This led, in 1981, to a further eighteen health councils being elected to monitor health centres in the eastern zone.

From 1989 on, the Movimento de Saúde da Zona Leste (Eastern Zone Health Movement) tried to increase its connection to health movements in other municipal regions, in an attempt to create a municipal health council. At this time, the struggle for a universal health system and against privatization was being waged by the militants of the movement, many of whom were workers in the state health department (ibid.).

The health movement's trajectory has much in common with other popular movements born during the period of Brazil's redemocratization. It was organized around priests in the Catholic Church, neighbourhood societies of friends, the *comunidades eclesiais de base* (basic Christian communities), mothers' clubs, popular education groups and movements against poverty (Singer and Brant, 1983; Sacardo and Castro, 2002). The Partido dos Trabalhadores (PT – Workers' Party), which was a new political actor in the early 1980s, also collaborated with the health movement by providing places for meetings, opening up institutional space for popular movements and supporting candidates connected to communities and the health movement (Bógus, 1998; Machado, 1995). Furthermore, there was a coming together of intellectuals, students and artists, all of whom played an important role in 'creating, with their work and social influence, the political conditions and infrastructure for popular causes', and so formed 'a support network for the movement' (Neder, 2001: 94).

When considering the group of *sub-prefeituras* selected for this study, it is worth noting that São Miguel was among those originally involved in this popular movement. Cidade Tiradentes is also in the eastern zone, and although social mobilization here gained traction more recently than in São Miguel, it has done so above all through the movement to guarantee the construction of the Cidade Tiradentes hospital. The third of the *sub-prefeituras* selected for a strong history of social mobilization is in the southern zone. M'Boi Mirim had high indices of homicide and violence some years ago, but the presence of associations in the area that have the power to mobilize the community – such as the Sociedade Santos Mártires (Society of Sainted Martyrs) and the Fórum de Defesa da Vida (Life Defence Forum) – was a decisive factor in forging processes of social mobilization aimed at improving living conditions. The battle for the construction of the M'Boi Mirim hospital also provided an impetus towards mobilization. One distinctive element of the health movements in these areas is that they do not lose track of the importance of maintaining their autonomy, which, for them, means a guarantee that an autonomous space will be maintained in which to plan and implement political action.

Of the *sub-prefeituras* selected for their relatively weak history of social mobilization, Parelheiros, together with other localities of the southern zone, did play a central role in the emergence of social mobilization in the second half of the 1970s, long before democracy returned to Brazil. But this mobilization contracted, at least partly because of the difficulties suffered by the progressive Church during the latter years of military rule, which resulted in suppression of the support it had been offering social movements in the southern zone.

By contrast, Vila Prudente, which borders the eastern zone, historically had closer relations with the East Zone Health Movement but lost these connections during the 1990s. Finally, in the northern zone, in the *sub-prefeitura* of Casa Verde, today's movement for health reform relies heavily on the participatory mechanisms provided by the state for its organization and operation.

By setting out the trajectory of the popular health movements, we hope to improve understanding of the dynamics of the CLSs in each *sub-prefeitura*. However, it should not be forgotten that other forms of mobilization and organization also make their presence felt on the CLSs.

The conselhos locais da saúde*: dynamics and debates* In this section, we compare the dynamics in, and the proposals generated by, the six selected CLSs during the study period. We analyse each of the three dimensions that form our assumptions about CLSs and their mobilization histories: inclusion, connections and participation. We then go on to present a fourth dimension: the debates that took place in the councils during this time.

In order to clarify how the indicators that will be presented in this section have been calculated, we provide a brief explanation of the steps that enabled us to convert continuous variables into dichotomous ones (0 or 1).[8] For the first three dimensions, a value of 1 is assigned to councils that have presented more: (i) inclusion; (ii) participation and (iii) connections. For the fourth dimension, a value of 1 is associated with more interventions made in a given council on three themes: (i) addressing policy problems; (ii) expanding political influence; and (iii) defining procedures. The criteria that allowed us to judge what should be recognized as, for example, more inclusion or more connections are presented and discussed at the start of each sub-section, with a brief literature review.

The methodological procedures that allowed the conversion of continuous variables into dichotomous ones varied depending on the available data. Nevertheless, the following examples cover the two procedures that were used in most of the cases:

For population characteristics such as gender, age or skin colour, we identified the profile of the population in the area covered by each council and measured the extent to which the distribution observed in the councils and the 'normal' distribution observed in the population converged ('normal' ranged from 10 per cent above or below this distribution). If a council's profile was in line with the population profile, we assigned a value of 1.[9]

In order to assess the connections between the CLS and the health managers, we took all the managers cited and assigned a value of 1 to those councils with more than the average number of managers (calculated across the six councils, where cited).

We now turn to an analysis of the six local health councils.

Inclusion in CLSs What is it that enables us to describe, compare and evaluate participatory processes in terms of the inclusion that they promote? There is no simple answer to this question, since there is considerable debate as to what type of inclusion is the ideal outcome of a participatory process. Some authors highlight the need to actively promote the inclusion of groups that have been traditionally marginalized from political processes and that may be poorly mobilized and organized (Gaventa, 2006a; Cornwall, 2007). Others call for the use of random selection as a way of guaranteeing that the socio-demographic profile of the councillors mirrors that of the population (Fishkin and Luskin, 1999). This method, it is argued, avoids favouring those with more resources, and should ensure that debates are not monopolized by politicized collective actors with strongly polarized positions.

Each of these perspectives contains a different understanding of what 'a greater degree of inclusion' actually means. Those who argue for random selection suggest that the more closely the socio-demographic profile of the councillors mirrors that of the population, the more inclusive is the council. For those who argue for a need to include the most marginalized, greater inclusion ultimately means that the neediest are 'over-represented'. From the legal perspective, however, the regulations of Brazilian health councils talk of guaranteeing adequate representation of organized civil society. From this point of view, then, there is greater inclusion when more CSOs are represented.

In this study we adopted, from among the many possible criteria, indicators that reflect a profile of associational and political plurality;

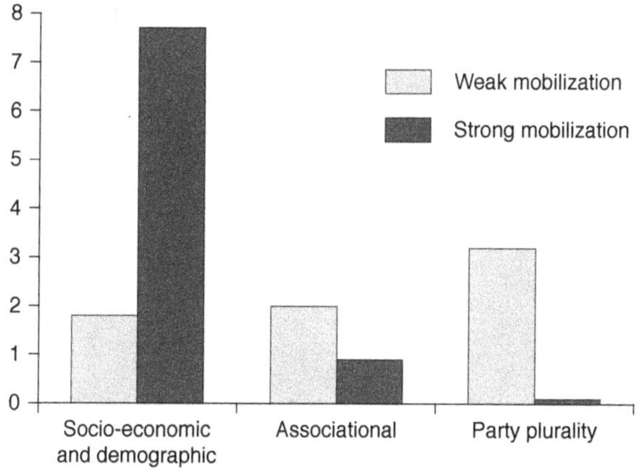

Figure 9.2 Types of inclusion in six CLSs located in areas with different histories of mobilization (*Source*: Health Policy and Public Involvement in the City of São Paulo project, 2008 – CDRC/CEM/NCD)

TABLE 9.1 Indicators of inclusion in local health councils (score of one indicates greater)

History of mobilization		Weaker			Stronger		
Indicator	Criteria	Vila Prudente	Casa Verde	Parel-heiros	M'Boi Mirim	Cidade Tiradentes	São Miguel
Gender	similarity to distribution in the population.	1	0	0	0	1	1
Skin colour	similarity to distribution of whites and non-whites in the population.	0	0	0	1	0	1
Education	representation of councillors with low level of education.	0	0	0	1	0	1
Income	representation of councillors with low income.	0	1	0	1	0	1
Party plurality	presence of representatives across the political spectrum.	1	1	1	0	0	0
Associations	number of types of association represented.	1	0	1	0	1	0

Note: Councillors reported themselves as representatives of popular health movements, health units, religious associations, neighbourhood associations, unions, civil rights groups, participatory forums, homelessness movements, the landless peasants movement, community or philanthropic groups, disabled persons associations, or as non-affiliated representatives.

Source: Health Policy and Public Involvement in the City of São Paulo project, 2008 – CDRC/CEM/NCD

a demographic profile that mirrors that of the population; and a socio-educational profile that has a significant presence of the poor and less well educated. Positive evidence of these indicators was coded as 1. Table 9.1 presents the scores of the six CLSs for this group of indicators. Figure 9.2 contains a synthesis of the information presented in Table 9.1.

In the case of the social, educational and demographic profiles, our indicators point to a relationship between more mobilized *sub-prefeituras* and greater inclusion. With respect to these characteristics, three observations should be made. The first concerns the notable participation of non-whites, particularly in Cidade Tiradentes, where 70 per cent of the councillors declared themselves to be black or brown. Second, 23 per cent of councillors had not completed even primary education. Third, there is a notable balance between the number of participants of both sexes. These observations suggest that the CLSs are able to reflect the socio-demographic profile of the population of their areas of the city, and that this type of inclusion is related to the trajectory of social mobilization in the *sub-prefeituras*.

With respect to the political profile, the data suggest a predominance of councillors affiliated or sympathetic to the PT in five of the six CLSs, but this presence is strongest in the *sub-prefeituras* with a greater background of social mobilization. The presence (albeit limited) of other parties was also reported in two of the *sub-prefeituras* with a weaker history of social mobilization. Similarly, *sub-prefeituras* with less background of mobilization show more types of association included in the council.

Connections between CLSs and other spaces and institutions What enables us to describe, compare and evaluate participatory processes in terms of the connections between the process and other spaces and institutions? Here again there is no simple answer, since there is considerable debate as to what type of connection and what level of coordination is important. Here we evaluate the existing connections between the CLSs and the policy processes that take place in the executive and legislative branches at the municipal, state and national levels. We also refer to the connections with other participatory forums, with other institutions in the health system and with other public and private organizations. A high level of reference to these other spaces and institutions in interviews and the minutes of meetings was coded as 1. Figure 9.3 contains a synthesis of the information analysed for this dimension in Table 9.2.

The number of health groups (971), state bodies (126) and partici-

TABLE 9.2 Indicators of connections between local health councils and other spaces and institutions (score of one indicates greater)

History of mobilization		Weaker			Stronger		
Indicator	Criteria	Vila Prudente	Casa Verde	Parel-heiros	M'Boi Mirim	Cidade Tiradentes	São Miguel
Manager	mentioned by councillors in questionnaire.	0	0	1	0	1	0
Politician	mentioned by councillors in questionnaire.	0	0	0	0	1	1
State body	cited in council minutes.	0	1	0	1	0	0
Executive and Legislature	identified by councillors as having a relationship with the organizations they represent.	1	0	0	0	1	1
Health Unit	cited in council minutes.	0	1	0	1	1	0
Organization	cited in council minutes.	0	0	1	0	1	1
Association	councillors representing an association.	0	0	1	0	1	1
Participatory Forum	cited in council minutes.	0	0	0	1	1	0

Source: Health Policy and Public Involvement in the City of São Paulo project, 2008.

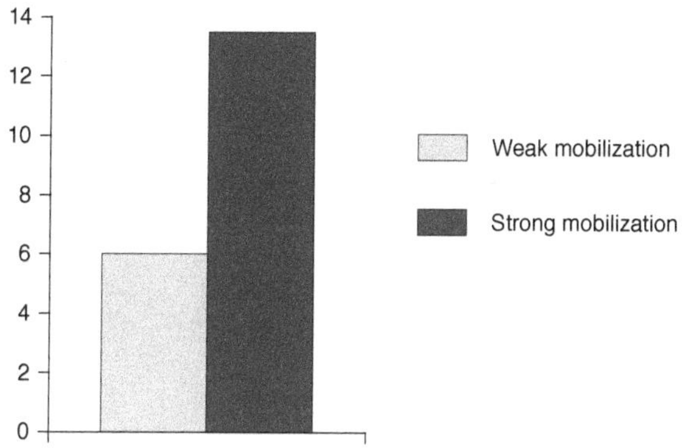

Figure 9.3 Connections by six CLSs located in areas with different histories of mobilization (*Source*: Health Policy and Public Involvement in the City of São Paulo project, 2008 – CDRC/CEM/NCD

patory forums (36) cited in the minutes is remarkable. Councillors representing associations reported that nearly half of the associations they represented had relationships with branches of municipal executive and legislative authorities. In addition, thirty-seven politicians and 264 organizations were referred to by councillors. The scores for these indicators point clearly to a relationship between a stronger history of social mobilization and a higher density of connections between CLSs and other spaces and institutions.

Participation Various authors who have analysed participative experiences highlight the fact that relationships between actors are marked by huge asymmetries, that state agents have excessive power, and that participatory forums are often captured by political parties (Avritzer and Navarro, 2003; Ziccardi, 1994; Coelho and Nobre, 2004).

Previous studies have suggested that certain design features contribute to minimizing these asymmetries, facilitating the deliberative process. Here we aim to evaluate the presence of these features and the effectiveness of the relations suggested in the literature. The first four indicators concern the way in which the CLS is designed: its selection procedures, the way meetings are facilitated, and how its agenda and themes are coordinated. The next four indicators concern the dynamics of who speaks in the CLS and how they do so. Finally, the last two indicators concern the accountability of the councillors to their constituencies, and the councillors' own satisfaction with the CLS process. Figure 9.4 synthesizes the information analysed for this dimension and presented in Table 9.3.

TABLE 9.3 Indicators of participation in local health councils (score of one indicates greater)

History of mobilization		Weaker			Stronger		
Indicator	Criteria	Vila Prudente	Casa Verde	Parel-heiros	M'Boi Mirim	Cidade Tiradentes	São Miguel
Selection procedure	transparency in selection of councillors.	0	0	0	0	0	0
Facilitation	presence of facilitator.	0	0	0	0	0	0
Agenda	% of meetings coordinated by non-manager councillors.	0	1	0	0	1	0
Themes	balance of themes on council agenda.	0	0	1	1	0	0
Right to speak	participation of non-manager councillors.	0	1	1	0	0	1
Right to speak	participation of non-councillors.	0	1	0	0	0	1
Environment	number of councillors contributing in council meeting.	0	1	0	0	1	0
Environment	number of times a single councillor contributed in a council meeting.	0	1	1	1	0	0
Accountability	number of media used by councillors to keep constituencies informed.	0	0	0	1	1	1
Satisfaction	councillor satisfaction about running of council.	0	0	0	1	1	1

Note: The value 1 was attributed to the councils where the agenda presents an equilibrium between issues concerning health policies; specific problems in the local health units; regional problems and procedures connected to the functioning of the forums.

Source: Health Policy and Public Involvement in the City of São Paulo project, 2008 – CDRC/CEM/NCD

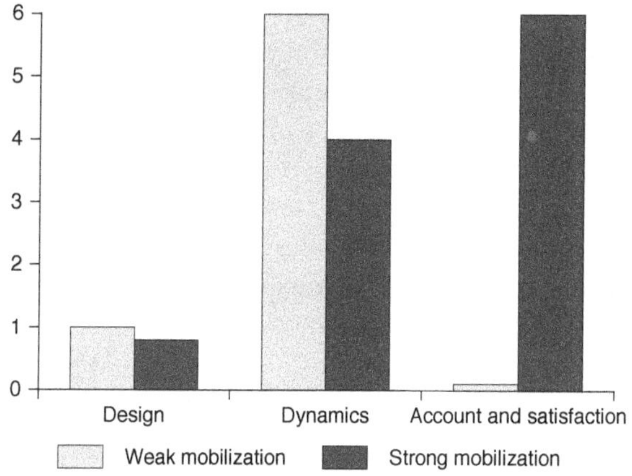

Figure 9.4 Features of participation in six CLSs located in areas with different histories of mobilization (*Source:* Health Policy and Public Involvement in the City of São Paulo project, 2008 – CDRC/CEM/NCD)

With respect to the design variables, the results show that all CLSs present poor design features. In terms of the discursive dynamics, the number of contributions made by councillors to CLS meetings suggests that debate is limited, with only a few councillors raising issues. Moreover, in 60 per cent of these cases, councillors speak only once, suggesting that they are not participating in sustained discussions. With respect to accountability and satisfaction, councillors who participate in councils located in areas with stronger trajectories of mobilization use a greater variety of media to keep their constituencies informed, and are themselves better satisfied with the performance of their CLSs than are councillors in areas with weaker trajectories of mobilization.

Debates The eighty-three sets of minutes analysed show that the discussions that took place in the CLSs were not simply the presentation of 'shopping lists', with councillors just complaining and demanding. On the contrary, at the meetings there were various types of issues debated. Those that we classified as health issues included discussions about health policies and programmes, and problems with service delivery. Participation issues dealt with procedures for elections and meetings. And local problems included water supply, infrastructure and security. We will focus on the first two of these themes, giving brief examples of the debates held during the research period.[10]

One of the principal health policy discussions that we observed in the council minutes during this period centred on outsourcing, which was strongly favoured by the state and municipal governments of São Paulo. This focused on the contracting of *organizações sociais* (OS – health organizations) to manage public hospitals, and outpatient medical care units to provide rapid treatment of patients with problems of low and medium complexity. Some 700 health councillors rejected the use of OSs at the municipal health conference held in December 2005 (Teixeira et al., 2007), but this did not stop the municipal government of São Paulo from passing a municipal law implementing the outsourcing of hospital and outpatient unit management to OSs in January 2006.

The CLSs of Casa Verde, Cidade Tiradentes, São Miguel and Parelheiros strongly criticized the OSs, calling them part of the process of privatization of health in the country. The CLS of Parelheiros went to court to denounce the move. The M'Boi Mirim CLS, however, acted in a different way, giving support to the OS that works in its area and congratulating its workers on their performance and on the excellent service they had provided to the population. All CLSs discussed the lack of representation in the new structures for outsourcing patient care.

In terms of health issues, São Miguel and M'Boi Mirim CLSs discussed how to reduce patient absenteeism for specialist consultations, and suggested a range of solutions. The M'Boi Mirim CLS also organized a process of monitoring hospital construction.

In terms of the political participation and influence of different ethnic groups, in Cidade Tiradentes reports were given about the meeting for Black Consciousness Day, the Black Population Health Fair, the Second Conference on the Health of the Black Population and the proposal for a seminar on sickle-cell anaemia. Meanwhile, in São Miguel a report discussed the situation of the Indigenous Population's Health Sub-System.

In terms of the electoral and participatory processes of CLSs themselves, in Vila Prudente CLS meetings were organized in health units, so that the councillors could be in more direct contact with the reality of the hospitals and health units. It was decided that the coordinator of each meeting would be chosen from among the participants at the previous meeting. This meant that each meeting was coordinated by a different person and increased the chance that everyone participated.

Figure 9.5 below summarizes the information for this dimension. Table 9.4 presents the frequency with which each council included in its debates discussion of particular demands, planning, monitoring, recognizing cultural and ethnic diversity, expanding political influence and design of electoral processes. A value of 1 was assigned to those councils that made more interventions in a given indicator.

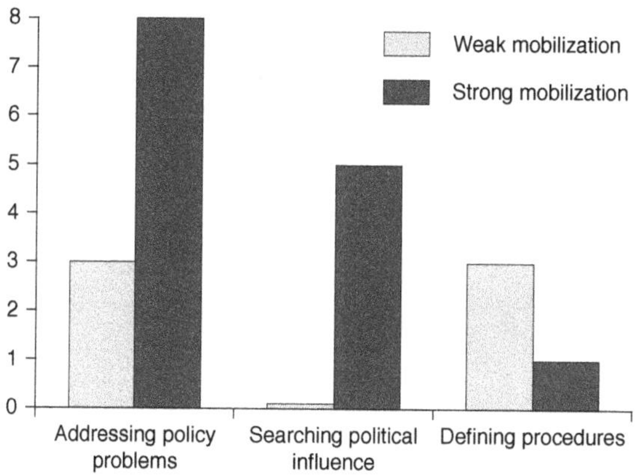

Figure 9.5 Types of theme debated in six CLSs located in areas with different histories of mobilization (Source: Health Policy and Public Involvement in the City of São Paulo project, 2008 – CDRC/CEM/NCD)

Looking at the quality of the minutes, we can distinguish two groups: one consists of Casa Verde, Vila Prudente and São Miguel, whose minutes were less detailed and report a more limited number of issues under discussion; the other consists of M'Boi Mirim, Parelheiros and Cidade Tiradentes, whose minutes are more detailed and refer to a wider range of issues. It is worth remembering that the level of detail in the minutes depends on the discretion of the executive secretary, and so these figures may not reveal accurately the content of the debates.

Either way, an analysis of the available data reveals important differences in the conduct of debates. We found a strong predominance of the three aspects most directly associated with tackling policy problems in the minutes of those CLSs located in areas with a greater background of social mobilization.

The aspects associated with political influence are also more frequently mentioned in the debates held in the CLSs of more mobilized areas. Particularly interesting is the presence of interventions related to programmes that call for cultural and ethnic recognition. This finding reinforces the hypothesis that, in Brazil, identity politics and affirmative policies are taking shape through a complex political process, in which participatory governance – and councils in particular – play an influential role.

Finally, aspects associated with procedures – design and election themes – appeared more frequently in the group with a weaker background of mobilization, suggesting that these CLSs are seeking to change their dynamics.

TABLE 9.4 Content of local health council debates (score of one indicates greater)

History of mobilization	Weaker			Stronger		
Criteria	Vila Prudente	Casa Verde	Parel-heiros	M'Boi Mirim	Cidade Tiradentes	São Miguel
Positioning about policy issues or making demands.	0	0	1	1	1	1
Planning, partnership or innovation.	0	0	1	1	1	1
Monitoring.	0	0	1	1	1	0
Recognizing cultural and ethnic diversity.	0	0	0	1	1	1
Expanding political influence.	0	0	0	1	1	0
Defining procedures for participation and electoral processes.	1	1	1	1	0	0

Source: Health Policy and Public Involvement in the City of São Paulo project, 2008 – CDRC/CEM/NCD

Discussing the assumptions

Four major assumptions have been assessed in this research: that, in those areas with a stronger history of social mobilization around health issues, we are likely to find CLSs that present: a) greater inclusion; b) broader participation; c) a higher degree of connections; and d) more proposals aimed at addressing policy problems. These topics were mainly assessed earlier in the chapter, and the results are mixed.

A background of social mobilization proved an important factor in promoting more vibrant CLSs, as well as in increasing the participation of the most vulnerable. As previously shown, there is greater inclusion of women, non-whites and councillors with less education on those councils located in the *sub-prefeituras* with a stronger background of mobilization. The indicators presented in Table 9.4 suggest that the way in which debates are conducted is very different, depending on whether an area has a greater or a lesser history of mobilization. In this sense, CLSs in areas with a stronger background of mobilization presented more contentious and demanding debates, but performed better on the indicators of planning, monitoring and innovation. These CLSs also reported more connections, especially with politicians, political institutions, health units, public managers, associations and other participatory forums – a result that calls attention to the way in which the CLSs are embedded in the political scene. It also suggests the importance of social mobilization in the process of creating links that connect the poor to the state and to other social organizations.

However, it was also shown that 'vibrant' participation is limited, inasmuch as few councillors raise issues or sustain discussion about them. In this sense, the creation of these CLSs, which are testament to an impressive institutional process of building participatory forums, was not accompanied by innovation in the day-to-day operation of these spaces. In many cases, they contributed, in the more mobilized areas, to simply reproducing the positions of health movements. The greater satisfaction felt with CLS performance and the greater accountability of councillors to the organizations they represent in those CLSs located in areas with a stronger background of mobilization might simply mirror this bias. In that sense, when we look at the political and associational profile of the councillors, we find a broader range of associations and greater political plurality in the CLSs that are located in areas with less history of mobilization. These CLSs are also the ones that drew up proposals to change the procedure for selecting councillors and running meetings, and this might be regarded as an attempt by those not politically connected to the health movements to introduce new dynamics.

These results reinforce the need to consider the distinction between the variables discussed and to be aware of the possible limitations of a number of studies that take participant satisfaction as a primary indicator of the performance of participatory forums.

From a theoretical perspective, these results call attention to the non-linearity of gains from participatory processes. The dimensions – inclusion, participation and connections – and the indicators that we have chosen to represent them run in different directions. We have achievements in some variables, and reversals in others – results that highlight the complexities of the democratization process. They also highlight the strong explanatory capacity of the concept of 'social mobilization', inasmuch as, despite the small number of cases, it opens up the possibility of predicting the kind of inclusion and participation and the number of connections that will be found in areas with stronger backgrounds of mobilization.

Final remarks

In this study, we worked to develop a model that enables institutionalized experiences of social participation to be compared and evaluated. As we saw early on, there is a highly normative debate about the role that social participation can play in the democratization of access to politics and policies. There is also a set of empirical studies that discuss the conditions for participation. However, there are no methodological instruments that allow us to move towards a systematic comparison of these experiences. The model of analysis presented here aims to fill this gap, moving towards an empirical study of the relations between these different variables and dimensions, and investigating more precisely the role that social participation has been playing in the democratization of access to debates and decision-making processes.

It is important to stress that the effort made here was directed more towards defining, setting up and testing the possibilities of this model, rather than drawing conclusions as to the behaviour of the variables being studied. It is worth remembering that we worked with a small number of CLSs, that the number of councillors was different in each and that the level of detail in the minutes depended on the discretion of the executive secretary – factors that limit the scope of the study. Despite these limitations, we have managed to present a set of indicators that are coherent with the variables described in the literature and allow an overview of the performance of the CLSs.

The data pointed to the richness of the CLSs' experience both in promoting political access for those worse off and in working out proposals that address health problems. As we saw, six CLSs operating on the periphery of the city combined possibilities for activism (strong positions, litigation and monitoring) and partnership (planning, redesigning the councils and deepening technical knowledge). This is new and different from the more usual technocratic way of discussing health policy in the municipality. It remains to be seen to what degree this novelty is translated into better services for the poor. A good indicator that this could be the case, however, is the recent action by the office of the Public Defender of São Paulo, which was prompted by complaints sent to it by the Parelheiros CLS, asking it to make a detailed study of the number of people in the southern zone of the city who are seeking specialist consultations and medical examinations, and the amount of time they spend on the waiting list.

Our study also calls attention to the relationship between the processes of mobilization and institution-building. While the creation of CLSs opened up a regular channel for those organizations fighting for health issues in the *sub-prefeituras*, the very existence of the organizations increased the chances of survival and the effectiveness of the participatory mechanisms. The results indicate a win-win game, as mobilization and participation prompt the democratization of health politics along the axes of inclusion of participants, themes and effective control. Nevertheless, the risk of 'capture' of the process by more organized groups is real: in areas with a stronger background of mobilization we found less political and associational plurality. Accordingly, we suggest that the gains could be maximized if the processes of mobilization and institution-building that occur at different times (the opening of spaces, followed by their occupation) were synchronized with experimentation with design features.

Thus it is suggested that those who are interested in citizen engagement with a view to democratizing politics and policies should look systematically (and simultaneously) at the three fronts: mobilization, design of participatory forums and training of public officials to deal with the challenges of facilitating participation.

Notes

1 This chapter presents results from the 'Participation and Health Policy in the City of São Paulo' research programme carried out by the Centro Brasileiro de Análise e Planejamento (CEBRAP, Brazilian Centre for Analysis and Planning) and the Centro de Estudos da Metrópole (CEM, Centre for Metropolitan Studies), funded by the Fundação de Amparo à Pesquisa do Estado de São Paulo (São Paulo State Foundation for Research Support) and the Citizenship DRC-DFID. We

would like to thank the Health Coordination Team, councillors of the *sub-prefeituras* and Carlos Neder for their support and interviews, as well as John Gaventa, Mark Warren, Naila Kabeer, Celestine Musembi, Chris Tapscott, Laurence Piper and Bettina von Lieres for their valuable comments and suggestions. Frederico Menino revised, discussed and extensively edited this paper, helping to improve the earlier versions with his careful and precise comments.

2 The constitution defined health as a right of all citizens and a responsibility of the state, and established the Sistema Único de Saúde (Unified Health System), the fundamental tenets of which are accountability, decentralization and popular participation.

3 The HDI varies from 0.74 to 0.95 across all the *sub-prefeituras* of São Paulo.

4 This classification, based on secondary research, was checked in interviews with Carlos Neder, ex-councillor, state deputy and a specialist on social health movements in the city of São Paulo, and Nabil Bonduki, an ex-municipal councillor and a research specialist on social movements in São Paulo.

5 A standard form was created to guide the analysis and the collection of data from these minutes. To see the distribution of the minutes in the sub-districts, as well as the data gathered and used in this research, see www.centrodametropole.org.br/v1/dados/saude/Anexos_Artigo_Saude_CDRCCEM.pdf.

6 According to the Municipal Law 13,716 from 2002, regulated by the Municipal Decree 44,658 from 2004, CLSs should have twenty-four effective and twenty-four substitute councillors; half should represent civil society and the other half should be split between government and service providers, and health workers.

7 More about this model can be found in the working paper presented by the Citizenship and Development Group in the Cape Town meeting, May 2008.

8 A more detailed presentation of how each variable was calculated can be found at www.centrodametropole.org.br/v1/dados/saude/Anexos_Artigo_Saude_CDRCCEM.pdf.

9 As explained later, for socio-economic variables we adopted different criteria: 1 was assigned to councils that had a socio-educational profile with a significant presence of the poor and less well educated.

10 A more complete presentation of the debates can be found at www.centrodametropole.org.br/v1/dados/saude/Anexos_Artigo_Saude_CDRCCEM.pdf.

10 · The dynamics of political change and transition: civil society, governance and the culture of politics in Kenya

DUNCAN OKELLO

> People wrongly assume that when you are in government you speak for civil society, yet the dynamics have changed. You have to play by the rules or lose the game. People wrongly assume that the values you had in civil society are the same values you'll continue to exercise in government. But sometimes you are forced to use strategies that people outside might consider underhand, yet the goal you are seeking is justifiable (Lawrence Mute, Commissioner, Kenya National Commission on Human Rights, interview, 2006)

Introduction

Since 1990, substantial changes have taken place in Kenya: the economy has been significantly liberalized, plural politics has taken a firm hold and four relatively successful multiparty elections have been held since 1992.[1] New actors have emerged on the scene, greatly changing the architecture of power. Civil society organizations (CSOs), broadly defined to include non-governmental organizations (NGOs), churches, professional bodies, grassroots organizations and trade unions, have been instrumental in the push for political reform. Notwithstanding their lack of homogeneity (Ngunyi, 1996), NGOs, churches and professional bodies have been central in fashioning the intellectual arguments at the heart of CSO mobilization. In the second half of the 1980s, leadership was provided by church organizations. Between 1989 and 1991 it passed to professional associations, and was then – from 1992 onwards – appropriated by NGOs (Nzomo, 2003). In the first multiparty elections, held in 1992, some civil society leaders were elected to parliament, but they managed to retain a strong and active presence in and membership of CSOs, effectively straddling the government and CSO spheres.[2]

Even though democratization and good governance have formed the overall defining agenda for civil society struggles, their form, style and focus have continually changed. Activities have ranged from simple calls and agitation for minor constitutional reform to allow the reintroduction of multiparty politics, to a mass push for a complete constitutional overhaul. Civil society has also shifted away from its hitherto cardinal and sacred principle of 'non-partisanship', taking sides in electoral contests and openly courting the support of voters – and thus moving from the mere provision of civic education to direct political mobilization.

In this chapter, I seek to assess the effect that civil society has had on improving the culture of governance in Kenya – by which I mean the values, conduct, institutions and structures of political life. I will look, in particular, at the aftermath of the 2002 general elections, when many civil society actors became part of the government for the first time.[3] I will argue that the culture of politics before this time was largely regressive, undemocratic, unresponsive and unaccountable, and that the raison d'être for civil society to intervene (whether as educator, competitor or mobilizer) was to reverse this situation. This orientation is explicit and implicit in the work of various CSOs and, particularly, NGOs, which, in Michael Bratton's terms, 'help to pluralise the institutional environment and promote a democratic political culture ... [as they help to] reconstruct state–civil society relations along democratic lines' (1989: 568). This is a view shared by many (Pietrowski, 1994; Nyangoro, 1999); but it has also been aggressively contested by others, such as Stephen Ndegwa (1996), who, in examining two Kenyan NGOs, argues that the actions of civil society are not necessarily democratizing. He suggests that they exhibit tendencies towards 'benevolent personal rule' and 'personality politics', and, because of a lack of proper institutionalization, that organizational actions correlate strongly with the preferences and actions of individual leaders. CSOs thus become merely 'resourceful platforms for the elite who are not immune to entrenched interests (such as class or ethnicity)' (1996: 5) and are therefore incapable of improving on the culture of governance and politics.

Bratton and Ndegwa provide us with an analytical spectrum through which to assess the contribution of civil society to improving the culture of politics and governance in Kenya. In this chapter, I take the view that, whereas the notion of civil society is broad (and the actors within it many and diverse), there is a category of civil society that – whether because of the advantages of 'learned' leadership, the ability to command resources or a high level of institutionalization – has been more visible in reform politics. It is from this high-profile category that the political establishment has actively recruited. I do not equate civil society with these elite groups, but I do recognize the significant influence that they have had in transforming Kenyan politics.

Civil society: between agency and structure

During the era of active political mobilization, civil society actors have taken the view that both structure and agency have been the cause of poor governance. Consequently, both of these notions have been the focus of civil society interventions. In the early part of the 1990s, a greater emphasis was placed on the importance of agency,[4] while the importance of changing structure gained prominence in the late 1990s, as expressed through the constitutional reform struggles of that time.

The agency argument assumed a managerial view of the decay of governance and politics in Kenya, positing that a 'change of guard' was the best cure for the existing governance malaise, as characterized by a leadership that was innately undemocratic and unaccountable, and that privileged personal survival, rather than performance, as a basis for legitimacy. The agency argument was also supported by the nascent opposition parties in 1992 which, convinced of their imminent victory in the elections, believed that a focus on constitutional reform would only allow the incumbent Kenya African National Union (KANU) to prolong its hold on power and delay the task of replacing bad state managers. It came as a surprise to them that KANU used a defective constitutional order not only to win the elections but significantly to frustrate efforts to improve the culture of politics and governance in Kenya for the next ten years (Mutunga, 1999).

The 'structural school', on the other hand, argued that the poor state of governance in Kenya was a function of weak and poorly designed systems and institutions. While agency was important, it ceased to be sufficiently important as a factor, especially in terms of expanding the democratic space as rapidly as the structural school felt was desirable. Its advocates insisted on institutional and constitutional reform as necessary preconditions for an improvement in the culture of politics and governance. As long as institutions such as the electoral commission, parliament, the judiciary and the executive remained unreconstructed, they argued, even new agents would find it difficult to behave differently (ibid.).

Codifying the reform agenda: issues for civil society intervention

Informed by the realities surrounding structure and agency, civil society interventions were powered by two objectives: institutional reform and reform of the values of both leaders and citizens. Continued state authoritarianism and unaccountability were seen as a consequence of citizens being deliberately kept in ignorance of their rights (and so unable to exercise or lay claim to them) – hence the civic education initiatives. Similarly, state institutions had been seriously undermined and eroded by prolonged periods of personal rule and a slew of constitutional amendments – hence the constitutional and institutional reform agendas.

The Kenyan state remained autocratic and, even after the restoration of plural politics in 1991, was still characterized by personal rule (Oyugi et al., 2003). The fact that this situation continued even after 1991 proved that autocracy and personal rule were at the core of political culture: both the state and the political parties were seen as victims of these two tendencies. The mandate of civil society was, therefore, to democratize the state.

Single partyism and a command economy – in which the state controlled 30 per cent of GDP (Institute for Economic Affairs, 1998) – served to conflate and concentrate political and economic power in the executive branch. This allowed the executive to overwhelm all other institutions, subordinate other arms of government to the party, stifle political competition by outlawing political parties and create an imperial presidency. It also controlled an unparalleled patronage system that was used to reward and punish (Kanyinga, 1995). The system lent itself very easily to the sort of corrupt behaviour that became a defining feature of Kenya's governing culture.

CSOs argued that the dispersal and diffusion of political power was a sine qua non in curing governance defects.[5] At the same time, it was considered necessary to empower the citizenry, in order to improve their ability to claim power and to inject a sense of responsibility and political accountability into government at the local level. Civil society's intervention and rationalization were the actions of a pluralizing agent working to reverse the undemocratic tendencies that were evident in the state. Civil society actors identified some key themes around which to pursue this agenda: constitutional reforms, human rights, accountability and anti-corruption. These issues were developed and made more concrete in the period from the late 1980s until 2002, when power shifted from KANU to the National Rainbow Coalition (NaRC), a change that was considerably assisted by civil society mobilization efforts. Civil society gave content and strategy to the struggle for change, but the ascent of civil society actors to positions of political power did not necessarily lead to a successful reform effort.

Grappling with the reform agenda: an analysis of civil society's effect on governance and politics

The constitutional reform agenda Those who argued that a problematic constitutional order was the reason behind Kenya's crisis of governance provided many examples of defects as they made their case for constitutional change. These included weak checks on the presidency, the concentration of power in one individual office, structural deficiencies in the constitutional and legal systems, and a structure and practice of government that was not based on any theory of constitutional form or practice. Several arguments on this subject were advanced by civil society actors through various platforms and publications (Wanjala and Mute, 2002; Oloka-Onyango et al., 1996).

Civil society's own understanding of the problem – and the articulation of its own aspiration for a better culture of politics – was perhaps best captured in the 'Model Constitution', developed jointly in 1994 by civil society groups led by the Law Society of Kenya (LSK), the Kenya Human Rights Commission (KHRC) and the International Commission of Jurists (ICJ). This document proposed a fundamental reordering of the institutions of the state, in order to improve the overall culture of politics in Kenya. It began in its preamble, for example, by noting past violations 'by tyrannical, despotic, fascist, and authoritarian governments'; called for the establishment of 'institutions of good governance such as an independent judiciary, a professional civil service and a truly representative legislature'; and called for institutionalization of 'the democratic values of transparency, accountability, respect for human rights and social justice', in addition to other reforms (Law Society of Kenya et al., 1994: i).

NGO leaders played an important role in the constitutional reform process, engaging at both the elite and the grassroots level, through petitions, scholarship, civic education and finally mass action protests in the late 1990s.[6] These actions forced through minimal constitutional amendments in what became known as the 'Inter-Parties Parliamentary Group Agreements' (IPPG), which set the stage for one of the most extensive and participatory constitution-making processes in the world. Elkanah Odembo, a former chairman of the NGO Council who also played a pivotal role in NaRC mobilization and electoral training work in 2002, noted:

> NGOs have a rich legacy on constitutional reform. They have increased citizens' levels of political awareness through their civic education programmes on the electoral process and constitutional issues, for example. The period 1999–2002 constituted a paradigm shift in development work – from 'pure' implementation of projects to raising questions about the root causes of poverty and underdevelopment, hence the robust socio-economic and political Bill of Rights in the Draft Constitution. (Interview with Elkanah Odembo, 2006)

During the clamour for constitutional reform, a consensus emerged among civil society actors. This included the need to devolve power, effect land reform, establish equity and respect for ethnic diversity, expand the Bill of Rights to accommodate social and economic rights and entrench women's rights. Most of these elements were captured in the 1997 Constitution of Kenya Review Act and were subsequently included in the 2002 draft constitution, which NaRC had committed itself to implementing on its accession to power towards the end of 2002. NaRC's commitment to these issues played a significant role in the decision of civil society actors to mobilize for the party in those elections, based on the assumption that, by winning the elections on this platform, the structure–agency dilemma would be resolved.

However, on taking power, NaRC began to renege on some of its reform commitments. Some of the ex-civil society leaders now in government changed their positions and opposed issues that they had previously stood for. The case of Hon. Kiraitu Murungi illustrates this shift rather dramatically. A prominent human rights lawyer who had been forced into exile in the early 1990s, Murungi was an important member of the civil society movement, even after he was elected to parliament in 1992. He founded, led and worked with several CSOs, among them the Centre for Governance and Development and the ICJ. During the constitutional review process in 1998, Murungi argued that the root cause of Kenya's governance problem was a strong and centralized executive, and he proposed that executive power be shared by creating the post of 'executive prime minister'. He observed that 'the enormous powers vested in the presidency have transformed the Kenyan president into an authoritarian imperial monarch, exercising feudal powers' and proposed that 'the powers of the president be drastically reduced and that powers of the head of government be exercised by a prime minister'.[7] This was in line with the manifesto of the Democratic Party (for which he was the shadow attorney general) for the design of government, and was one of the bases on which he had secured civil society support in the 2002 elections.

As minister for justice and constitutional affairs, however, Murungi changed his view. In 2005, he argued that it was a constitutional impossibility to have two centres of power in a developing country, and maintained that this would be a recipe for negative power and political competition. His volte-face was informed by the power politics of the NaRC's partners – the Liberal Democratic Party (LDP) and the National Alliance Party of Kenya (NAK) – and the seductiveness of power at the time. As Maina Kiai, chair of the Kenya National Commission on Human Rights (KNCHR), observed:

following the victory against a common enemy, 'Moi's badness', there was more divergence of views and positions by civil society actors due to access to power as well as self-preservation based on both personal preference and ethnic alliances. (Interview with Maina Kiai, 2007)

Murungi also played a leading role in the collapse of the entire constitutional project, which undid fifteen years of hard work. Following its election, the NaRC promised Kenyans a new constitution 'within 100 days'. It was generally anticipated that this new constitution would be based on the draft of September 2002. Instead, the constitutional review process collapsed – the victim of a major rift over power sharing within the NaRC that pitted Murungi's party, the NAK, against the LDP. This was a very significant lost opportunity, as a new constitution had been one of the biggest elements of the partnership between civil society and the new government.

Human rights agenda Civil society in Kenya was founded on a very strong human rights platform. Arguably, human rights NGOs were the first of Kenya's governance NGOs. The KHRC was the first major human rights player to be registered, in 1991, and it provided legal shelter for a number of nascent NGOs that had difficulty in obtaining legal recognition. Even older but less visible NGOs, such as Kituo Cha Sheria (Centre for Legal Empowerment) and the Public Law Institute had a very strong orientation towards human rights in their work.

This focus on human rights was driven by the fact that Kenya had one of the world's worst human rights records, in spite of being a signatory to various international conventions on human rights. Torture, extra-judicial killings by police, detention without trial and other violations were common. Both in rhetoric and in practice, there were serious deficiencies in the Kenyan government's human rights agenda. In fact, a focus on human rights was considered virtually treasonable, and it took considerable persistence by human rights organizations to force the government to acknowledge (however grudgingly and obliquely) the language of human rights.

The first major sign of change was the appointment of Amos Wako, a long-serving UN human rights rapporteur, as attorney general in 1991. The second was the establishment of the Standing Committee on Human Rights. These two developments, significant as they were, did not go far enough, and remained grossly inadequate in seriously committing the KANU government to the human rights agenda. Thus, civil society work to further human rights continued unabated, and ultimately pushed the government into establishing, by statute in 2002, the KNCHR.

However, in spite of having secured this structural gain, civil society human rights activists remained distrustful of the KANU regime, considering its work incomplete until the agency side of the argument was also won. This is why civil society actors mobilized for NaRC and the KNCHR during the 2002 elections, marking a significant shift away from civic education and towards direct political action. One of the first agenda items of the NaRC government was to breathe life into the statute, by appointing KNCHR commissioners and establishing its offices. Predictably, most of the first-generation commissioners were drawn from CSOs.

Recognition of human rights undoubtedly increased as a result of the broader reform agenda between 2002 and 2006, even if the violations themselves did not end entirely. This process is illustrated by the opening up of the hitherto insular prison system to ideas and scrutiny by NGOs. The political transition enabled civil society actors to continue the reforms 'from within' (2006 interview with Mburu Gitu, former head of the NGO Legal Resources Foundation, subsequently executive director of the KNCHR). Changes in the Police Act and the Evidence Act and the closure of the Nyayo House torture cells in 2003 provided evidence of a strengthened official human rights agenda.

Further evidence of progress includes the acceptance and use by government of the idea and language of human rights. For example, the phrase 'human rights-based approach to development' is now used in the water, roads, governance, justice and law and order sectors – an important sign of the changes being made in the culture of politics and governance, despite the fact that the culture of public service remains anti-human rights.

Similarly, the fact that civil society's access to public offices has improved marks a major shift in the culture of governance. Previously, civil society agitation was based on demands for the right to an audience with government on questions of policy and law. However, the development of the NaRC's premier policy blueprint, the Economic Recovery Strategy for Wealth and Employment Creation (2003–2007), benefited from immense input by civil society. It made governance and institutional reform the single most important determinant of economic development – an earthshaking event in Kenya's policy development history. This historical recasting of Kenya's economic policy orientation was, in no small measure, the work of Prof. Anyang Nyongo, a former civil society actor who was the minister for planning when the strategy paper was developed. Similarly, the Ministry of Justice and Constitutional Affairs was at the time working with the KNCHR and selected civil society bodies to develop a national policy on human rights.

The desired changes have not, however, reached all agencies of government. Law enforcement agencies (and in particular the police) are the least changed or reformed, and remain insular, in spite of the pressure from civil society. Indeed, the police are abusive and hostile, and have even prevented the KNCHR from executing its statutory mandate. As illustration of the frustration this has caused, a KNCHR commissioner has remarked:

> The worst culprit is the police. Even discussions at the highest level do not make a difference. For instance, when the current police commissioner was appointed, we exchanged nice letters, we dined the man; he would say yes to things but do nothing in the end. For instance, we had agreed that we would have billboards outside every police station setting out citizens' rights and what services they should expect from the police. He agreed to impromptu visits from the KNCHR commissioners to verify that the police were doing certain things, e.g. displaying their name and number badges more clearly for members of the public to see, that they were recording all complaints brought to them, treatment of people in police holding cells, etc., but none of this was ever implemented. Another recent example: when the recent Miscellaneous Amendments Bill included the reintroduction of 'Alcoblow',[8] we wrote to the Attorney General with our advice on the human rights issues it raises and how to deal with them. In his reply to us, the Attorney General copied the police commissioner into the correspondence. The next thing I knew was that I received this nasty letter from the police commissioner, telling me that I was busy-bodying and had no business making recommendations on the issue. (Personal communication)

There is evidence that the influence of former civil society actors within the government has given human rights reform a higher general profile. However, the experience of ex-civil society leaders so far has been that career government officers do not take human rights as seriously as they should. As one KNCHR commissioner put it: 'It's as if the government set up the KNCHR but did not expect to hear from us – not in criticism of the government anyway' (interview with Lawrence Mute, 2006). Success cannot be achieved without the cooperation and foresight of leaders within government and the bureaucracy.

Most ex-civil society leaders in government are of the view that there are simply not enough of them in government itself to influence change in a significant way; nevertheless, to some extent the reforms have come about thanks to them. At the KNCHR, for instance, programming is inspired and shaped by the experience that its officers bring from their backgrounds in civil society. These officers are able to share or transfer this knowledge (and their agenda) into mainstream government. There is recognition that any success within government is determined less by sheer numbers than by the individuals, their qualities and their sense of responsibility towards their role.

While the challenges that those civil society actors now in government have faced are many, there has been a good start in terms of shared language, ideas and programming based on human rights. It is important to note, however, that the success or failure of the civil society agenda also depends on the progress being made on the broader reform agenda.

Accountability and corruption The other major manifestation of the governance problem has been corruption, with its attendant problems of an absence of accountability and a culture of impunity. Before 2002, many civil society actors took the view that corruption was endemic and urgently needed to be tackled through the establishment of anti-corruption agencies with powers to investigate and prosecute corruption, provide for stronger disclosure requirements and guarantee punishment for offenders (Kibwana et al., 1998).

Consequently, 'zero tolerance for corruption' became one of the cardinal principles of civil society action and subsequent partnership with NaRC in the 2002 elections. Among the earliest laws the new government passed were the Public Officer Ethics Act (which emphasized disclosure requirements such as wealth declarations) and the Economic Crimes Act, and there were other high-profile anti-corruption initiatives. To their credit, the anti-corruption agenda was aggressively pursued by ex-civil society leaders and, in particular, by Minister Kiraitu Murungi and Permanent Secretary John Githongo, who had been director of Transparency International and who was appointed by President Kibaki to be his 'governance and ethics adviser' in the new NaRC administration.

It can be argued that, by demonstrating early interest through the passage of laws and the creation of institutions, the civil society leadership that joined the ruling government did an outstanding job. They created many avenues for speaking about accountability and attempting to remedy lack of accountability; but challenges nonetheless remained. In 2004, the NaRC regime faced a major corruption scandal – the Anglo Leasing scam – which was exposed by Githongo at great personal risk. The fact that Murungi was himself implicated in this scandal represented a major blow to the standards of governance that civil society had come to be associated with. These ethical standards fell even lower when the president, under pressure from representatives of Murungi's ethnic group, reinstated him in his ministerial position before any investigation had been conducted to clear his name.

The government's rather mixed record in fighting corruption has not been for lack of will or interest. Ex-civil society actors, particularly those in semi-autonomous governmental anti-corruption or accountability agencies, have had to confront serious practical challenges: how to deal with unfulfilled (and sometimes unrealistic) public expectations, especially since managing those expectations depends on other arms of government; the lack of institutional cohesion, especially at the operational level; and the obvious need to seek partnerships with other agencies to execute their mandates (and the difficulty in finding such partnerships).

The existence of multiple avenues of accountability has created a gap between expectations and capability. Public complaints attract wide media attention, but not all get addressed. A culture of impunity still remains, as commissions investigate issues and make their reports, but no prosecution follows.

On the issue of accountability, Maina Kiai, who was founding executive director of both the civil society-based KHRC and the government-sponsored KNCHR, believed that the standing of the NaRC government was higher than that of KANU, largely as a result of internal and external pressure and a widening democratic space that has led to greater scrutiny and demands for greater accountability. Kiai cited the establishment of 'active, strong and independent' institutions, such as the KNCHR, which has a binary effect on government: when it suits its purposes, the government lauds the KNCHR as a 'trophy' of success and evidence of government commitment to human rights; when KNCHR speaks out against the government, the government attacks it for being too harsh and for acting beyond its mandate (interview with Maina Kiai, 2007).

Electoral reform Kenya's electoral culture has been characterized by violence, ethnicity, bribery, hate speech, low voter turnout and the misuse of public resources. Because of its centralized nature and winner-takes-all structure, electoral politics has also been full of ethnic competition and manipulation (Kanyinga, 2003). As Murungi observed rather resignedly:

> We can no longer pretend that ethnicity is not an important factor in Kenyan politics. It is part and parcel of our historical and social reality ...

> the family, clan, and the tribe are the basic forms of political socialisation and the characteristic mode of our political expression. We cannot avoid the objective fact by reference to abstract theories of human nature, the categorical imperatives of enlightenment philosophers or the laws of historical materialism. (Murungi, 2000: 159)

CSOs have sought to correct this state of affairs. Smokin Wanjala, a former civil society leader who became deputy director of the Kenya Anti-Corruption Commission in 2003, argued that the key dangers to the electoral process are manipulation of the outcome of the process, money and ethnicity. Of these three, the greatest danger lies in the manipulation of votes, as that is the hardest behaviour to overturn. In trying to control these illegitimate influences on the electoral outcome, Wanjala acknowledged the role played by civil society in electoral reform. He noted that change had been incremental and had significantly decreased the opportunities for the manipulation of electoral results (interview with Smokin Wanjala, 2006). In the 1992, 1997 and 2002 general elections, CSOs provided the Kenyan citizenry with civic education. In 2002, however, CSOs not only pushed for unity on the part of the opposition to enable it to mount a strong and successful challenge to the ruling party KANU, but also provided a structure for the achievement of this unity, in the form of the National Alliance for Change, a conglomeration of the three main opposition parties that was the precursor of NaRC. It also pushed for electoral reform, which resulted in votes being counted at the polling stations.

Civil society leaders who joined government oversight institutions in 2003 made some effort to address various aspects of the negative electoral culture. The KNCHR did monitoring work on electoral violence, sectarianism and misuse of public resources in the 2005 referendum. The effect of this work was largely positive, even if it did not run its full legal cycle. As Mute observed:

> With regard to the work on hate speech, we recorded the speeches in question, and recommended prosecution of the people making them. The Attorney General never prosecuted, and so we went to court to initiate the prosecution ourselves, but then the AG entered a nolle prosequi and that was the end of the matter. With regard to abuse of public funds [during the campaigns that preceded the national referendum of 2005], our report was balanced, in that we investigated both sides and found that the abuses were on both sides. (Interview with Lawrence Mute, 2006)

The KNCHR's report on the referendum did indict ex-civil society leaders in one form of electoral malpractice or another. Three former civil society leaders and cabinet ministers, for example, were mentioned as having misused government vehicles and aeroplanes in the campaign (Kenya National Commission on Human Rights, 2006) yet they remained unapologetic.[9] They also mobilized to influence the vote in the referendum on a sectarian basis. The Hon. Kivutha Kibwana, one of the leading civil society leaders, was recorded as saying that a NaRC party membership card was the equivalent of a certificate of good conduct, which would determine people's access to economic opportunities; this harked back to the days of single partyism, when access to public services such as markets and bus stops would often be made conditional on possession of a KANU membership card.

The outcomes of the 2002 general elections and the 2005 national referendum demonstrate the importance of an independent electoral commission. They also confirm that Kenya has widened its democratic space, with less executive interference in the democratic process, especially at the ballot box, and that the premium placed on democracy is now higher than before. In a 2006 interview, Wanjala considered that the non-interference of the executive in 2002 and 2005 made the Electoral Commission of Kenya (ECK) bolder and more confident. Moreover, there were almost no incidents of serious violence.[10] There are still loopholes in the electoral process that must be plugged, however. For instance, although the independence of the ECK has been enhanced, it can still be manipulated by the incumbent, since its commissioners are appointed by the president, who is not obliged to consult parliament or any other stakeholders on his appointees.

In furthering the agenda for good governance, citizens have a role to play. However, Kepta Ombati, a former executive director of the National Convention Executive Council, the leading civil society group for constitutional reform, argued that they have not been playing it. He notes that voter turnout, particularly among young Kenyans, continues to be poor, despite tremendous efforts on the part of civil society. He attributes this, in part, to a political culture that discourages good ideas and promotes 'criminals' who possess the resources needed to attain political office. Ombati has pointed out that, for elections to be fully 'free and fair', the environment in which they are conducted must be taken into consideration. For instance, the existing political system is hostile to women and young people participating in the political process, as both groups often lack the necessary patronage and resources needed for their ideas to be heard (interview with Kepta Ombati, 2006).

Civil society in government: a steep learning curve for agency

Civil society as bureaucrats and with bureaucrats: culture clash and bad strategy In the 2002 elections, civil society mobilized politically and succeeded in creating a government. The expectation in return was for a fundamental shift in the culture of government. The strategy adopted called for the recruitment of large numbers of non-traditional bureaucrats, mainly drawn from civil society, to inject new values, methods and pace of doing government work into the system.

This strategy rested on faulty assumptions about the legitimacy of civil society actors and their ability to effect instant government-wide change, as well as about the willingness of the bureaucracy to embrace reform quickly. A culture clash occurred, compromising the speed of reform. There was mutual frustration, as traditional bureaucrats viewed the style of civil society actors and the content of their agendas with constant suspicion, hostility and cynicism. When bureaucrats worked out that not much was going to change, the bureaucracy lapsed into its old ways, facilitated by NaRC's internal rifts.

Civil society leaders had a weak grasp of the ways of government, while demands piled up for them to deliver 'civil society trophies'. The goals of civil society leaders became easier to frustrate because of their failure to build alliances among themselves once they were in government. Civil society leaders had come into government as individuals, in the tradition of 'personality politics' (Ndegwa, 1996: 14). Personal stardom was considered a sufficient qualification to push for reform in government – a patently wrong-headed approach within bureaucratic operations. Consequently, not only were civil society leaders few in number, but also lacking in strategic thinking. As Kiai observed:

> some ex-civil society actors who came in on a platform of reform became enamoured by the new positions and eventually stopped consulting with fellow ex-civil society leaders in government or even those outside it. (Interview with Maina Kiai, 2006)

Civil society leaders took a long time to find a happy balance between agitation and governing. Even in instances where some thought they had succeeded in their goals, their view was not shared by others. Reflecting on his civil society and government experiences, Mute observed:

> Being on the other side you discover that some civil society positions are simply impractical and unsustainable. For instance, when the Terrorism Bill was published, civil society people had a simple line: this Bill is bad, throw it out. But being in the Commission [for human rights], our

task is to advise the government, and do so in great detail because while human rights were important, the security concerns are valid too. We would hold meetings with our civil society friends and at these meetings we would appear to disagree violently. We tried to show them that outright rejection of the Bill would not be in fulfilment of our mandate. We had to offer the government practical, implementable [sic] advice. You see, there is a difference between simply criticizing, and contributing to shaping public policy. When I was in CLARION [Centre for Law and Research International], we would write a book and make twenty-odd recommendations; but in policy making, you have to prioritize. You can't present the government with twenty recommendations. (Interview with Lawrence Mute, 2006)

While the objectives of former civil society actors were clear – to change the way in which government works and reorient it towards service delivery – strategies for pursuing these objectives were weak. Ill equipped to participate in the political warfare of bureaucratic processes, undermined by a civil war within the government coalition and unable to forge alliances within or outside government, their objective of fundamentally changing the way government performed was significantly undermined.

Values deficits or betrayals? Weak partnerships It was expected that civil society actors who joined the government would continue to pursue the reform agenda, but this proved not always to be the case. Some were unable to navigate their new bureaucratic environments, while others perhaps did not have very strong commitments to reform in the first place.

In itself, opposition to the regime during the KANU era was regarded as an indication of progressiveness. This meant that the undemocratic and self-serving tendencies of CSO leaders were routinely overlooked, as when individuals pushed for change for personal or organizational benefit. Thus, people whose reasons for allying themselves to a progressive agenda were questionable were allowed to thrive. As Odembo observed:

> Many CSOs and NGOs are not well governed, transparent or accountable, which poses the question as to why we expect them to insist on these standards once they are in government. After all, an individual's worldview is determined by where one sits. If an individual is only playing a lobbying and advocacy role for personal gain, it is unlikely that they will espouse any of the values or stand for any of the positions of civil society. (Interview with Elkanah Odembo, 2006)

Generally, ex-civil society actors in government remain largely inaccessible to their former allies. When clear opportunities for partnership did emerge – such as at the National Constitutional Conference in 2003–04 – some former civil society leaders-turned-ministers were found to be remarkably elusive. As Mburu Gitu observed:

> [T]here [are] apparently more divergences than alliances or partnerships having developed between ex-civil society actors while in government. Individuals have shifted positions and seem to have less commonality. They became politicians and the objective for them is self-preservation. In their view, their survival may be in doubt if they continue playing the civil society role. This is not in tandem with the previously held value system on which positions were articulated. We must acknowledge that values change and bureaucracies also change people. Independent institutions have more or less survived and remained faithful to their original calling because they operate in insulated environments. (Interview with Mburu Gitu, 2006)

There are points both of convergence and of divergence between ex-civil society actors within government. They seem to agree on the importance of government remaining faithful to legal instruments and processes when executing its mandates, and on the need to be guided by ideals and values. However, they seem to disagree on the extent of the mandate of semi-autonomous government agencies. The existence of the KNCHR, for example, continues to generate tension between its staff, who are largely ex-civil society actors, and the minister for justice, who has frequently questioned the manner in which KNCHR interprets its mandate, especially with respect to inquiries into the misuse of state resources.

Those reformers who remained in civil society, outside government, were greatly weakened after the election of the NaRC. Their weakness was a result not so much of the exodus of their leaders into government, but of the redirection of donor funds away from civil society's governance initiatives and towards directly supporting the budgets of a government perceived to be reform oriented. Weak transition and succession plans in CSOs also had a destabilizing effect in the period immediately following the NaRC win. The shift in focus by international development partners exposed CSOs and resulted in a decline in their ability to lobby and check government. This turn of events also caused friction between ex-civil society leaders in government and the remaining leadership. NGOs saw the agencies that were created (and mostly headed) by ex-civil society leaders as taking funding away from them, which caused friction and made the task of building alliances for reform very difficult. Whereas civil society had in fact worked its way into government, those not in the public service did not establish the means to develop and form creative partnerships with those in government.

Conclusions

What, then, has been the effect of civil society on the culture of politics and governance in Kenya? Results are mixed. There have been advances and reversals, but it may require an empirical study to determine whether these constitute a net loss or a net gain.

However, it is arguable that, generally speaking, ex-civil society leaders in government have tried to move the country towards a progressive culture of politics. Even though one may argue about whether reform efforts have occurred because of or in spite of civil society actors in government, it is clear that the intellectual contributions of individuals in civil society have borne fruit, even if operational limitations still obtain. Various individuals have positively influenced decisions and operations within the government itself, and new laws, institutions, philosophies and practices have been initiated.

However, this view is not shared by all civil society leaders, and especially not by those that remained outside government. And for good reason: most question the blanket general acceptance that there is 'reform taking place' without any investigation of the quality of that reform. Using the establishment of the Kenya Anti-Corruption Commission as an example, in a 2006 interview Elkanah Odembo argued that there had been no demonstrable impact on the fight against corruption; that judicial reform had not followed due process of law; that the establishment of numerous commissions and committees was not evidence of actual reform; and that the review of laws and regulations did not constitute reform unless these were actually implemented.

However, at the sub-national level, Odembo concedes that public administration and resource allocation may slowly be becoming more accountable. Even though civil society investment in civic education over time may have led to greater engagement at the grassroots levels with these initiatives this should not be attributed solely to the work of the elite ex-civil society leaders (Nyamu Musembi, this volume).

Different sectors or areas of reform show different results or effects. Human rights constitute the sector in which civil society has made the single biggest impact. In terms of both content and style, the human rights credentials of ex-civil society leaders in government have remained largely intact. However, in the accountability/anti-corruption sector, the successful legislative work of early 2003, which saw the enactment of two important pieces of anti-corruption legislation, has not always been followed up with consistent political action. This may be because, in contrast to the KNCHR, the head of the anti-corruption agency was a judge rather than an ex-civil society leader. It may also be due to the unique political problems that fighting corruption presents to the Third World.

Similarly, the effect on constitutional reform has been mixed – the discourse on rights and devolution/dispersal of power has advanced, but Kenya still does not have a new constitution. When the new constitution is finally completed, however, it is likely to include most of the ideas already developed by civil society, such as an expanded bill of rights. It is also significant that ex-civil society leaders campaigned on different sides in the constitutional referendum. The electoral arena is one place in which the ex-CSO leaders who plunged into direct electoral politics have had no impact in changing the culture of politics: ethnic/sectarian mobilization, patronage and abuse of state resources have remained notable features, even among this group. However, the ex-CSO leaders who went into government human rights work have made remarkable strides in trying to limit impunity and foster electoral accountability.

However, reform has also happened despite rather than because of the inclusion of civil society actors in government. On this score, it has been argued that the context determines the extent of civil society's effect in realizing reform. Ndegwa points out that:

> The necessity for political opportunity, which is evident in actions of NGOs in Kenya, underscores that civil society activity does not cause political liberalization, but that the democratic movement is a larger force engulfing the whole society to which civil society actors respond. Even though NGOs occupy an influential position in civil society, command considerable resources and voice, and have leverage against developing states such as Kenya, they are not the originators of reform movements. Indeed, they are respondents to both the repressive capacities of the state and the reformist backlash against the state from sectors of civil society (most prominently displaced elites). The resurgence of civil society and its political activity in Africa therefore reflects a social movement of which it may be only a belated but nevertheless significant sign. (1996: 111)

While one can understand Ndegwa's contention, it is too sweeping to place the origins of reforms entirely outside NGO circles. To confine the meaning of the word 'origin', as he seems to do, to some dramatic peasant or grassroots initiative is to exclude the power of cognition and intellect. The fact that the NGOs are able to 'think it' rather than 'act it' is, in my view, not a sufficient reason to conclude that they cannot be the 'originators' of reform. The struggle for reform has a division of labour, which assigns different responsibilities to different groups in different sets of circumstances, and this division is not always perfect. The success of the civil society reform agenda is dependent on alliances. In Kenya, it appears that civil society actors have been most successful in pushing reforms only when they have sought partnership with politicians, who have the capacity to organize citizens.[11]

The lesson that civil society actors have learned over this period, and particularly between 2002 and 2007, is that the success of reform depends on the partnerships for mobilization that one builds, even when in government. Part of the reason why the civil society record is mixed is that few ex-civil society members have built creative and strategic partnerships once they have got into government. These partnerships were missing in relationships with the bureaucracy and with other civil society leaders, both in and outside government.

The difficulty of building partnerships with the segments of civil society that remain outside government was related to conflicts over funding and perception. When donors shifted direct support for civil society to government, the relationship between these erstwhile partners degenerated, sometimes into open hostility. This was further compounded by a crisis of expectation and perception. As one ex-civil society leader in government reflected:

> The greatest challenge is having to justify yourself to former peers in civil society. They always express concern that you have become 'one of them'. They don't understand how government works. It is difficult for us to talk to each other because our civil society colleagues have the impression that we have lots of powers that we are not using. But again they have got to understand the calculation that goes into making any move. (Interview, December 2006).

The Kenyan experience shows that it is not enough for ex-civil society leaders to troop into government and hope that reform will happen. For civil society reform agendas to succeed, there is a need to investigate the goals and values of all actors, and also to establish both the extent to which they diverge or are shared and a plan of action based on this knowledge. While goals and values may appear the same, if everyone takes what they feel to be the best approach then they are in danger of ending up fragmented, inefficient and ineffective. If this happens, the bureaucratic bulwark will stymie the good intentions that exist within individual civil society actors.

Furthermore, the success that civil society will have in changing the culture of governance is still determined considerably by the environment in which it operates. Where there is a weak socio-political environment, with weak accountability structures and no deterrents to wayward behaviour or means to hold leaders to account, even those with the best intentions may find themselves simply swimming with the tide for their political survival. The post-2002 period has demonstrated a 'national naivety' – the belief that investing either in individuals (agency) or in institutions and laws (structures) is all that is needed to ensure good governance. The challenge lies in trying to find a happy balance that works, and this requires simultaneity of, and connection between, interventions directed at structure and agency.

It is evident that, even as civil society actors have – in a Brattonian sense – tried to improve on the culture of governance and politics in Kenya, civil society itself is a product of its environment (in the Ndegwan sense). The lack of immunity from social fission, and the lures of class and ethnicity, is what led Ndegwa to caution that:

> the potential or demonstrated abilities of civil society organizations to pursue democratizing actions must therefore be examined in the context of the broader politics of any state, and assumptions regarding their uniqueness or immunity to usual political proclivities must be abandoned. (1996: 5)

Indeed, as this chapter has shown, ex-civil society leaders did not always behave any differently from traditional politicians in dispensing ethnic patronage or in circumventing accountability rules and standards, thus further undermining the emergence of a positive culture of politics.

Notes

1 This includes the 2005 constitutional reform referendum, which we are treating as an 'election' but was strictly not one. This chapter is based on a paper that was originally written before the 2007 general elections, which were disputed and led to unprecedented violence.

2 Examples here include Paul Muite, chairman of the Law Society of Kenya (LSK), and Kiraitu Murungi and Martha Karua, both members of the LSK Council who were also active in other NGOs.

3 Some of those who joined the government became ministers; others became part of semi-autonomous agencies, such as the anti-corruption and human rights commissions.

4 I refer to this as 'third-party agency', in the sense that civil society actors still did not want to engage directly in competitive politics, not seeing themselves as agents. This is in contrast to the second phase of engagement, where the struggle for structural reconstruction was also informed by the realization that there cannot be reform without reformers. It was at this point that civil society actors decided to become first-party agents.

5 This was such an article of faith in civil society activism that the struggle for constitutional reform in Kenya came to be defined by it. The curbing of executive power became one of the six principles of the 1997 constitutional review process.

6 These protests were organized and led by the National Convention Executive Council, a network of civil society organizations that was established primarily – indeed exclusively – to fight for constitutional reforms.

7 www.newsfromafrica.org/articles/art_8160.html (accessed 10 November 2009).

8 'Alcoblow' is a shorthand reference to the breathalyser test used to detect drunk drivers. The police introduced it and then had to withdraw it because a citizen successfully argued in court that it was a violation of their rights, as no measures had been taken to ensure that communicable diseases, such as tuberculosis, would not be passed on through the device.

9 They retaliated by arguing that a minister is a minister twenty-four hours a day and is therefore entitled to use his or her official vehicle all the time, and that the referendum was not a private venture. As reported in 'We Will Use State Resources to Win Vote, Ministers Vow', *East African Standard*, 23 October 2005.

10 However, in view of the interference of the executive with the Electoral Commission in the 2007 elections, this salutary view no longer remains valid.

11 Examples include the shift to multipartyism and constitutional reform. In both cases, civil society actors were vocal campaigners and advocates, and in both cases their engagement was made effective only by the inclusion and participation of politicians.

12 This interview respondent requested anonymity.

PART FOUR

Where and how to participate?

11 · Passivity or protest? Understanding the dimensions of mobilization on rights to services in Khayelitsha, Cape Town

LISA THOMPSON AND NDODANA NLEYA

Introduction

> Here in Khayelitsha, we often hold meetings and when government fails to respond to us we take further steps. I think meetings come up with good solutions. To protest is the best solution because our parents used to do that in the past and look, now we have a democratic country. (Interview respondent, Khayelitsha, 2007)

Protests around service delivery have been a source of discussion and debate in South Africa in recent years, following a series of demonstrations – some violent – over lack of housing, water and sanitation. This chapter examines how violent protest forms part of a continuum of participatory strategies used by the poor to claim their socio-economic rights. As the quotation above highlights, various methods of participation can be viewed as progressive steps on a ladder. Drawing on mobilization and social movement theories, we explore how resource-deprived communities weigh up the different forms of participatory involvement with the state that are available to them, and choose their course of action in trying to claim what they are entitled to but may not actually receive.

We examine the findings of a survey on perceptions of governance and service delivery, which was undertaken in 2007 in Khayelitsha, a poor township some 35km from Cape Town. The survey was designed to obtain a comprehensive understanding of the diversity of participatory strategies employed by individuals and communities. Drawing on an eclectic mix of approaches, we argue that communities in Khayelitsha are highly aware of the political opportunities and the political opportunity structures available to them, and also of the relative power of protest action in yielding results from government.[1] This chapter illustrates that, while mobilization and collective action form the loosest definition of social movement action (in the sense that street committees and other groupings come together as needed in order to act collectively), the range of actions is very carefully chosen, and protest is a means of last resort.

The study shows that, throughout Khayelitsha, grassroots forms of political and social organization are part of daily life. Street committees – a form of organization with its origins in the struggle against apartheid – have been rejuvenated and are a key self-created or 'invented' space in which political and socio-economic rights and entitlements are discussed and in which decisions affecting the wider community are made. We are cognizant of the fact that, as Kabeer has pointed out, not all forms of associational politics are democratic. She reminds us that:

> there is nothing inherently democratic about associations and not all groups promote democratic rights ... Equally, however, others can help expand the space available for democratic activity. These groups may not necessarily operate in the political sphere, but they become 'democratically relevant'. (2005: 35)

In the light of what has been said, it is worth remembering that at this stage little is known about how democratic the internal decision-making processes of the new-style street committees really are. It is clear that these forms of organization (and the platform for social movement activism they represent) provide a basis for challenging the state on rights and entitlement to basic services that have been promised but are not forthcoming (Thompson and Nleya, 2008).

'Thicker' forms of democracy – where civic engagement extends beyond voting – are not a given, but are something that emerges through contestation (Tapscott, 2007). To explore the forms of contestation that emerge in the light of the survey, the remainder of this chapter is divided into four sections. The first section examines some of the analytical and conceptual issues we have used to frame the study. The next section describes the study area and the methodology of the study. The third section focuses specifically on some of the main findings of the study in relation to three areas: community concerns about service delivery, perceptions of institutional democratic practices and participatory strategies for approaching issues of community concern. The final section brings together the findings and draws some conclusions.

Understanding mobilization strategies in Khayelitsha: analytical considerations

Since the adoption of a liberal democratic form of government in 1994, the evolution of state–society relations in South Africa has been closely observed by academics, policy think tanks, development agencies and the local and international press. One view is that the 'marginalized' poor (or 'underclass') have still not bought into the liberal notions of citizenship that are embodied in current institutional manifestations of liberal democracy. Tapscott (2005) attributes this to the top-down governance processes driven by the ruling classes and state bureaucrats. Others argue that the poor are variously perceived as apathetic and reluctant to take advantage of the fresh opportunities available to them, especially now that apartheid has gone (Thompson and Matheza, 2005). Meanwhile, the violent forms of protest that break out sporadically around lack of service delivery have caught both academic and media attention (Ballard et al., 2006). Our survey findings indicate that, while everyday forms of community expression are mostly ignored by the media, this does not mean that they are not at the heart of any conception of democracy. As Bracking states:

> the chronically poor express agency, notably through informal self-organization, religious organizations, clientelism, populism, authoritarianism, insurrection, criminality, and war ... Then, while the poor are performing live, unnoticed, at another venue, they are identified as 'failing' to act in accordance with a script which expects them to 'join in' the structures of the relatively privileged (feeding elite prejudice that the poor are 'not trying enough'). The result is an unrealistic, judgemental and ultimately disempowering expectation of how the poor should behave. (2005: 1014)

By arguing that the poor fail to participate in the new 'participatory state', proponents of a virtuous notion of citizenship in the civic republican tradition (Hill, 1994; Kofman, 1995) provide a restricted vision of how the poor should act. The language they employ is illustrated by Leslie Sklair's definition of active citizenship:

> The good democratic citizen is a political agent who takes part regularly in politics ... Active citizens keep informed and speak out against public measures that they regard as unjust ... Although they do not refrain from pursuing their own and their reference group's interests, they try to weigh the claims of other people impartially ... They are public meeting-goers and joiners of voluntary organizations. (Cited in Hadenius, 2001: 17)

It is clear that perceptions of the 'active citizen' derived from this tradition create a view of the 'poor' that is both static and idealized. MacKian (1995) also cautions against over-romanticization of active citizenship, for, as well as seeking the positive effects of citizen action, so-called 'active citizens' are often on the look-out for positions of influence for themselves. We argue instead that there is a range of mobilization strategies that show how communities redefine citizenship and the notion of democratic action in ways that challenge the sanitized notion of active citizenship, and that enable us to view this concept as one that must be contextualized if it is to have any real meaning. In much the same way, understandings of democracy or democratic practices are largely context specific, once certain basic conditions (such as free and fair elections) are met.

Analytically, it is just as important to bear in mind the larger context within which community action or active citizenship plays itself out. Debates around participation have led to a rich diversity of perspectives on how to understand the ways in which spaces of participation are constructed, how different actors construct identities and power relations within institutionalized spaces, and how alternative spaces are constructed to circumvent power hierarchies and disempowering institutional dynamics (Cornwall and Coelho, 2007; Robins et al., 2008). What is at stake ultimately is the extent to which the state, operating at different levels, is conditioned over time into stronger relationships of social accountability (Joshi, 2008). Following Skocpol (1992), Joshi argues that changing state–societal power dynamics are reflected through the polity, defined as 'the space within which political struggles across the public–private divide take place and through which both state and societal capacities and natures are shaped' (2008: 15). This approach focuses on the interplay between the state-led processes of participation and social dynamics both within and outside these processes, and helps retain a sense of the importance of less visible forms of participation and mobilization, which can ultimately lead to reconfigurations of social accountability. Our study of Khayelitsha shows the strength of community organization in forms that are less visible (to the public media). Street committees, in particular, are a longstanding form of social organization, and although more established in some areas of Khayelitsha than in others, these street-level forms of organization and communication often serve as the building blocks for other forms of institutional participation with the state as well as with non-governmental organizations (NGOs), and for mobilization across a broad spectrum of governance issues – from basic services like water and sanitation to demands for better policing and housing (Conradie and Thompson, 2010).

In order to make sense of the complexity of civil society agency, activism and state interactions, we must be mindful of the fact that, as Cornwall and Coelho point out '"the state" and "civil society" [are] heterogeneous and mutually constitutive terrains of contestation' (2007: 7). Neither necessarily has the moral high ground in terms of democratic processes, nor even a common understanding or commitment to a common democratic project.

Skocpol (1979, 1994) argues that social revolutions and social transformation can be understood as a particular historical configuration of state and non-state actors, highlighting the critical role of the state and state bureaucracies in shaping social conditions that allow for the mass mobilization and popular leadership that characterize revolutionary social movements. While we focus here on a democratic state context and on the interplay between state and non-state actors that creates the conditions for certain forms of participation and mobilization, we acknowledge that these are rooted both in how the state shapes citizen identities through a range of legal and policy instruments and in how they are constructed by individuals and communities themselves. When we evaluate the range of participatory action taken by communities, we need to remember that self-created spaces like street committees are necessary because of the failure of the state to provide spaces of meaningful participation and effective (as well as accountable) decision-making, and not necessarily because people feel compelled to participate as 'new citizens' in the recently formed democracy.

Indeed, while there are a number of complex factors that give rise to the importance of street committees in Khayelitsha, one of the main reasons why they have undergone a resurgence of organizational commitment and energy is that local forms of state–societal institutional participation are seen as inadequate and ineffective. Mobilization occurs because there is a need for it, and because there is sufficient knowledge of the commitments made by government for communities to insist on fulfilment of the bold promises made by politicians at election time. Mobilization and the formation of local social movement activity through street committees and local community-based groups and organizations are both initiated and continually reconfigured by policy processes and participation (or the lack thereof) at higher levels of decision-making.

The next section traces the origins of social organization and mobilization in Khayelitsha, against the backdrop of its location and spatial design, originating in apartheid city planning.

Exploring participation in Khayelitsha: context and methodology

Khayelitsha is a sprawling township located to the south-east of Cape Town, between the northern shoreline of False Bay and the N2 highway. The term 'township' is popular parlance for any area that lacks such basic infrastructure as proper roads and storm water drainage; the general feel, as McDonald (2000: 3) puts it, is 'dry and dusty'. Now, as in the past, 'township' is also understood to imply racial and socio-economic segregation, with poor black communities continuing to reside in these areas, while middle-class black families have moved to the historically white suburbs. While there are some wealthy families still living in places like Khayelitsha, this is increasingly the exception rather than the norm.

The construction of Khayelitsha was unveiled in parliament in March 1983, against a background of strict influx control legislation[2] and the 'coloured' labour preference policy that applied in Cape Town and large parts of the Western Cape.[3] Articulating issues related to citizenship and human rights, Khayelitsha requires an understanding of the 'native question' – a phrase that refers, in a sanitized way, to the exercise of state power to emasculate indigenous populations in settler colonies (Mamdani, 1996). The history of Khayelitsha is bound up with the struggle of black South Africans for urban permanence in Cape Town; as Conradie (1992) points out, this historical struggle epitomizes the lot of black people in the Western Cape, past and present. Service issues in Khayelitsha should thus be interpreted as the culmination of a series of historical continuities, which have embedded poverty along racial lines in distinct geographical areas.

In the original plans for Khayelitsha, there was more than one type of housing and service arrangement. In addition to formal housing, there were 'site and service' areas – essentially a form of controlled squatting, with the provision of rudimentary services. These areas would be developed in a confined section of Khayelitsha – Site B and Site C – but they marked the beginning of a far wider phenomenon of 'planned informal settlements'. Initially, site and service areas were intended to provide temporary shelter for residents, but a report by the engineering company originally responsible for site planning warned that the development of the site and service settlement option would 'have far reaching and long lasting implications' (VKE, 1985: 11). True to this prediction, the sites that were developed for housing in serviced plots have fewer service delivery problems, while site and service settlements are experiencing the most severe strain in the service delivery arena. To understand the socio-economic differences that are prevalent in Khayelitsha, it is important to distinguish between the areas that constitute it. Approximately 70 per cent of residents live in informal housing, and the conditions in informal and formal housing vary widely. To illustrate this, we refer briefly to the differences between the five areas in which we conducted interviews: Site C, Site B, Endlovini, Ilitha Park and Khaya.

Site C is a largely informal settlement, located on a site that was originally intended to become the commercial district of Khayelitsha, but that was eventually allocated to 'illegal' residents from KTC squatter camp and Crossroads, two squatter communities in the Cape Town area. These 'illegals' initially resisted settlement in Site C, because it meant longer journeys to work and a perceived loss of their right to resettlement in New Crossroads, a township closer to Cape Town. This resistance collapsed when vigilante warfare in Crossroads and KTC left many homes destroyed (Burman and Schärf, 1990). Site C was conceived as a 'site and service' settlement. It was made up of so-called 'double' plots, which consisted of a yard measuring 90 square metres, a tap and a toilet to be shared by every two households. Eventually, however, squatting occurred on virtually all the open land of Site C.

A report compiled by the City of Cape Town (CCT), based on the results of the 2001 Census, indicates that Site C has the worst socio-economic profile of all the different parts of Khayelitsha (City of Cape Town, 2005). It lags behind on formal education achievements, employment indicators and the delivery of housing, water, sanitation and electricity services. The upgrading of Site C has been hampered by the existence of the double plots, although there is evidence that the municipality has been trying to 'decongest' these by moving one of the households to new housing in some other part of Khayelitsha. During our fieldwork, it was apparent that a major reconstruction was in the offing (as evidenced by survey pegs and brick stacks placed at various points). By the time of writing (November 2008), this reconstruction was in full swing.

In some ways, Site C and Site B are quite similar. When first settled, Site B consisted of yards measuring 160 square metres, each with an individual toilet and adjacent water point. As with Site C, uncontrolled squatting emerged on the edges of Site B. However, given that each household had its own yard, upgrading has been rapid in recent years, with many residents applying for government housing grants. Accordingly, (apart from in the uncontrolled, squatted areas) Site B has seen rapid change since 1994.

Endlovini is very different from Sites C and B, in that it is an uncontrolled, informal settlement. Services here are generally less than adequate, and the area is known for its high levels of crime. It is worth noting that Endlovini has been in existence for some time now, but because of its marginal location it has not received basic services as rapidly as other, newer, informal settlements. In the view of local government officers, both the formal and the informal areas of Khayelitsha already have basic services (interviews with Ramsay and Van Niekerk, 2004).

Ilitha Park stands in stark contrast to Endlovini, in that it is a relatively new and middle-class area of Khayelitsha. Most houses have tiled (rather than asbestos) roofing. The yards are larger and lack any visible squatting within their boundaries. In terms of services, all houses are either already connected or are potentially connectable to the electricity, sewerage and water distribution systems. Home owners in Ilitha Park are mostly employed.

Finally, Khaya is the original settlement in Khayelitsha. While several of the houses have been extended, most remain unaltered. As in Ilitha Park, all houses are either connected or are potentially connectable to the electricity, sewerage and water distribution systems. A large proportion of the heads of household are pensioners – consistent with the fact that these houses were acquired over twenty years ago, at a time when most people were already well into their working lives. Between them, Ilitha Park and Khaya constitute the middle-class section of Khayelitsha.

These differences within Khayelitsha affect the identities and perceptions of the communities that live there. To some extent, they also affect the notions of quality of life, as well as propensity for certain types of social action.

A sample of 300 randomly selected interviewees were surveyed between June and November 2007.[4] Contact interviews were preferred to methods, so that a questionnaire (and the quantitative data that generated) could be augmented by open questions designed to stimulate discussion (which generated qualitative data). To provide a degree of comparability with service delivery and governance issues and with grievances outside the Khayelitsha context, the survey used some of the questions on democratization from the multi-country Afrobarometer survey,[5] though a number of specific contextual questions were also added. For reasons of space, this chapter does not examine the broader South African context, but instead looks in some detail at the issues and problems that give rise to various forms of citizen action in Khayelitsha.We chose Khayelitsha as our case study area in the full knowledge that it is said to be one of the most protest-prone suburbs of Cape Town. Studies that specifically target an area simply because the phenomenon of interest is known to occur there may fail to explain it adequately because they provide a one-sided version of events (Olzak, 1989). However, since there is no official detailed breakdown of protest action in the different township areas of Cape Town, our survey questions and methodology examine perceptions of a range of participatory strategies (including protest), and we included a wide range of areas within Khayelitsha in order to try to obtain a comprehensive understanding of the full diversity of participatory strategies that individuals and communities employ.

As has been mentioned, Khayelitsha is not a homogeneous area: housing, for example, ranges from underserviced informal settlements, through serviced informal settlements, to mixed areas and formal brick housing. Since many socio-economic variables in the 2001 Census are correlated with type of housing, this factor was adopted in stratifying the sample. The ratio of shack dwellers to those in formal housing in the sample (73:27) corresponded quite closely to the 2001 Census for Khayelitsha (68:32).

Main findings of the study

Community challenges, democratic practices and participation in service delivery The findings of the study are revealing: they indicate clearly that, across different levels of service delivery and socio-economic position, most residents of Khayelitsha utilize similar forms of participation. Before detailing this, though, we present some information on the core participatory issues facing the community. We show here that, although the African National Congress (ANC)-led government has, over the years, made various attempts to address the structural socio-economic inequalities of the urban and rural poor, levels of service remain unsatisfactory for many poor people.

Respondents were asked to rank the three most important problems facing them in order of their importance or severity. This question was asked early on in the interview, before questions about particular services. The responses were collated, in order to find the problem mentioned most frequently by respondents, without regard to perceived severity. It emerged that housing was the most important problem facing Khayelitsha, with 64 per cent of respondents mentioning it; this was followed closely by unemployment and crime – both 61 per cent.[6] Water supplies (22 per cent) and sanitation (17 per cent) complete the top five. The top three areas of concern coincide with those listed in the CCT's 2006/07 integrated development plan (IDP).[7]

As well as engaging citizens on matters that affect their lives, the survey drew responses on perceptions of specific forms of service delivery: provision of housing, water supply and sanitation, refuse removal and cleaning and electricity. These are shown in Figure 11.1. In terms of housing, only 22 per cent assessed the municipality's performance positively (fairly good or very good). A similar picture emerges for sanitation, with only 30 per cent of respondents positive about the performance. It emerges that the municipality is performing better with the water supply – 52 per cent of respondents described the CCT's performance as adequate. Surprisingly, given the levels of refuse pollution in Khayelitsha, most

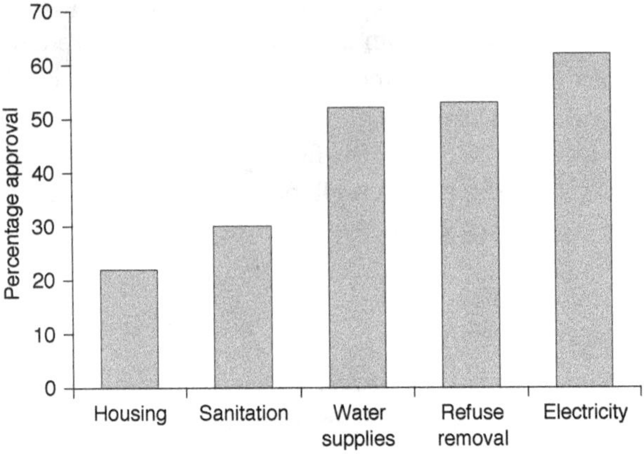

Figure 11.1 Perceptions of the City of Cape Town's performance in service delivery

people were happy with the CCT's job of removing waste – 53 per cent responded that the municipality was doing fairly or very well. Up to 62 per cent of respondents were satisfied with the municipality's performance in providing electricity.

These data suggest a critical attitude on the part of most people in the community to key aspects of service delivery that might be expected to engender greater civic engagement in an effort to solve the problems. The importance of citizen participation in processes of governance is widely acknowledged, but there are discrepancies in people's views of what the different forms of participation entail and which of them might yield the greatest success in influencing governance processes. The data presented below indicate a complex interaction between mainstream and unconventional channels of participation, with an unmistakable skew towards the latter.

Knowledge and perceptions of representative democracy As we have already suggested, the Constitution of South Africa and several other pieces of legislation engender a system that promotes greater citizen involvement in the affairs of government than just periodic elections. For example, at the level of the ward – the smallest electoral district in South African politics – ward committees are expected to play an important role in promoting greater participation. Even though turnout in South African elections is generally high, this does not translate into knowledge of representatives; thus accountability of representatives is low. Our survey tried to elicit from Khayelitsha residents both a quantita-

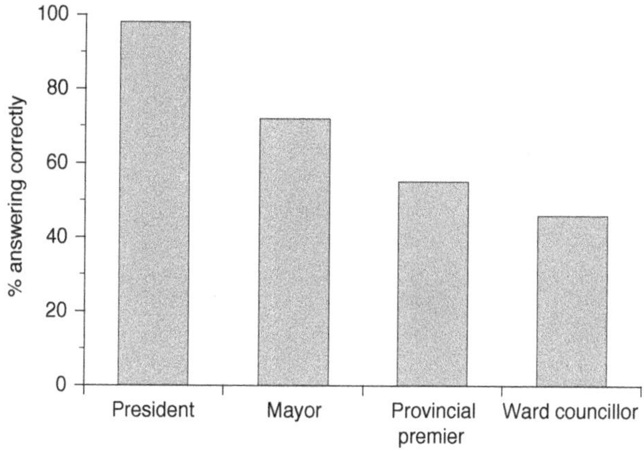

Figure 11.2 Recognition of elected representatives

tive and a qualitative assessment of the success of local government's efforts to foster increased participation (as it is obliged to do by national legislation).

Although ward councillors are based in the community, Figure 11.2 indicates that only 46 per cent of respondents in Khayelitsha could name their ward councillor correctly. By contrast, 72 per cent could name the mayor of Cape Town, and 55 per cent knew who the premier of the Western Cape was. This indicates a higher level of political awareness of more senior figures, which may be a symptom of the centralization of power in South African political governance systems. This undermines autonomous decision-making at the ward level, and thus local democracy (of which citizens are keenly aware).

If we look at non-executive representatives, then, as the data below indicate, disenchantment with representative democracy is more apparent. Figure 11.3 indicates that only 22 per cent of respondents believed ward councillors to be consistently receptive to the concerns of their constituents, and a mere 8 per cent felt that MPs listened to their constituents.

The picture that emerges from the data above is one of a community that has little confidence in representative democracy. The accountability of elected representatives gravitates towards the party bosses responsible for the party lists, rather than to voters. The ANC, however, remains popular with the electorate – partly because of its history of leading the liberation struggle. Thus, while Tapscott (2005) argues for delivery failures to be viewed as failures on the part of the ANC, it would seem that, in apportioning responsibility, the electorate still largely looks elsewhere.

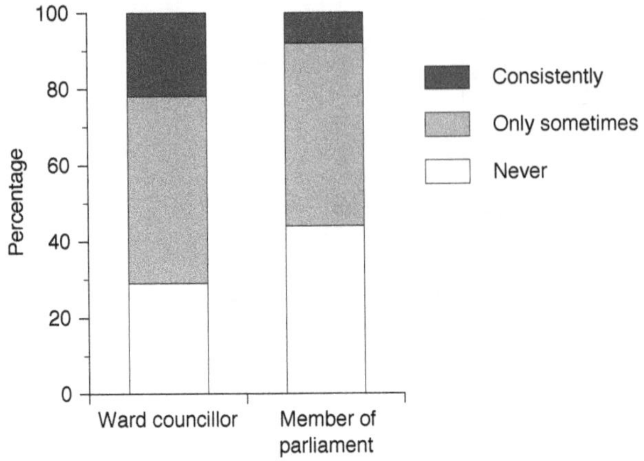

Figure 11.3 Perception of receptiveness of elected representatives

The search for effective alternative forms of engagement The legal framework for citizen participation in South Africa promotes accountability of government through various systems that ostensibly permit the voice of the governed to be heard. In fact, 'citizen voice' is caught up in a bureaucratic maze of politicians and officials, each of whom competes for a say in decision-making. For the residents of Khayelitsha, the decision-making apparatus of the state is very remote, and the quest for change to the status quo seems painstakingly slow, even though Khayelitsha enjoys special status as part of the national government's

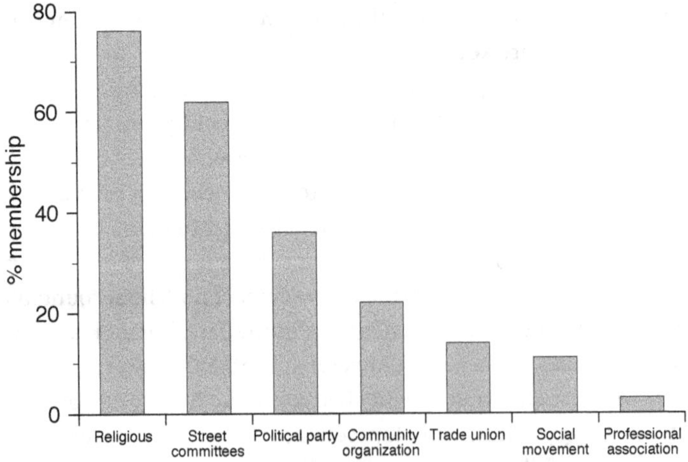

Figure 11.4 Membership of associational groups

Urban Renewal Programme. So how do the residents of Khayelitsha seek to resolve their problems? What forms of organization are utilized in the quest to resolve service delivery issues? The survey data show that many groups attracted only a low level of patronage in Khayelitsha, as Figure 11.4 shows. The exceptions were religious groups (with 76 per cent of respondents being involved) and street committees (which involved 62 per cent).

The relatively high levels of membership of street committees – a localized form of residents' association referred to earlier – prompted further research into the nature of this organizational form. It emerged that street committees enjoy wide mandates, covering issues such as fighting crime, solving family disputes, service delivery issues and facilitating employment. Although street committees are informal organizations, they establish links with formal state organs such as the police and ward councillors in order to increase their effectiveness and legitimacy. The following quotations from interviewees capture some of the positive sentiments about what street committees do:

> We try by all means to meet as a community and find some solution to problems that are reported and involve the police and neighbourhood watch. (Interview respondent, Khayelitsha, 12 September 2007)

> When we have problems in our community we report them to the street committee because they know the channels [through which these problems can be solved]. (Interview respondent, Khayelitsha, 20 August 2007)

> We take our problems to the street committee and they come up with solutions. (Interview respondent, Khayelitsha, 11 August 2007)

Although most people seem to view street committees in a positive light, negative sentiments were also proffered in interviews:

> They do nothing; they're uneducated so they know nothing. (Interview respondent, Khayelitsha, 20 August 2007)

> People are tired now there is no progress. Sometimes they [street committees] listen to our problems but when it comes to action they do nothing. (Interview respondent, Khayelitsha, 20 August 2007)

> They [street committees] are also waiting for the government to come and solve our problems; there is nothing they can do. (Interview respondent, Khayelitsha, 20 August 2007)

It has been suggested that street committees also 'take the law into their own hands' (Ismail Davids, Policy Workshop Presentation,

26 November 2007). Nominally, street committees are non-partisan civic bodies, but they are also grouped under the banner of the South African National Civics Organization (SANCO), which has strong links to the ANC. The separation of civic and political battle lines is, therefore, not always clear and unambiguous – either within or outside the ruling party.

In dealing with community problems within the available organizational framework, two major forms of action emerge – participation in self-organized community meetings and protests. We employed a number of strategies to analyse these two forms of participation. First, we asked about their perceived ranking, relative to the overriding framework of representative democracy; and second, we asked how they relate to different forms of delivery. We also tried to ascertain the extent to which community members are willing to participate in unlawful and violent acts to achieve their aims.

The form of engagement that was perceived as most effective was participation in community meetings, with 42 per cent of respondents favouring this form of action; 40 per cent favoured engaging elected representatives, such as ward councillors and MPs; 15 per cent favoured protest; and 3 per cent preferred to do nothing at all. Clearly deliberative forms of engagement were regarded as the most viable means of finding solutions to problems in the community. Responses often bordered on a romanticized sense of the community's ability to resolve its problems:

> The community can come up with solutions. (Interview respondent, Khayelitsha, 27 August 2007)

> We must solve our problems as a community; nobody can do it for us. (Interview respondent, Khayelitsha, 23 August 2007)

Those who advocated protest seemed to be motivated by the success of this method in other areas:

> People of Luzuko didn't have electricity but through protesting they have electricity now. (Interview respondent, Khayelitsha, 15 September 2007)

The relatively high level of the perceived effectiveness of engaging with elected representatives is surprising, in light of the lack of confidence in elected representatives (see above). This may, however, indicate that respondents have faith in the system itself, but not in the incumbent representatives. This may also explain the consistently high voter turnout and the continuing support for the ANC.

In the context of a dysfunctional representative system, two forms of engagement with government remain – meetings and protests. In theory,

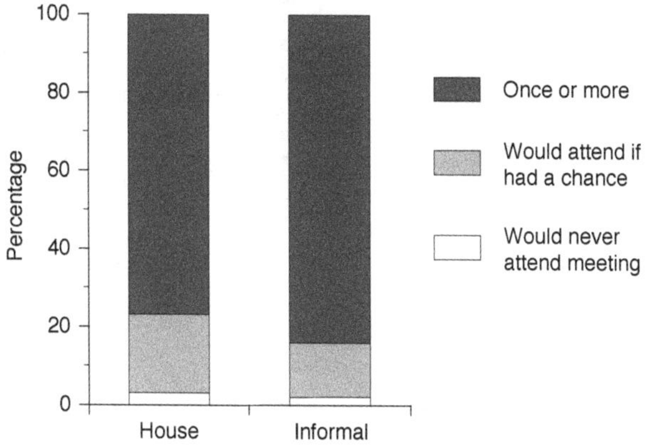

Figure 11.5 Participation in meetings by house and shack dwellers

these two forms of participation would seem to be poles apart; yet in practice they may coexist – at times symbiotically. Figure 11.5 shows that attendance at community meetings was high for the residents of both informal settlements and formal brick houses – 84 per cent and 77 per cent, respectively. We found that the combination of a sense of neighbourliness and familial encouragement has a big impact on attendance at community meetings. The marginally higher rate of attendance among people from informal settlements is statistically insignificant.

Although only 15 per cent of respondents argued that protest is the most effective method of engagement, the actual incidence of protest showed that 45 per cent of respondents had been on a protest march at least once in the preceding year. The disaggregated data shown in Figure 11.6 show that the residents of informal settlements are much more likely to participate in protests than are those living in brick houses. This alerts us to the importance of service delivery (as typified by housing) in protest mobilization.

One of the hallmarks of public protest in South Africa is its association with unlawful conduct and violence. It is well established that violence during protests is a result of provocation by the authorities, especially the police; but it is also important to understand that violence is actually seen as a constituent element of civic action. We wanted to understand how violence and unlawful conduct operate within this context. Respondents were given two statements and asked to choose which was closer to their own view.

The first statement was: 'It is better to find lawful solutions to problems even if it takes longer'; the second statement was: 'It is sometimes

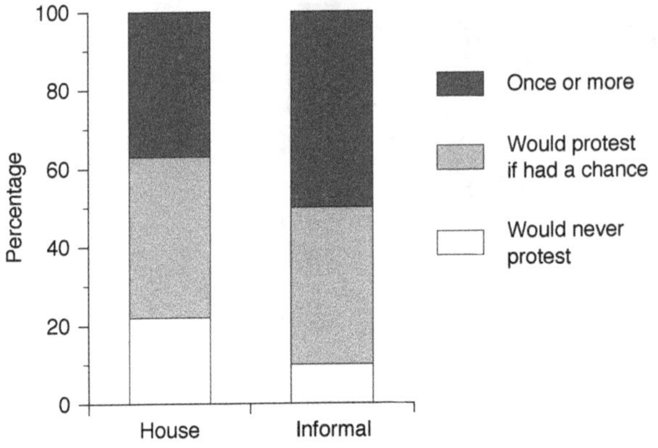

Figure 11.6 Participation in protests by house and shack dwellers

necessary to disobey the law to solve problems immediately, using other means'. Some 74 per cent agreed with the first statement and 25 per cent agreed with the second (1 per cent agreed with neither). The more open-ended questions on this subject generated responses on the illegality and cultural inappropriateness of violence, its retrograde nature, property damage and death. Further, legal methods – invariably meetings – were widely discussed as the appropriate way of solving problems, often in romantic terms. The following quotes highlight some of the points above:

> I think it's wrong to take law into our own hands. (Interview respondent, Khayelitsha, 22 September 2007)

> We can solve anything by talking. (Interview respondent, Khayelitsha, 28 August 2007)

> We can sort things out by talking; we need to do that, it's part of our culture. (Interview respondent, Khayelitsha, 23 September 2007)

> It's because words are more powerful than violence. (Interview respondent, Khayelitsha, 28 August 2007)

> There is no need to disobey the law at all [besides] we cannot build our country in a day. (Interview respondent, Khayelitsha, 5 August 2007)

> It is a good idea to wait because if you have patience you will gain something. We didn't even know our country would become a democracy. (Interview respondent, Khayelitsha, 15 September 2007)

However, those who believe in violent action invoke the violent ethos of the anti-apartheid struggle, which ultimately brought down the system.

While violent action is not the first option, it is seen as one that is available, should other methods fail to yield appropriate results – although some of the comments show high levels of anger over the rate of delivery. Violent action is proposed as a method of attracting government attention:

> Here in Khayelitsha, we often hold meetings and when government fails to respond to us we take further steps. I think meetings come up with good solutions. (Interview respondent, Khayelitsha, 23 August 2007)

> To protest is the best solution because our parents used to do that in the past and look, now we have a democratic country. (Interview respondent, Khayelitsha, 17 September 2007)

> Our government is very slow; we need to wake it up. (Interview respondent, Khayelitsha, 2 August 2007)

Respondents were given two more statements that related to the use of violence as a political tool. They were again asked to choose which statement was closer to their own view. The first statement was: 'The use of violence is never justified in South African politics'; the second was: 'In this country, it is sometimes necessary to use violence in support of a just cause'. In this case, 70 per cent of respondents agreed with the first statement, while 29 per cent agreed with the second.

The most dominant responses justifying opposition to violent politics were that violence was destructive, cost human lives and dialogue was a more useful way to solve problems. It was obvious, though, that protest was often equated with violence – a reasoning that is understandable, given the high incidence of violent protests. The argument in favour of violent methods tended to be made in historical terms:

> Violence helped us during the anti-apartheid struggle; why not now? (Interview respondent, Khayelitsha, 19 September 2007)

> It is to show anger towards government. (Interview respondent, Khayelitsha, 14 September 2007)

Overall, it seems fairly clear that unlawful and/or violent forms of community action and protest are eschewed in favour of approaches that promote community unity, although, for historical reasons and efficacy, a sizeable proportion favours these violent forms of action. This willingness to engage in violent and unlawful action forms the justification for repressive state action when dealing with protests. However, it is important to realize that the expectation of repression by the state (and indeed the reality of this) in itself feeds the propensity to engage in violence and unlawful conduct, in a vicious cycle of causality.

In summary, the data presented here reveal a complex set of dynamic relationships between formal institutions of democracy and forms of community participation – a picture that does not conform to the stereotypes of either the 'active citizen' or the 'passive marginalized'. The linkages between community action and social accountability on the part of the state emerge to show some revealing trends in terms of power relationships and participatory trends – most notably a strong trend to self-organize and mobilize around issues and grievances that stem from weaknesses in state-sponsored forms of participation and deliberation on the delivery of public goods and services, as well as on pro-poor policy initiatives, such as subsidized housing for the poor. (In South Africa, all of this is referred to collectively as 'service delivery'.)

Conclusions

This chapter started by stating that there is a diversity of participatory strategies geared up to resolving the problems affecting people living in Khayelitsha. It proceeded to demonstrate some of the complex interactions and choices employed by grassroots community organizations in choosing between these methods. The dominant problems facing Khayelitsha are housing, unemployment and crime, water supplies and sanitation. The study shows that there is a dominant collective opinion in the predominantly poor community of Khayelitsha that, at some point, government abandoned the poor, since its policies have been so gradually transformative. In response to these grievances, the residents of Khayelitsha organize themselves in several ways, though deliberative community meetings are the overwhelmingly predominant choice. The favoured method seems to operate by encouraging community agreement on issues, which are then passed on to elected representatives, such as ward councillors. However, these elected representatives, most respondents alleged, are out of touch with their constituents, which disrupts effective transmission of grievances to higher-level decision-makers. It may be expected that such disruptions would lead to a loss of faith in the representative system. However, the representative system still enjoys high levels of electoral participation.

Although deliberative forms of engagement such as community meetings and communicating with the ward councillor were favoured over protest, 45 per cent of respondents had been on at least one protest march or demonstration in the year of the survey – three times the proportion (15 per cent) of those who indicated that protest was the most effective method. Protest, it seems, is regarded as a means of last resort – one that, given its association with violence and unlawful conduct, attracts the attention of the authorities. At play here are contradictions between optimism with the democratic era and a desire to support it, and anger at the pace of the delivery of services. Such contradictions have encouraged communities to take to the streets as part of a multi-pronged strategy, underpinned by new-found democratic freedoms in the quest for socio-economic advancement. The move to claim socio-economic rights through collective action that is organized at the grassroots level and that feeds into loose forms of social movement is, we argue, central to any understanding of citizenship and participation in South Africa.

Democracy – and the rights that are supposed to go with it – is being demanded by those people who find themselves neglected by the state because their lack of power, education and economic resources makes it hard for them to influence state behaviour (Thompson and Tapscott, 2010). It remains to be seen whether these forms of localized resistance and mobilization can, in time, bring about significant change to government policies.

It is also fair to say that we gain a false picture if we link the measures of the extent of achievement of socio-economic rights to development indicators: South Africa's apparent success in meeting its Millennium Development Goal targets obscures the relative resource deprivation of the huge population of the urban poor, and the figures themselves fudge the often inadequate services that are provided (Thompson and Nleya, 2008).

In many respects, Khayelitsha epitomizes the situation in many black townships in South Africa – inadequate to non-existent services, further compounded by a high crime rate (Thompson and Nleya, 2009). The deterioration of the global economy (to which the South African economy is inextricably linked), compounded by a rapid reorganization of the political landscape of the country,[8] creates a fertile environment for greater mobilization in the future.

The residents of Khayelitsha are not necessarily passive or mute beneficiaries of government programmes; they are a vibrant community that is negotiating between different forms of engagement. A loose social movement is emerging, based on smaller collective forms of action that have their origins in the street committees.

It important to note that participation occurs within a context; and while it is clear that the residents may lack the specific linkages and resources required to engage effectively in complex knowledge-based governance debates, they select various modes of operation that make best use of the resources they do have. These involve complex interconnected methods of choice and collective action. As such, they serve to epitomize the type of contested terrain referred to in the polity by Skocpol (1992) and others. While these contestations are not always democratic, ultimately they are necessary for democracy, as they underline the linkages between the accountability of the state and its citizens to a mutual project: political liberty and individual freedoms, underpinned by democratic and responsive state and non-state institutions, and both individual and collective political and socio-economic security.

Notes

1 See Thompson and Tapscott (2010) for a discussion of social movements and political opportunity theory.

2 This entailed a plethora of legislation, the primary goal of which was to restrict the number of blacks in urban centres. Given the nature of demand for black labour in urban areas, this was one of the most obvious of the contradictions embedded in the policies of apartheid and the earlier segregation.

3 As part of the spatial planning strategy of apartheid, in 1955 the Western Cape was designated as the 'traditional' place of residence of the white and coloured communities. Proof was needed that coloured labour was unavailable before a black person was employed, and blacks were to be gradually removed from the Western Cape.

4 The sampling interval used was determined by the date of the interview; for example, on the 5th, 14th and 23rd days of the month, the day code (and sampling interval) is five. So the fifth dwelling structure on the right is chosen. On the 6th, 15th and 24th days of the month, the sampling interval is six.

5 The Afrobarometer is an Africa-wide survey. See www.afrobarometer.org/.

6 The relative importance of crime as a source of hardship in Khayelitsha debunks the notion that the social outcry about high levels of crime in South Africa is led by disaffected whites.

7 All municipalities in South Africa must produce an annual IDP.

8 Thabo Mbeki's resignation from the presidency and the departure from government of a number of loyalists in his cabinet led to the formation of the Congress of the People (COPE) which won 7.42 per cent of the votes in 2009 election.

12 · How styles of activism influence social participation and democratic deliberation

ARILSON FAVARETO, CAROLINA GALVANESE, FREDERICO MENINO, VERA SCHATTAN P. COELHO AND YUMI KAWAMURA

Introduction: Why study styles of activism and participation?[1]

In Brazil, as in the rest of the world, participatory governance is a means of improving the distribution of social services and facilitating the implementation of development projects. As participatory governance has grown more popular as an idea, so it has grown beyond the decision-making and representative structures of democratic states and has begun to be part of the more interactive democratic spheres that are the domain of social movements. In the process, a series of crucial questions has been posed, concerning the association between participation, democracy and development. How can marginalized sectors of society be included in decision-making processes? How can they engage in politics? How can democratic spaces and institutions be strengthened so that diverse people can effectively and fairly express their opinions and particular needs?

The main argument in this chapter is that social movements can develop different styles of activism, even when functioning in the same sorts of institutional frameworks. These different styles may, in turn, confirm or refute the expectations presented by the normative ideal of democratic deliberation. Once it is assumed that the performance of participatory governance is influenced by the conditions present when participatory spaces are established, it becomes essential to look at and combine various aspects of the trajectories taken by social actors. These include the networks and ties they have established and prioritized over the years; the role of the state in framing the group's opportunities and claims; the role of non-institutionalized norms and cultural habits; and the characteristics of the leaders who have coordinated social action within particular groups.

The better to understand these connections, our research developed two combined approaches. The first was to investigate the styles of four social action groups whose roots originated in conflicts involving land issues, and the trajectories of activists working within them. The second was to analyse how these styles and trajectories relate to greater or lesser support for the participatory governance project being pursued by the organizations representing these groups. In this way, we expect to go beyond the typical limits imposed on structural, institutional or contextual studies, which are usually strong in their descriptive analysis but weak when it comes to explaining dynamic aspects linked to the innovation and transformation of collective action. The model does not completely ignore the structural determinants of collective action; rather, it moves towards merging them with rationalist and constructivist approaches.

This chapter is organized into three sections. The first presents a theoretical framework and a system of hypotheses for the analysis of activism styles, the reasons for their existence and their repercussions for participatory governance. The second is a discussion of the main findings of the study, which examines the styles and trajectories of four local organizations and their leaders as representatives of different styles and types of activism in a poor and socially diverse area of Brazil. Finally, a relationship is depicted between the trajectories of the groups, the styles of activism they practise and the role of the state in its greater or lesser support for the project of participatory governance.

We chose as our case study the Ribeira Valley, an area in south-eastern Brazil with a regional population of around 350,000 (Instituto Brasileiro de Geografia e Estatística, 2000). We did so because it is unusual in combining a low level of economic dynamism and poor social indicators with an active social movement and a reasonable history of initiatives aimed at sustainable development of the region. In terms of social organization, the region has a large concentration of traditional communities, such as the *ribeirinho* (riverside), *caiçara* (artisanal fishermen and smallholders of mainly indigenous descent) and *quilombola* (rural Afro-Brazilian) communities. The identities of all these groups are closely linked to their land and environment, not only through their cultural roots but also through their dependence on local natural resources.

In this area, there are at least two different types of citizen activism. On the one hand there are organizations and social movements that oppose a particular policy or event; on the other there are organizations and social movements concerned with economic and environmental issues, formed on the basis of common community identity. Of the four organizations and movements that are the focus of the study, the Movimento dos Ameaçados por Barragem (MOAB – Movement of Those Threatened by the Dam) falls firmly into the first type: it was created amid the conflict that grew up over a proposal to build a series of dams along the Ribeira river.

At the other end of the spectrum are two other groups – the Associação dos Residentes de Mandira (ARM – Mandira Residents' Association) and the Associação dos Residentes de Guapiruvu (ARG – Guapiruvu Residents' Association). These come from communities where part of the land falls in a designated conservation reserve. The ARM and ARG have their roots in a discourse that emerged from the legal formation of conservation reserves during the 1970s and 1980s, which associated household economic production with environmental conservation. These two residents' organizations access organized markets for their natural resource-based products, and are applying the principles of sustainable natural resource management to their productive activities.

The fourth organization, the Sindicato dos Trabalhadores na Agricultura Familiar do Vale do Ribeira (SINTRAVALE – Union of Farming Families of the Vale do Ribeira) brings family farmers and producers together in defence of their common interests.

The two most important participatory forums in the Vale do Ribeira operate at the regional level: the Comitê de Gestão de Recursos Hídricos (Committee for the Management of Water Resources in the Ribeira river basin) and the Consórcio de Segurança Alimentar e Nutricional e Desenvolvimento Local (CONSAD – Consortium for Food Safety and Local Development). They discuss local development plans, accompany the implementation of the public policies to which they are connected, and allocate a considerable percentage of available resources to projects that are considered priorities and in line with the development plans. Previous research that we carried out with local leaders (Coelho et al., 2007) left no doubt in our minds that these forums are part of everyday life in the region, and that, given the intensity of political debate, it is important for leaders to guarantee space for their own activist group within them. Nonetheless, the forms of mobilization and organization in these forums vary considerably. While all four of our case study organizations have their origins in social conflicts involving access to land and natural resources, they have very different positions with respect to the ways in which they view the forums and how they act in them. Consequently, each social group and its respective organization have different possibilities for its own practices to be coherent with expectations of democratic deliberation. What could explain the differences observed in the style of activism of each of these organizations and, by implication, of social movements more broadly?

What determines styles of activism and their effects?

The issue of mobilization has been dealt with at length in the literature on social movements, but there is no literature about different styles of activism per se. However, a good starting point is Charles Tilly's thesis, based on his critical review of the literature (Tilly, 1998), in which he makes a two-fold contribution. First, he proposes a typology of collective action, classifying social movements into three groups: a) those where competitive action predominates and groups compete for the same resources; b) those where reactive action predominates and groups attempt to maintain or reiterate already established demands when challenged by an external actor; and c) those where proactive action predominates and groups make new demands. Second, he provides a synthesis of the fundamental elements that need to be taken into account when analysing the structure and dynamics of social movements. In spite of different sources and emphases in the literature, there is general agreement that, to understand content, one needs to take into account the way in which the content itself was generated. Consequently, one must look at: a) the social networks that surround movement participants; b) the identities created in collective conflicts; c) the structures created by the accumulation of shared understanding; and, finally, d) the structures of political opportunities, as they are important to the history of the social movements while simultaneously being transformed by the actions of those selfsame movements.

The literature contains a broad debate around these four themes and raises two principal theoretical problems. The first recognizes the need for a conceptualization of the individual that is not restricted to what is compatible with behavioural psychology, which takes the approach that an action would be determined completely by sanctions and stimuli emanating from the medium. Rather, this new conceptualization would be more akin to the manner in which such things are viewed by social scientists – from Durkheim to Goffman, Elias and Bourdieu – where individual behaviour is understood through the ways in which innate and indistinct impulses take on social content and drive different trajectories. Viewed thus, we effectively are dealing not with choices but with how social energy generated by conflict is perceived – as deprivation, possibility, estrangement, injustice, passivity and desire for power. We also need to deal with how that energy is directed in specific ways – as negation, conformism, confrontation, cooperation, representation, alliances and oppositions, to list just some of the possibilities.

The second problem centres on the necessity to postulate a mediating body that can function as a kind of membrane between an individual and society. It also describes the way in which relations are established: not in a random or completely open way, but rather in a simultaneously structured and structuring way. Thus, the emphasis is not on the conflict or the mediators, but on how interactional structure is formed, mediates conflicts and then transforms them into social actions.

Our proposition is that styles of activism are the result of factors that can be understood through the idea of structured interactions. In the case of social movements, there are three principal components to the structure of interactions:

1 The leader's trajectory, through which it is possible to understand how an agent's social properties can translate into categories to classify the social world, be disposed to action and be injected into stocks and resources to mobilize.
2 The networks through which it is possible to understand how the relations and the resources that can be channelled through them can stretch.

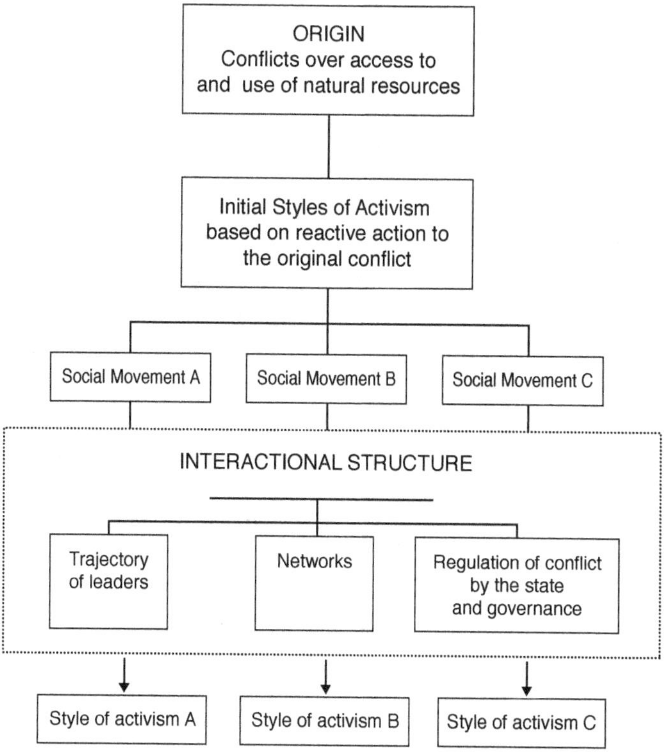

Figure 12.1 Interactional structure and styles of activism

3 The trajectory of the social conflict motivating these movements and the way the state regulates this conflict. Calculating the trajectory of conflict makes it possible to understand the fields of opposition engendered by the conflict, on the one hand, and, on the other, how much room there is for demands to be absorbed into the way that the conflict is drawn up.

This general analytical framework is represented in Figure 12.1. Each of the three principal components of interactional structure can be schematically represented by two opposing axes, one of which shows the structural determinants and the other the possibilities for interaction. We now go on to discuss how our theoretical framework applies to each of these three components in turn.

About the trajectories of leaders Leadership trajectories show how historically formed social properties are transformed into what Bourdieu (1985/2007) has described as a social agent's system of dispositions, which has undeniable impact upon the forms of collective action with which the agent engages. Systems of character do not come about by chance or mere interaction, but are exchanges structured by systems of classification. Utilized by individuals, they are situated in the overlap between structural constraints and the opportunities for interaction, which are themselves opened up by such exchanges.

The structural axis of these social properties of leadership is determined by how 'uprooted' these individual agents are. In other words, the socialization of people who become group leaders could follow a trajectory whereby they maintain proximity to the spheres of autonomy of their group of social origin (local education, marriage within the same social group, similar employment opportunities to those typical of the group of origin); or it could take place in a more heterogeneous way (education outside the local area, exogamous marriage, different employment opportunities). We hypothesize that there will be a greater display of relations and categories of rationalism in situations where socialization is more heterogeneous. Conversely, where the socialization is closer to the autonomous circles of the group of origin, there would be a greater tendency to establish relations based on strong ties, which would contain greater similarity, and a convergence of values and interests between agents and mediators, for example. This axis is labelled structural because it deals with the way social structures are incorporated into individual trajectories.

The interactional axis of the social properties is determined by the forms of rationalization that follow the experience of 'uprootment'. They can be further influenced by mediation based on conceptions more strongly supported by traditions or values, or by forms based on more instrumental interpretations. Our second supposition, which will be tested by the hypothesis in this chapter, is that the predominance of traditions may have a greater connection with conceptions of the world where the relation with conflicts is oriented to their suppression, implying a form of activism more oriented to confrontation. Conversely, where action is a rational instrument, or is related to ends, there will be a greater stimulus to bargain or to use the possibilities of interaction pragmatically, thus opening up the propensity to participation. This axis is labelled interactional because it deals with the interaction between the social structures present in individuals as they react to and experience conflict.

About the structure and dynamics of networks Networks reveal the structure and reach of those resources that individuals and social groups can mobilize. They can decisively influence the meaning, as well as the outcomes, of collective action.

How do the resources mobilized by social groups and their leaders acquire social significance? According to the classic formulation by Mark Granovetter (1973), networks are more effective when they are based not only on strong ties (understood as those relations permanently mobilized by the agents), but also on weak ties (or those relations that can be accessed secondarily and through the mediation of strong ties). The particular blend of strong and weak ties in any given network tends to determine, or at least strongly influence, the hierarchy of identities that is established between agents. They are therefore the result of exposure to common constraints.

On the structural axis, our hypothesis is that the predominance of strong ties in a particular agent's range of relations structurally limits the field of political action. This tends to have a direct effect on the type of activism promoted by the group of which the agent is part. We suggest that a predominance of strong ties tends to stimulate the formation of practices and strategies of action oriented towards intransigence when dealing with social conflict. A predominance of weak ties, infused with a certain degree of plurality, tends to conform to styles of activism that are more open to dialogue and negotiation with different groups. This axis is labelled structural because it deals with the stock of relations that an individual and his or her organization have available.

On the interactional axis, the hypothesis considers that the pattern of relations established by this same agent contains a relation of mutual determination with the more or less politicized character of this network. Here politicization is understood as the predisposition of a group to orient its actions in the political sphere to obtain and exchange political resources. If the group's relations are markedly politicized, there will be a tendency to take sides with its strong allies, conferring a strong ideological component to the forms of classification of the conflicts. In the opposite direction, it appears that, if the action of the actors is more plural or informed more directly by a more than purely political character, the influence tends to translate into more pragmatic interpretations of the social conflicts and of the collective action surrounding them. This axis is labelled interactional because it shows the different ways in which resources can be mobilized and the types of reciprocity implied by this.

About the state and the institutional place of conflict as unfolded in forms of governance The structure of political opportunities is strongly related to the way in which the state regulates conflicts between different interests. It does this either through its own mechanisms (such as legislation, policies and programmes) or through the way in which it directs political dissension in a particular configuration of forces (Tarrow, 1994). As with the previous two hypotheses, these suppositions and the way they affect forms of collective action are expressed in terms of axes of structural and interactional determinants.

The hypothesis here is that structural determinants can be understood in terms of whether the state acts in a more targeted fashion or in a universalist way concerning the social group in question. More universalist policies will permit a greater number of groups to access the benefits of those policies, while more targeted policies restrict the beneficiaries. Thus, the predominance of universalist elements in these policies would not presuppose a distinction between the actors involved in the process, and would understand them as equals. This would stimulate dialogue on a normatively egalitarian basis, and the result of these supposedly horizontal conditions, at least from the point of view of the state, could translate into acts tending towards negotiation that would enable access to policies. Conversely, where the predominant element of the policies or programmes distinguishes between different groups, protecting some to the detriment to others, this would stimulate the activity of target groups aimed at protecting their rights to special benefits, situating them in the political arena in a way that is potentially more confrontational. This axis is labelled

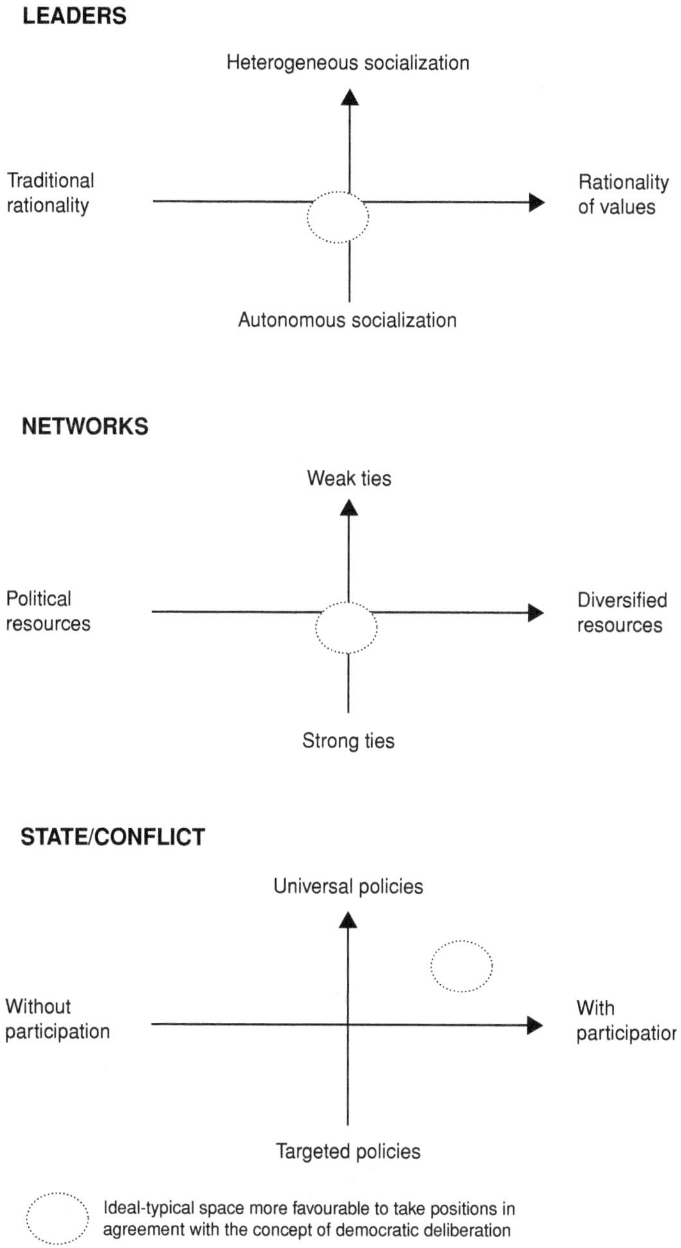

Figure 12.2 Schematic representation of the variables from which the system of hypotheses is composed

structural because it involves the institutional role that conflict is given by the state.

On the one hand, the hypothesis suggests that the propensity to participate will be stronger where there are institutionalized spaces that allow dialogue and that promote access by different groups. On the other hand, the hypothesis also suggests that targeted policies and programmes that dispense with institutionalized spaces to access policies tend to make dialogue between different groups more difficult, and favour a style of activism that dispenses with plurality and dialogue. This axis is labelled interactional because it deals with the action that individuals and their organizations can build within this institutional space. The three hypotheses can be schematically represented in the diagrams of Figure 12.2.

Explaining styles of activism: common origins, different trajectories

1 The trajectory of the leaders – evidence on the first hypothesis

common origins ... As part of the case study, nine different leaders of the four groups introduced above – ARG, ARM, MOAB and SINTRAVALE – were interviewed, and their trajectories compared.[2] The similarities and differences between them are shown in Figure 12.3.

The leaders have certain origins in common: almost all were inspired to become politically active by left-wing Catholic activists (who are very active in the region) and by their backgrounds, which exposed them to land conflicts and restricted access to ancestral natural resources. The individual histories of the leaders frequently revealed a number of points where they had veered away from the expected trajectories to pursue paths that were unexpected within the limits of their social groups.

... unexpected trajectories None of those interviewed was, strictly speaking, significantly distant from their social group of origin, and all had a strong connection to their group. But two leaders, Gabriel Oliveira of ARG and Hélio Bastos of SINTRAVALE, have adopted non-traditional discourses, which indicate their external connections and influences.

Oliveira comes from an educated family: his mother completed secondary school (albeit late) and Oliveira himself went to secondary school in a large urban centre – something that distinguishes him from his peers. His father occupied important political positions in the district. In Oliveira's professional trajectory, he has experience of working in various qualified jobs, and was once elected a councillor.

Unlike the other interviewees, Oliveira had no religious influence in

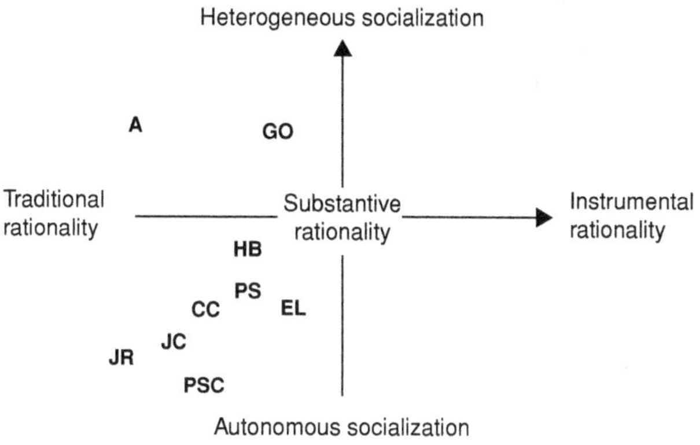

HB: Initials of Sintravale's leader
JR, PS, A: Initials of MOAB's leaders
CC, JC, PSC: Initials of ARM's leaders
EL, GO: Initials of ARG's leaders

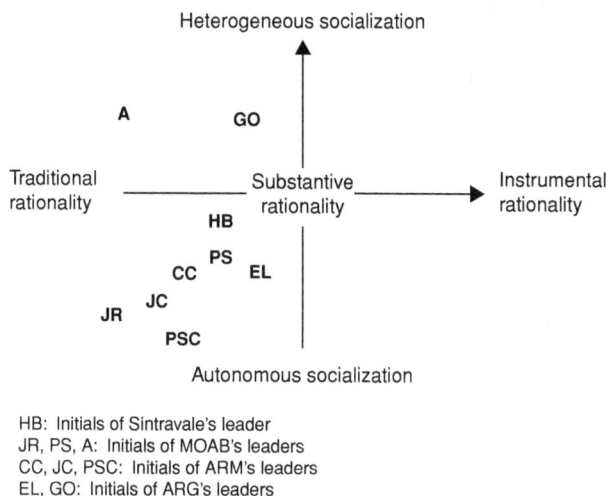

Figure 12.3 Representation of the trajectories of the leaders

his socialization. He structures himself in terms of his desire to distance himself from his family group because of differences in ideology and values. He has made diverse personal investments that have yielded a significant increase in his cultural capital and rendered him independent of the religious groups that have been responsible for the increase in the cultural capital of the other leaders. It is Oliveira's cultural capital – associated with his personal network of relations in the business and non-governmental organization (NGO) world – that has been converted into political and economic capital. As a result, he enjoys a prestigious position among ARG representatives, and clearly orients his action to making the economic enterprise of the ARG viable. He combines social and environmental values with economic activities, seeing them as an important element of cohesion and meaning in the social life of the group. His narrative often emphasizes the environmental content associated with quality of life and products produced.

Like Oliveira, Hélio Bastos of SINTRAVALE has various characteristics that distance him from his group of origin. Nonetheless, his socialization was very different from Oliveira's because it was dependent first on church groups and later on political parties. Consequently, the terms 'politics' and 'religion' crop up regularly in his narrative. This translates into a more polarized view of the world than Oliveira's. There is a clear emphasis on political determinism in all the spheres of social life.

The discourse of the MOAB leaders Pedro Silva, Ana Lemos and João

Ricardo differs from that of the two leaders of ARG and SINTRAVALE. They make no mention of the modernization that is found on both the ARG and the SINTRAVALE agendas; instead, their focus is on justice, rights and the defence of elements of ethnicity and identity. MOAB has several leaders, all of whom have a high level of education. Like Bastos of SINTRAVALE, Silva has become part of educational and professional circles that are different from his group of origin. In contrast to Bastos, however, he depended very little on the Church to help him into these new arenas. Once his education was completed, he continued to exercise his external connections. This part of his trajectory diverges from that of fellow MOAB leader Ana Lemos, who, after completing her external education, returned to the community. A third MOAB leader, João Ricardo, maintains a considerable degree of similarity with the community he represents, and has always done so. A combined analysis of the trajectories of the three MOAB leaders suggests that it is important to understand their complementarity. While Ricardo is the leader who symbolically merges with the group of origin, Silva exemplifies the kind of leader who mobilizes external resources that are capable of putting the group in contact with the political sphere, where its disputes can be resolved.

Finally, Carlos Chaves, João Cordeiro and Paulo Cunha, leaders of the ARM, have very similar trajectories to that of Ricardo: there is only fairly little distance from their group of origin, though there are relatively significant differences in terms of their forms of rationality. While ARM leaders structure their discourse in a relatively restricted, bipolar fashion, and the Church was very strong in their socialization, the presence of moral arguments in their approach is less noticeable than in the case of the leaders of MOAB. There is a greater degree of pragmatism, which is hard to explain solely in terms of the trajectory of the leaders; here it is necessary to look at the networks they mobilize.

None of the leaders has a profile that can be clearly described as conducive to participatory governance. Even though many of them experienced forms of socialization that could potentially have provided cognitive elements and relationships to be mobilized that would favour participation in the available forums, the interactional axis of socialization is marked significantly by the politicization and ideologization of conflicts, which distances them from this possibility. It remains to be seen how this variable works in combination with the other two: dealing with networks and resources mobilized, and dealing with the institutional role in conflict.

2 The networks: evidence for the second hypothesis

Characteristics in common ... In different ways, all four organizations have their roots in conflicts involving land issues, yet they have metamorphosed since their founding. In each case, strong network ties predominate, with the early presence of the left-wing Catholic Church, which subsequently provided access to other ties that, in later stages, became more important. Equally, in each case, links with the state are very strong.

... heterogeneous networks If the basis of all four organizations was the question of land rights, then each went off in a different direction after its initial founding. In the case of SINTRAVALE, connections with other political spheres, particularly with unions and political parties, meant that, by the mid-1990s, land issues had been included in the wider discourse about family farming. This discourse lay at the heart of the public policies of the Partido dos Trabalhadores (PT – Workers' Party) whose rise to power coincided with SINTRAVALE's consolidation of itself. The organization built strong ties with the PT and union factions allied to it, as well as with NGOs linked to land and environmental issues.

In the case of MOAB, land issues were the focus of the conflict surrounding the Tijuco Alto dam. The 1988 Constitution enshrined possession by the *quilombola* of the very land that would be inundated by the dam. Organizational ties that favoured the rationalization of MOAB's discourse of opposition to the dam grew increasingly important – such as its links with the Instituto Socioambiental (Socio-Environmental Institute), an NGO with origins in investments by the left-wing Catholic Church, and the broader social movement specializing in the fight against large-scale hydroelectric projects.

The ARG and ARM engage in similar activities in support of the livelihoods of their members. They are connected to land issues by the relationship between environmental conservation and economic production based on natural resources. Their networks, however, show different characteristics. The ARG has favoured ties with public organizations (such as the Forest Foundation), NGOs (such as Vitae Civilis) and investment funds in productive and environmental projects (such as the Funbio or Biodiversity Fund), while the ARM has favoured organizations that are mainly linked to the state.

In each of these groups, the organizational profile and methods of dealing with the issue of participation vary, too. MOAB has diversified and mobilized its ties and resources least. At the other extreme, the ARG has accessed a greater number of agents and organizations. The

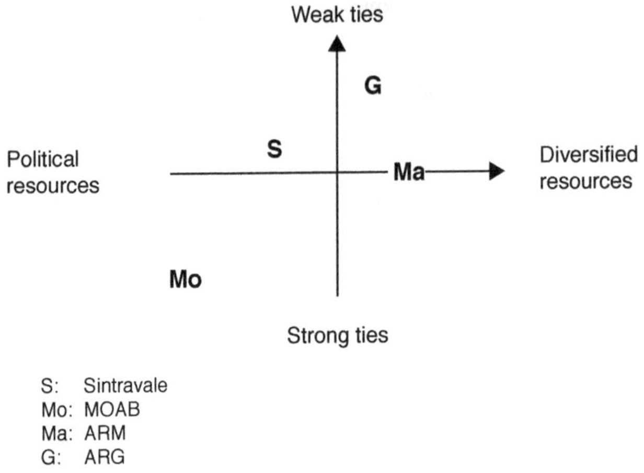

Figure 12.4 Representation of the networks

same variation can be seen if we analyse the types of resources that are mobilized through these ties: MOAB mobilizes resources that are predominantly political, while the ARG's members are more diversified; the ARM and SINTRAVALE are somewhere in between. While MOAB is dependent on donations from the public and civil society organizations, the ARG is financed through a wide range of sources.

Another type of differentiation occurs with respect to the definition of the social bases of these organizations. While the ARM and ARG make direct references to the local community, MOAB and SINTRAVALE base themselves on wider categories, such as family farming, black movements and the *quilombolas*. With the ARG and ARM, the main issues are linked to projects aimed specifically at the economic development of the community. This is in contrast to MOAB and SINTRAVALE, whose predominant themes are political and organizational.

The first element to be highlighted in our evaluation of the system of hypotheses has to do with the clear correlation between the diversification of ties and the mobilization of resources beyond the political: the more diverse the ties, the wider and more diverse the resources mobilized. The second element concerns the disposition of the organizations to participate and negotiate. The two organizations based on local identities and the need to combine environmental conservation with economic production, ARG and ARM, showed a greater disposition to participate and negotiate. By contrast, MOAB, which is supported principally by political resources mobilized by a limited range of ties, appeared the least disposed.

Our analysis will be completed by a review of the third hypothesis. This centres on the ways in which the state encourages or blocks this disposition.

3 The state and conflict: evidence for the third hypothesis

Common conflicts ... The land conflicts that form the basis of the history of these four organizations have not just been rationalized in different directions by each organization's discourse. They have also been absorbed into the institutional environment of public policies and programmes in different ways.

The Mandira community benefits from federal laws guaranteeing the protection and special treatment of areas designated as 'productive reserves'. The classification 'productive reserve' guarantees that the ARM and those it represents have access to government credit provision and specific government programmes. Second, the Mandira community benefits from the provisional classification of 2,000 hectares of its land as *quilombo*, and recognition of sixteen families as *quilombolas*. This classification guarantees Mandira residents access to public policies and programmes that are designed specifically for the *quilombolas*. These forms of recognition give them the right to access particular public concessions, and one effect of this is that there is no need for the ARM to take part in participatory forums or deliberative processes.

MOAB, with its equally strong identity as a *quilombola* organization, is similarly dependent on state laws and programmes. Recognition of the *quilombola* classification has guaranteed resources that today support some of the principal projects that reach out to the community, such as the Política Nacional de Desenvolvimento Sustentável dos Povos e Comunidades Tradicionais (National Sustainable Development Policy for Traditional Peoples and Communities), the Programa Brasil Quilombola (Brazil Quilombola Programme) and the programme of technical assistance by the Instituto de Terras (Land Institute).

For ARG and SINTRAVALE, the state is also important. For ARG, whose work takes place in the environmental protection areas of three national parks, it is vital to obtain licences from public bodies. It is even more vital when concessions are made in the form of land settlement in those parks. This is an important connection when the ARG is looking for funding, since it has a diverse profile of action, with projects that involve commercial production, community organization and the sustainable use of natural resources. In the case of SINTRAVALE, state recognition of the condition of family farmers is necessary for its members to gain access to the Programa Nacional de Fortalecimento da Agricultura Familiar

(PRONAF – National Programme for Supporting Family Farmers), the main credit programme that is available. It is likewise necessary in terms of public policies, such as the sale of their products to the state. SINTRAVALE also needs each year to negotiate these resources in the regional participatory forums, such as CONSAD – an important difference between it and the other groups that is discussed below.

... differentiated institutionalization For SINTRAVALE, participation in regional forums is essential, since legislation requires it to meet at CONSAD to agree annually how investments in infrastructure that are made available through PRONAF will be distributed. For the ARG, these forums are also important as places in which to negotiate resources: settlers, family farmers and residents in conservation areas are guaranteed special status, but it requires negotiations to secure the resources for projects that involve them (unlike the *quilombolas*). Investment in these areas also includes a number of loans. In order to create viable projects that can compete with those of other (often private) entities, organizations such as SINTRAVALE and ARG have been obliged to diversify their ties and abilities.

The incentive to obtain funding has also had an impact on whether organizations are closer or farther away from the deliberative spaces. Thus the ARM only occasionally participates in the forums, and its degree of involvement is limited. For MOAB, participation holds a modicum of importance, allowing it to glean information and forge alliances in its principal political dispute – the fight against the dam.

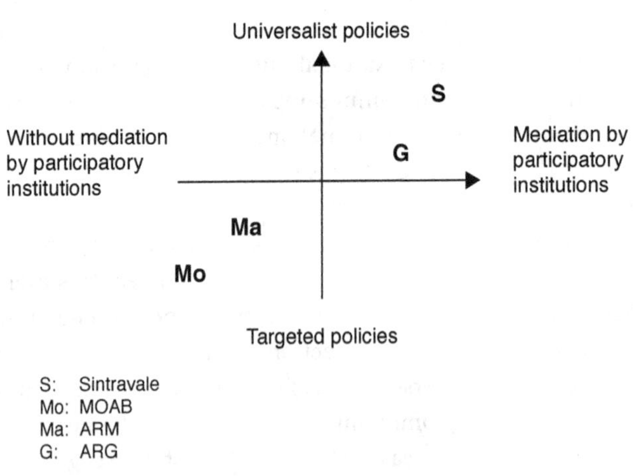

Figure 12.5 Representation of the state forms of conflict regulation

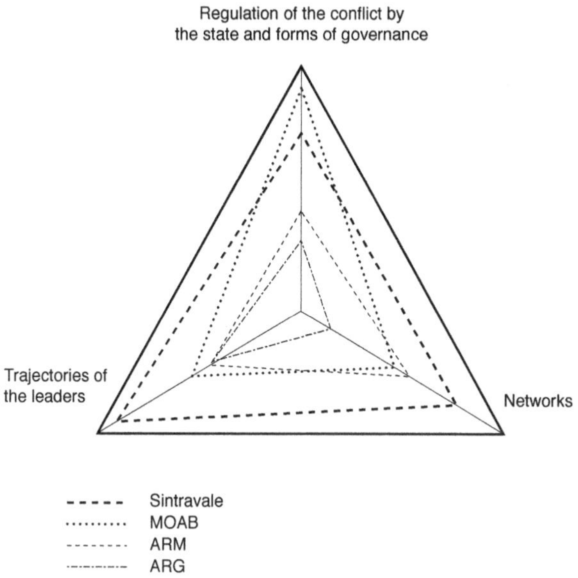

Figure 12.6 Triangle-synthesis to compare the configuration of social movements' attributes and the ideal-typical configuration favourable to democratic deliberation

For the ARG, participation is important, since that enables it to negotiate resources. While for SINTRAVALE, participation is fundamental and occurs in a relatively structured way. It is through participation that each organization exerts its political force and guarantees, at the same time, access to the material resources for its base.

Figures 12.5 and 12.6 summarize the arguments in this section. Figure 12.5 highlights two points: first, it charts the presence of more targeted or more universalist policies; second, it plots the existence of rules that require participation and negotiation in forums and councils. It was noted from the data collected that the way in which the state recognizes and absorbs the condition of family farmers has translated into a greater incentive to participate and negotiate. Meanwhile, the 'hybrid' position of members of the ARG places them in an intermediate position. The two *quilombola* organizations are located at the other extreme.

Figure 12.6 sketches the position of each organization on a schematic, where the outside triangle represents the ideal conditions for engagement in the deliberative processes in the participatory forums, according to the evidence available.

Taking stock of the evidence: one original conflict, three styles of activism

Taking stock of the above hypotheses helps us identify the social conditions that relate to the readiness of groups to take part in the processes of participatory governance that are in place in the Ribeira Valley. This idea is presented in Figure 12.7 below. The study shows the strong relationship between the trajectory of an organization and the way it positions itself in the participatory processes – a situation that is very similar to the three types of collective action set out by Tilly.

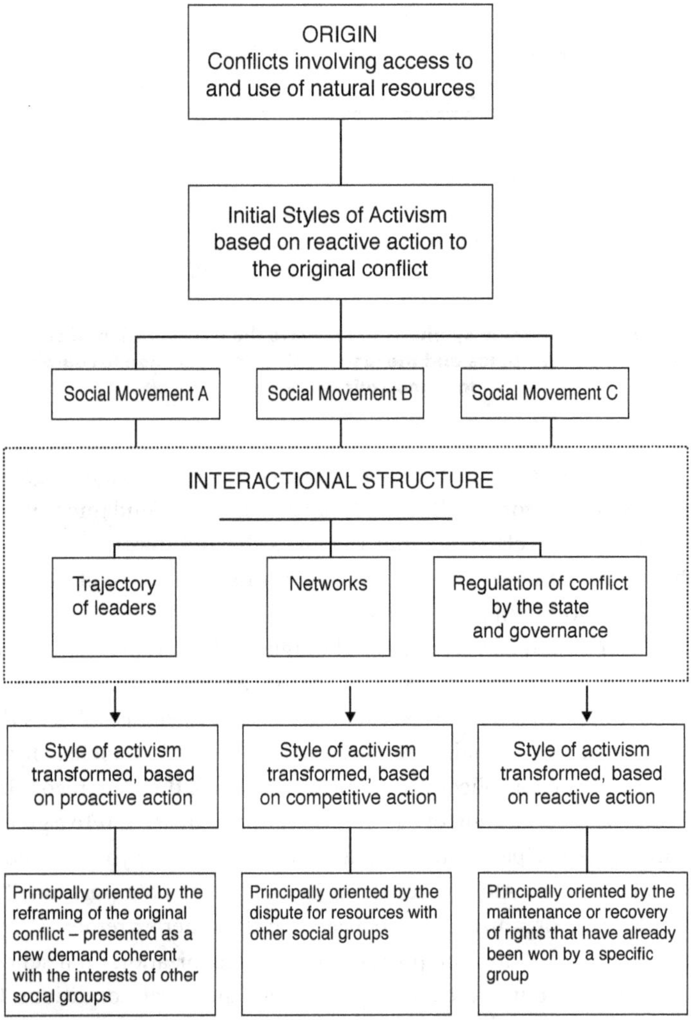

Figure 12.7 Styles of activism transformed by the interactional structure

SINTRAVALE presents a pattern that is similar to the type classified as competitive action: involving groups in a dispute with other groups over natural resources. In this pattern, the participatory forums for regional development are seen pragmatically as spaces where resources can be obtained, and the validity of each organization is based on fulfilling this criterion. MOAB shows a pattern of reactive action: involving groups that try to maintain or recover rights that are already established when an external actor threatens them. Participatory forums are seen as possible sources of information and as a place for the mobilization of political resources, together with other agents.

The ARG's pattern differs subtly from the previous two, with a position close to proactive action: involving groups that make new demands. 'New' is not used here in the sense of being innovative, but to indicate the search for a social and political place that has yet to be defined, and that differs from the position of the family farmers or *quilombolas*. The ARG is trying to obtain social recognition of the importance of its members as farmers who can offer environmental conservation and healthy produce in a way that is derived from their ethnic identity.

Finally, the ARM can be seen as being halfway between proactive and reactive action, since its proactive condition is now mixed with the demand for its classification as *quilombola*, with all that the status of this special group permits and implies in terms of activism.

The styles of activism above reveal themselves to be the result of a combination of factors that can be expressed as the idea of structured interactions: that intermediary instance between structure and action, and between the formation of perceptions and the propensity to action.

Analysis of the trajectory of the leaders of these four organizations has enabled the authors to gain an understanding of how the social properties of agents have been translated into a disposition to action and into stocks of resources to be mobilized. It is possible to see how better education, the diversification of professional investments and the experience of living in an urban area were converted into resources to be mobilized and social abilities to deal with conflicts and to rationalize them into discourses that guided action. The more diverse the options of the individuals, the more heterogeneous their ties and the less polarized their view of the world.

An analysis of the networks reveals the number of ties mobilized and the resources channelled by them. In the cases under analysis, the more concentrated or diversified the content of the ties, the more or less dependent are the organizations on political resources. The networks provide a kind of 'web' of resources that are mobilized by the actors.

The state regulates the conflicts in a way that depends on the trajectory of both the individuals and the groups.

Moreover, analysis of how conflicts are regulated by the state has enabled us to recognize the centrality of the state in defining the identities assumed by the groups; their proximity to (or distance from) the participatory forums; and their belief (or not) in deliberative processes. These terms appear in the calculations of the costs and benefits of participation, compared to other, competing political and cognitive investments.

When the possibility of participation and deliberation are seen in this way – through social groups and their organizations, rather than from the normative suppositions that support the participatory and deliberative discourse – it is evident that these participatory and deliberative spaces make up only a handful of the many that are open to the strategies and political projects of groups and organizations.

Conclusions

Using the concept of structured interactions, our aim has been to combine in the same interpretative model three vertices that are usually treated separately in the scientific literature. The formulation of networks is often contrasted with the functionalist explanation, which emphasizes the relationship between conflict and the state, while the emphasis on trajectories traditionally aims to distance itself from networks and to accentuate structural permanence and character. By taking each of these explanations as a hypothesis to be tested, we have shown that a combined study of fields, networks and institutions provides a more fruitful approach than does a separate analysis of these elements.

The leaders of the organizations do not just replicate structures and social conditioning. How they understand and intervene are a result of their trajectories: social structures translate into social properties of the leaders, who respond in turn to the forms of rationalization and position-taking, creating the idea of structured interactions. How this works can better be understood by comparing the trajectories of the organizational leaders presented here with one another. In spite of their common origins, the social trajectories of the group leaders reveal different possibilities of socialization for each. As a result, their experiences offer them different ways of classifying their conflicts, different ways of accessing their organizational work and a diverse range of options in selecting their modes of action.

Just as important as the trajectory of the leaders is the way in which the state regulates the conflict and translates it into forms of governance that are more or less open to participation and deliberation. Recognition of the *quilombolas* as a 'special group' was enough to guarantee their access to certain rights and resources, while the family farmers have found funding for their projects by negotiating in participatory forums. Here two marginalized groups have two different ways of getting the state to absorb their claims and, consequently, two different levels of stimuli for the groups to take part in participatory institutions. These two dimensions – the social trajectory of the leaders and the absorption of conflict by the state – determine the identities of the mediators and the resources that will be mobilized by the network.

The first contribution of this study, then, has been to formulate this framework of analysis. Its second contribution can be summarized in two normative elements that proceed from these interpretative findings. First, those who bring to attention the role of the state in guaranteeing the performance of the participatory sphere place their emphasis on systems of incentives, and so tend to ignore the fact that the capacity of agents to react to the stimuli and sanctions depends on how they themselves classify these rules and sanctions. This classification process, in its turn, depends considerably on the past experiences of these agents – their historical trajectory. Second, the diversification of ties seems to be decisive in enabling agents to set out and negotiate their conflicts in the institutional environment. This diversification of ties strongly influences the capacity of agents to interact with institutional environments. From here, one of the main challenges to the democratic agenda for the coming years will lie in how to make participatory institutions more prepared to deal with conflict, social diversity and asymmetry.

Notes

1 This chapter presents results from the 'Styles of Activism and Social Participation' research project carried out by the Centro Brasileiro de Análise e Planejamento, with the support of the Development Research Centre on Citizenship, Participation and Accountability, based at the Institute of Development Studies (University of Sussex) and funded by the UK Department for International Development. The study received additional funding from the Brazilian National Council for Scientific Research. Earlier versions of this chapter were presented at a meeting of the Deepening Democracy Research Group of the Institute of Development Studies, held in Cape Town, South Africa, in 2008, and also at the Congress of Latin American Political Science Association in San Jose, Costa Rica the same year. We would like to acknowledge all the comments and suggestions made at those two meetings, as well as the contributions received from the reviewers.

2 Actual names have been changed to protect the identities of the people interviewed.

About the contributors

Samuel Egwu is currently the governance adviser for the United Nations Development Programme in Nigeria and professor of political science at the University of Jos. He has published extensively on topics including the impact of structural adjustment programmes, agrarian change in rural communities and federalism.

Fabiola Fanti is a research assistant at CEBRAP in São Paulo. She specializes in human rights law and has a masters degree in political science from the University of São Paulo.

Arilson Favareto is professor of economic analysis at the Centre of Engineering, Modelling and Applied Social Sciences of the Federal University of the ABC Region, Brazil, and a researcher with CEBRAP. He has published on rural development, participation and public policies for sustainable territorial development, and his current interests include new forms of the social use of natural resources.

Alexandre Ferraz has a PhD in political science and is currently working as research analyst at the Inter-Union Department of Statistics and Socio-Economic Studies in São Paulo. His research interests include comparative democracy, interest groups, democratic participation and democratic institutions.

Idaci Ferreira is a social activist and has worked in communities in Brazil and Angola. She has been a trainer and adviser on the participatory planning, monitoring and evaluation of development projects. Her areas of research interest include collective action, participation and empowerment.

Carolina Galvanese is a researcher at CEBRAP, and also works at the Cooperativism and Associativism Institute, Vale do Ribeira. She has a masters degree in energy and regional development, and her work focuses on environment, collective action and regional development.

Jibrin Ibrahim has a PhD in political science from the Institut d'Etudes Politiques, France. He is the director of the Centre for Democracy and Development, an NGO doing research, advocacy and training work across the West African region. His areas of specialization are democratization, the political economy of poverty reduction, comparative federalism and religious and ethnic identities.

Naila Kabeer is a professorial fellow at the Institute of Development Studies, Sussex. The main focus of her work has been gender, poverty and social exclusion in developing countries, particularly in Asia. She has extensive experience of research and training and has had work commissioned in these fields.

Yumi Kawamura is a PhD student at the Federal University of the ABC Region, Brazil, researching the National Biodiesel Programme. Her research interests and experiences as a consultant are on the interface between public policies, territorial development and innovation.

Simeen Mahmud is currently research director at the Population Studies Division of the Bangladesh Institute of Development Studies. She studied statistics at Dhaka University and medical demography at the London School of Hygiene and Tropical Medicine. Her past research has focused on demographic estimation, the relationship between women's work, status and fertility, and demographic transition in conditions of poverty. Her current research focuses primarily on women's work, pathways of women's empowerment, participation and mobilization for citizenship and rights.

Frederico Menino is a member of the Citizenship and Development Centre of CEBRAP, and has a masters degree in political science. He is currently involved with rural and ethnic social movements in Brazil, and has been involved with research on participatory budgeting, international immigration and the African-American diaspora.

Ranjita Mohanty has a doctorate in sociology from Jawaharlal Nehru University, New Delhi. She is an independent scholar and works as a consulting sociologist with national and international organizations. Her research addresses the grassroots issues of development and democracy, and her abiding interest is in studying the politics of the powerless, and the contestation and negotiation of power that take place between civil society and the state.

Celestine Nyamu Musembi is a fellow at the Institute of Development Studies, Sussex, currently on leave of absence at the University of Nairobi's School of Law. She holds both a masters and a doctoral degree in law from Harvard Law School, and is an advocate of the High Court of Kenya. Her areas of research and teaching include human rights and development, property relations, gender equality in governance reforms, and citizen participation in formal and informal local governance forums.

Ndodana Nleya is a PhD candidate and research assistant at the African Centre for Citizenship and Democracy in the School of Government, University of the Western Cape. He worked in various capacities in industry in Zimbabwe before pursuing an academic career.

Duncan Okello is the eastern Africa regional director for the Society for International Development, based in Nairobi, Kenya. He holds a masters degree in international studies from the University of Kent at Canterbury. He has worked extensively with research and civil society organizations in eastern Africa, including the Institute of Economic Affairs, Green Belt Movement and Youth Agenda.

Meire Ribeiro is a research assistant at CEBRAP, where she is also member of the Citizenship and Development Group.

Steven Robins is a professor in the Department of Sociology and Social Anthropology at the University of Stellenbosch. He has published on a wide range of topics, including the politics of land, 'development' and identity in Zimbabwe and South Africa; the Truth and Reconciliation Commission; urban studies; and, most recently, on citizenship and governance.

Sandra Roque is a PhD candidate in social anthropology at the University of Cape Town, South Africa. She is also the consultancy director of AustralCOWI, a consultancy company working on social and economic issues in Mozambique and southern Africa, and a member of the Angolan development NGO Acção para o Desenvolvimento Rural e Ambiente (ADRA). Her research has covered issues related to the relationship between state and society, and issues referring to social development, in particular in urban areas.

Alex Shankland is a social scientist who has worked extensively in Brazil, Peru, Angola and Mozambique as a researcher, NGO manager and social development consultant. His doctoral research examined representation and health policy in the Brazilian Amazon. His research interests have centred on rights, democracy, participation and policy, particularly in the health sector.

Lisa Thompson is professor of international relations and development and director of the African Centre for Citizenship and Democracy at the

School of Government, University of the Western Cape. She continues to focus on issues of socio-economic development in the context of the global political economy, and has published widely on research pertaining to regional development and democratization processes.

Bibliography

Abelson, J. and F. Gauvin. 2006. *Assessing the Impacts of Public Participation: Concepts, Evidence and Policy Implications*, CPRN Research Report No. P06. Ontario: McMaster University.

Abers, R. 2001. *Inventing Local Democracy: Grassroots Politics in Brazil*. Boulder, CO: Westview Press.

Ake, C. 1996. *Democracy and Development in Africa*. Washington, DC: Brookings Institution.

Ake, C. 2005. *The Feasibility of Democracy in Africa*. Dakar: CODESRIA.

Alexander, N. 2002. *An Ordinary Country: Issues in the Transition from Apartheid to Democracy in South Africa*. Pietermaritzburg: University of Natal Press.

Alves, A. 2007. 'Florestania', *Biblioteca da Floresta*. www.bibliotecadafloresta.ac.gov.br/index.php?option=com_content &view=article&id=85:florestania&catid=50:antonio-alves&Itemid=256 (accessed 20 May 2010).

Ansell, C. and A. Gash. 2008. 'Collaborative governance in theory and practice', *Journal of Public Administration, Research and Theory* 18(4): 543–71.

Appadurai, A. 2002. 'Deep democracy: urban governmentality and the horizon of politics', *Public Culture* 14(1): 21–47.

Arens, J. and J. van Beurden. 1977. *Jhagrapur: Poor Peasants and Women in a Village in Bangladesh*. Amsterdam: Third World Publications.

Athias, R. 2007. 'A Luta dos Povos Indígenas: 500 Anos de Uma Outra História', in J. Romano and M. Antunes (eds), *Olhar Crítico sobre Participação e Cidadania: Trajetórias de Organização e Luta pela Redemocratização da Governança no Brasil*. São Paulo: Expressão Popular.

Avritzer, L. 2002. *Democracy and Public Space in Latin America*. Princeton, NJ: Princeton University Press.

Avritzer, L. and Z. Navarro. 2003. *A Inovação Democrática no Brasil*. São Paulo: Cortez.

Ballard, R., A. Habib and I. Valodia (eds). 2006. *Voices of Protest, Social Movements in Post-Apartheid South Africa*. Durban: University of KwaZulu-Natal Press.

Barroso-Hoffmann, M., M. P. Iglesias, L. Garnelo, *et al.* 2004. 'A Administração Pública e os Povos Indígenas', in D. Rocha and M. Bernardo (eds), *A Era FHC e o Governo Lula: Transição?* Brasília: INESC.

Bebbington, A., R. Abramovay and M. Chiriboga. 2008. 'Social movements and the dynamics of rural territorial development in Latin America', *World Development* 36(12): 2874–87.

Betteille, A. 2000. *Antinomies of Society. Essays on Ideologies and Institutions*. New Delhi: Oxford University Press.

Bittencourt, M. F. 2007. *Kulina do Envira: Resistência Cultural, Vulnerabilidade e Ausência do Estado.* Rio Branco: DERACRE (mimeo).

Björkman, M. and J. Svensson. 2009. 'Power to the people: evidence from a randomized filed experiment on community-based monitoring in Uganda', *Quarterly Journal of Economics* 124(2): 735–69.

Bógus, C. M. 1998. *Participação popular em saúde.* São Paulo: Anna Blume.

Bond, P. 2000. *Elite Transition: From Apartheid to Neoliberalism in South Africa.* London: Pluto Press.

Bourdieu, P. 1985/2007. *Algérie 60 – structures économiques, structures temporelles.* Paris: Seuil.

BRAC. 1983. *The Net: Power Structure in Ten Villages.* Dhaka: BRAC.

Bracking, S. 2005. 'Guided miscreants: liberalism, myopias, and the politics of representation', *World Development* 33(6): 1011–24.

Bratton, M. 1989. 'The politics of government–NGO relations in Africa', *World Development* 17(4): 569–87.

Bratton, M., P. Alderfer, G. Bowser and J. Temba. 1999. 'The effects of civic education on political culture: evidence from Zambia', *World Development* 27(5): 807–24.

Brazil. 1988. *Constituição da República Federativa do Brasil.* São Paulo: Atlas.

Brown, L. D. 2008. *Creating Credibility.* Sterling, VA: Kumarian Press.

Burman, S. and W. Schärf. 1990. 'Creating people's justice: street committees and people's courts in a South African city', *Law & Society Review* 24(3): 693–744.

Carothers, T. 2009. 'Democracy assistance: political vs. developmental?', *Journal of Democracy* 20(1): 5–19.

Centro de Estudos e Investigação Científica. 2007. *Relatório Econômico de Angola 2007.* Luanda: Centro de Estudos e Investigação Científica and Universidade Católica de Angola.

Chabal, P. 2006. 'Transições políticas em Angola: *E Pluribus Unum*', in N. Vidal and J. P. Andrade (eds), *O Processo de Transicao para o Multipartidarismo em Angola.* Lisbon and Luanda: Firmamento Ediçoes.

Chabal, P. 2008. 'Twilight Zone: sociedade civil e política em Angola', in N. Vidal and J. P. Andrade (eds), *Sociedade Civil e Política em Angola: Enquadramento Regional e Internacional.* Lisbon and Luanda: Firmamento Ediçoes.

Chabal, P. and N. Vidal (eds). 2007. *Angola: The Weight of History.* London: Hurst.

Chandhoke, N. 2003. 'Governance and the pluralisation of the state: implications for democratic citizenship', *Economic and Political Weekly* 38(28): 2957–68.

Chen, M., R. Jhabvala and R. Kanpur (eds). 2007. *Membership-based Organizations of the Poor.* New York: Routledge.

Citizenship and Development Group. 2008. *Policy and Social Participation in the City of São Paulo.* São Paulo: CEBRAP-CEM.

City of Cape Town. 2005. 'A population profile of Khayelitsha: socio-economic information from the 2001 Census'. City of Cape Town: Cape Town.

Coelho, V. S. 2006. 'Democratization of Brazilian health councils: the paradox of bringing the other side into the tent', *International*

Journal of Urban and Regional Research 30(3): 656–71.
Coelho, V. S. and A. Favareto. 2009. 'Conexões entre participação, democracia e desenvolvimento investigação dos impactos políticos e distributivos da participação social', in A. G. Lavalle, *El horizonte de la política. Cuestiones emergente y agendas de investigación.* México: CIESAS.
Coelho, V. S. and M. Nobre (eds). 2004. *Participação e Deliberação: teoria democrática e experiências institucionais no Brasil contemporâneo.* São Paulo: 34 Letras.
Coelho, V. S., A. Favareto, C. Galvanese and F. Menino. 2007. 'Fóruns Participativos e Desenvolvimento Territorial no Vale do Ribeira (Brasil)', in M. Chiriboga and J. Bengoa (eds), *Movimentos Sociais, Governança Ambiental e Desenvolvimento Territorial.* Santiago de Chile: Rimisp/IDRC.
Coimbra Jr., C. E. A., L. Garnelo, P. C. Basta, *et al.* 2006. 'Saúde: Sistema em Transição', in C. A. Ricardo and F. Ricardo (eds), *Povos Indígenas no Brasil 2001–2005*. São Paulo: ISA.
Comaroff, J. L. and J. Comaroff (eds). 1999. *Civil Society and the Political Imagination in Africa: Critical Perspectives.* Chicago, IL and London: Chicago University Press.
Conradie, C. 1992. 'Khayelitsha: interpreting a process of social transformation', unpublished Masters thesis, Cape Town: University of the Western Cape.
Conradie, C. and L. Thompson. 2010. *Democracy in Action? Women Leaders and Empowerment Processes in Khayelitsha*, ACCEDE Working Paper Series, forthcoming.
Cornwall, A. 2007. 'Negotiating participation in a Brazilian municipal health council', in A. Cornwall and V. S. Coelho (eds), *Spaces for Change? The Politics of Citizen Participation in New Democratic Arenas.* London: Zed Books.
Cornwall, A. and V. S. Coelho (eds). 2007. *Spaces for Change? The Politics of Citizen Participation in New Democratic Arenas.* London: Zed Books.
Cornwall, A. and A. Shankland. 2008. 'Engaging citizens: lessons from building Brazil's national health system', *Social Science & Medicine* 66(10): 2173–84.
Costa, S. 1997. 'Movimentos sociais, democratização e a construção de esferas públicas locais'. *Rev. bras. Ci. Soc.* [online] 12(35) ISSN 0102-6909. doi: 10.1590/S0102-69091997000300008.
Dagnino, E. 2008. 'Challenges to participation, citizenship and democracy: perverse confluence and displacement of meaning', in A. Bebbington, S. Hickey and D. Mitlin (eds), *Can NGOs Make a Difference? The Challenge of Development Alternatives.* London: Zed.
Dagnino, E. and L. Tatagiba. 2007. *Democracia, Sociedade Civil e Participação.* Chapecó: Argos.
Dagnino, E., A. Olvera and A. Panfichi. 2006. *A disputa pela construção democrática na América Latina*. São Paulo: Paz e Terra.
Dahl, R. A. 1971. *Poliarchy: Participation and opposition.* New Haven, CT: Yale University Press.
Damasceno, A. (director). 2008. *Fala Txai: Os Índios e a Saúde no Acre* (DVD). Brazil: SSL, 10 minutes.
Davis, P. R. and J. A. McGregor. 2000. 'Civil society, inter-

national donors and poverty in Bangladesh', *Commonwealth and Comparative Politics* 36(1): 47–64.

Devine, J. 2003. 'The paradox of sustainability: reflections on NGOs in Bangladesh', *Annals of the American Academy of Political and Social Science* 590: 227–42.

Diamond, L. 1989. 'Beyond autocracy: prospects for democracy in Africa', in R. Joseph (ed.), *Beyond Autocracy in Africa: Working Papers for the Inaugural Seminar of the Governance in Africa Program.* Atlanta: Carter Center, Emory University.

Dryzek, J. 2000. *Deliberative Democracy and Beyond: Liberals, Critics, Contestations.* Oxford: Oxford University Press.

Duprat, D. M. 2002. 'O Estado Pluriétnico', in A. C. de Souza Lima and M. Barroso-Hoffmann (eds), *Além da tutela: bases para uma nova política indigenista III.* Rio de Janeiro: Contra Capa.

Ebrahim, A. 2003. 'Accountability in practice: mechanisms for NGOs', *World Development* 31(5): 813–29.

Edwards, M. 2004. *Civil Society.* Cambridge: Polity Press.

Edwards, M. and J. Gaventa. 2001. *Global Citizen Action.* Boulder, CO: Lynne Rienner Publishers.

Elliot, C. M. 2006. 'Civil society and democracy: a comparative review essay', in C. M. Elliot (ed.), *Civil Society and Democracy.* Oxford University Press: New Delhi.

EU Election Observation Mission. 2003. *NIGERIA: National Assembly Elections, 12 April 2003; Presidential and Gubernatorial Elections, 19 April 2003; State Houses of Assembly Elections, 03 May 2003*, Final Report.

Ferguson, J. and A. Gupta. 2002. 'Spatializing states: toward an ethnography of neoliberal governmentality', *American Ethnologist* 29(4): 981–1002.

Finkel, S. 2002. 'Education and the mobilization of political participation in developing countries', *Journal of Politics* 64(4): 994–1020.

Fishkin, J. and C. Farrar. 2005. 'Deliberative polling', in J. Gastil and P. Levine, *The Deliberative Democracy Handbook: Strategies for Effective Citizen Engagement in the 21st Century.* San Francisco, CA: Jossey-Bass.

Fishkin, J. and R. Luskin. 1999. 'Bringing deliberation to the democratic dialogue', in M. McCombs and A. Reynolds (eds), *The Poll with a Human Face: The National Issues Convention Experiment in Political Communication.* New York: Erlbaum.

Fraser, N. and A. Honneth. 2003. *Redistribution or Recognition? A Political-Philosophical Exchange.* London: Verso.

Freire, P. 1972. *Pedagogy of the Oppressed.* Harmondsworth: Penguin.

FUNASA. 2002. *Política Nacional de Atenção à Saúde dos Povos Indígenas.* Brasília: Ministério da Saúde/Fundação Nacional de Saúde.

Fung, A. 2003. 'Associations and democracy: between theories, hopes and realities', *Annual Review of Sociology* 29: 515–39.

Fung, A. 2004. 'Survey article: Recipes for public spheres: eight institutional design choices and their consequences', *Journal of Political Philosophy* 11: 338–67.

Fung, A. and E. O. Wright. 2001. 'Deepening democracy: innovations in empowered participatory governance', *Politics & Society* 29(1): 5–41.

in Rural Nigeria, 1952–1990. Lagos: Malthouse Press.

Fung, A. and E. O. Wright. 2003. *Deepening Democracy: Institutional Innovations in Empowered Participatory Governance.* London: Verso.

Gastil, J. and P. Levine. 2005. *The Deliberative Democracy Handbook: Strategies for Effective Citizen Engagement in the 21st Century.* San Francisco, CA: Jossey-Bass.

Gaventa, J. 2006a. 'Finding the spaces for change', in *Power: Exploring Power for Change*, IDS Bulletin 37(6): 23–33.

Gaventa, J. 2006b. *Triumph, Deficit or Contestation? Deepening the 'Deepening Democracy' Debate*, IDS Working Paper No. 264. Brighton: Institute of Development Studies.

Gaventa J. and G. Barrett. 2010. *So What Difference Does It Make? Mapping the Outcomes of Citizen Engagement*, IDS Working Paper. Brighton: Institute of Development Studies.

Gaventa, J. and R. McGee (eds). 2010. *Citizen Action and National Policy Reform: Making Change Happen.* London: Zed Books

Gerrits, A. 2007. 'Is there a distinct European democratic model to promote?' in M. van Doon and R. von Meijenfeldt (eds), *Democracy: Europe's Core Value?* The Hague: Eburon Delft.

Gills, B., J. Rocamora and R. Wilson (eds). 1992. *Low Intensity Democracy: Political Power in the New World Order.* Boulder, CO: Pluto.

Government of Gujarat. 1972. *Zinabhai Darzi Committee Report.* Gandhinagar.

Granovetter, M. 1973. 'The strength of weak ties', *American Journal of Sociology* 78(6): 1360–80.

Guyer, J. 1994. *Representation without Taxation: An Essay on Democracy in Rural Nigeria, 1952–1990.* Lagos: Malthouse Press.

Habermas, J., C. Cronin and P. de Greiff. 1998. *The Inclusion of the Other: Studies in Political Theory.* Cambridge, MA: MIT Press.

Hadenius, A. 2001. *Institutions and Democratic Citizenship.* Oxford: Oxford University Press.

Heller, P. 2000. 'Degrees of democracy: some comparative lessons from India', *World Politics* 52(4): 484–519.

Heller, P. 2001. 'Moving the state: the politics of democratic decentralization in Kerala, South Africa and Porto Alegre', *Politics and Society* 29(1): 131–63.

Hemming, J. 1987. *Amazon Frontier: The Defeat of the Brazilian Indians.* London: Macmillan.

Hill, D. M. 1994. *Citizens and Cities: Urban Policy in the 1990s.* New York: Harvester Wheatsheaf.

Hossain, N. 2009. *Rude Accountability in the Unreformed State: Informal Pressures on the Frontline Bureaucrats in Bangladesh*, IDS Working Paper No. 319. Brighton: Institute of Development Studies.

House, E. and K. Howe. 2000. Deliberative Democratic Evaluation Checklist, Evaluation Checklist Project, available at: www.wmich.edu.edu/evalctr/checklist.

Houtzager, P. and A. Acharya. 2010. 'Associations, active citizens and the quality of democracy in Brazil and Mexico', *Theory and Society* (forthcoming).

Houtzager, P., A. Acharya and A. Lavalle. 2007. *Associations and the Exercise of Citizenship in New Democracies: Evidences from São Paulo and Mexico City*, IDS Working Paper No. 285. Brighton: Institute of Development Studies.

Howell, J. and J. Pearce. 2001. *Civil*

Society and Development: A Critical Exploration. Boulder, CO: Lynne Rienner Publishers.

Ibrahim, J. 2007. *Nigeria's 2007 Elections: The Fitful Path to Democratic Citizenship*, United States Institute for Peace Special Report No. 192, January.

Iglesias, M. P. and T. Valle de Aquino. 2005a. 'O "Movimento Indígena" no Acre', in M. P. Iglesias and T. Valle de Aquino (eds), *Povos e Terras Indígenas no Estado do Acre.* Rio Branco: SEMA (mimeo).

Iglesias, M. P. and T. Valle de Aquino. 2005b. 'Políticas Públicas Estaduais para os Povos Indígenas, 1999–2004', in M. P. Iglesias and T. Valle de Aquino (eds), *Povos e Terras Indígenas no Estado do Acre.* Rio Branco: SEMA (mimeo).

Ilaiah, K. 2001. 'Dalitism and Brahminism: the epistemological conflict in history', in G. Shah (ed.), *Dalit Identity and Politics.* Delhi: Sage Publications.

Institute for Development Studies. 2007. *The Size, Scope, Structure and Financing of the Non-Profit Sector in Kenya.* Nairobi: Institute of Development Studies.

Institute of Economic Affairs. 1998. *Our Problems, Our Solutions: An Economic and Public Policy Agenda for Kenya.* Nairobi: IEA.

Instituto Brasileiro de Geografia e Estatística. 2000. Censo Demográfico. Available at: www.ibge.gov.br.

Jacobi, P. 1993. *Movimentos sociais e políticas públicas: demandas por saneamento básico e saúde – São Paulo, 1974–84.* São Paulo: Cortez.

JMJ International. 2006. *The Enabling Environment for Local Governance in Angola: Strengthening the Links between Decentralization and Community Driven Development*, Report for the World Bank, Community-Driven Development Anchor and Angola Social Fund.

Joseph, R. 1987. *Democracy and Prebendal Politics in Nigeria: The Rise and Fall of the Second Republic.* Ibadan: Spectrum.

Joshi, A. 2008. 'Producing social accountability? The impact of service delivery reforms', in *State Reform and Social Accountability*, IDS Bulletin 38(2): 10–18.

Justice and Peace Development Commission. 2003. *Final Report on the Observations of the 2003 General Elections in Nigeria.* Lagos: Catholic Secretariat.

Kabeer, N. (ed.). 2005. *Inclusive Citizenship: Meanings and Expressions.* London: Zed Books.

Kabeer, N. with A. Haq Kabir. 2009. *Grassroots Narratives about Citizenship in the Absence of Good Governance: Voices of the Working Poor in Bangladesh*, IDS Working Paper No. 339. Brighton: Institute of Development Studies.

Kabeer, N. with A. Haq Kabir and T. Y. Huq. 2009. *Quantifying the Impact of Social Mobilisation in Rural Bangladesh: Donors, Civil Society and 'The Road not Taken'*, IDS Working Paper No. 333. Brighton: Institute of Development Studies.

Kanyinga, K. 1995. 'The changing development space in Kenya: socio-political change and voluntary development activities', in P. Gibbon (ed.), *Markets, Civil Society and Democracy in Kenya.* Uppsala: Nordiska Afrikainstitutet.

Kanyinga, K. 2003. 'Limitations of political liberalization: parties and electoral politics in Kenya, 1992–2002', in W. Oyugi, P. Wanyande and C. Odhiambo-Mbai (eds), *The Politics of Transition in*

Kenya: From Kanu to Narc. Nairobi: Heinrich Böll Foundation.

Kenya National Commission on Human Rights. 2006. *Behaving Badly: Deception, Chauvinism and Waste During the Referendum Campaigns.* Nairobi: KNCHR.

Kibwana, K., S. Wanjala and O. Owiti (eds). 1998. *Anatomy of Corruption in Kenya: Legal, Political and Socio-Economic Perspectives.* Nairobi: Claripress.

Kofman, E. 1995. 'Citizenship for some and not for others: spaces of citizenship in contemporary Europe', *Political Geography* 14(2): 121–37.

Lavalle, A., A. Acharya and P. Houtzager. 2005. 'Beyond comparative anecdotalism: how civil and political organizations shape participation in São Paulo, Brazil', *World Development* 33(6): 951–61.

Law Society of Kenya, Kenya Human Rights Commission and the International Commission of Jurists – Kenya (eds). 1994. *Kenya Tuitakayo, the Kenya We Want: Proposal for a Model Constitution.* Nairobi: Citizens' Coalition for Constitutional Change.

Lewis, D. 2004. 'On the difficulty of studying "civil society": reflections on NGOs, state and democracy in Bangladesh', *Contributions to Indian Sociology* 38(3): 299–322.

Luckham, R., A.-M. Goetz and M. Kaldor. 2000. *Democratic Institutions and Politics in Contexts of Inequality, Poverty, and Conflict: A Conceptual Framework*, IDS Working Paper No. 104. Brighton: Institute of Development Studies.

Luckham, R., A.-M. Goetz and M. Kaldor. 2003. *Democratic Institutions and Democratic Politics.* Governance and Social Development Resource Centre (GSDRC), University of Birmingham.

Machado, A. 2005. 'Tire Sua Conclusão', *Blog Altino Machado*, 7 October. Retrieved 9 May 2009 from http://altino.blogspot.com/2005/10/tire-sua-concluso.html.

Machado, A. 2007. 'Protesto Huni Kuin', *Blog Altino Machado*, 23 May. Retrieved 9 May 2009 from http://altino.blogspot.com/2007/05/protesto-huni-kuin.html.

Machado, M. V. 1995. *Atores Sociais: movimentos urbanos, continuidade e gênero.* São Paulo: Anna Blume.

MacKian, S. 1995. 'The great dust-heap called history: recovering the multiple spaces of citizenship', *Political Geography* 14(2): 209–16.

Mahajan, G. 1998. *Aspects of Liberal Democracy.* Delhi: Oxford University Press.

Mamdani, M. 1996. *Citizen and the Subject: Contemporary Africa and the Legacy of Late Colonialism.* Cape Town: David Phillip.

Manin, B. 1997. *The Principles of Representative Government.* Cambridge: Cambridge University Press.

Mansbridge, J. 2003. 'Rethinking representation', *American Political Science Review* 97: 515–28.

Marais, H. 1998. *South Africa: Limits to Change: The Political Economy of Transition.* London: Zed Books.

McDonald, D. 2000. *Municipal Bureaucrats and Environmental Policy in Cape Town*, MSP Background Research Series, Graduate School of Public and Development Management, University of the Witwatersrand.

Melo, M. A. and G. Baiocchi. 2006. 'Symposium: deliberative

democracy and local governance: towards a new agenda', *International Journal of Urban and Regional Research* 30(3).

Messiant, C. 1983. '1961 – L'Angola colonial, histoire et société, les prémisses du mouvement nationaliste', PhD thesis, Ecole des Hautes Etudes en Sciences Sociales, Paris.

Messiant, C. 2006. 'Transição para o multipartidarismo sem transição o para a democracia', in N. Vidal and J. P. Andrade (eds), *O Processo de Transição para o Multipartidarismo em Angola.* Lisbon and Luanda: Firmamento Ediçoes.

Mohanty, R. 2007. 'Gendered subjects, the state and participatory spaces: the politics of domesticating participation in rural India', in A. Cornwall and V. S. Coelho (eds), *Spaces for Change? The Politics of Citizen Participation in New Democratic Arenas.* London: Zed Books.

Moore, M. and J. Putzel. 1999. *Thinking Strategically about Politics and Poverty*, IDS Working Paper No. 101. Brighton: Institute of Development Studies.

Murungi, K. 2000. *In the Mud of Politics.* Nairobi: Acacia Stanteex Publishers.

Mutunga, W. 1999. *Constitution-Making from the Middle.* Harare and Nairobi: SAREAT and MWENGO.

Ndegwa, S. 1996. *The Two Faces of Civil Society: NGOs and Politics in Africa.* West Hartford, CT: Kumarian Press.

Neder, C. 2001. 'Participação e gestão pública: a experiência dos movimentos populares de saúde no Município de São Paulo', Masters dissertation, Faculty of Medical Sciences, Campinas State University.

Ngunyi, M. 1996. 'Building democracy in a polarized civil society: the transition to multiparty democracy in Kenya', in J. Oloka-Onyango, K. Kibwana and C. M. Peter (eds), *Law and the Struggle for Democracy in East Africa.* Nairobi: Claripress.

Nyamu-Musembi, C. and S. Musyoki. 2004. *Kenyan Civil Society Perspectives on Rights, Rights-Based Approaches to Development, and Participation*, IDS Working Paper No. 236. Brighton: Institute of Development Studies.

Nyangoro, J. (ed.). 1999. *Civil Society and Democratic Development in Africa: Perspectives from Eastern and Southern Africa.* Harare: MWENGO.

Nzomo, M. 2003. 'Civil society in the Kenya political transition: 1992–2002', in W. Oyugi, P. Wanyande and C. Odhiambo-Mbai (eds), *The Politics of Transition in Kenya: From Kanu to Narc.* Nairobi: Heinrich Böll Foundation.

Oloka-Onyango, J., K. Kibwana and C. M. Peter (eds). 1996. *Law and the Struggle for Democracy in East Africa.* Nairobi: Claripress.

Olukoshi, A. 2006. *Assessing Africa's New Governance Models.* Dakar: CODESRIA.

Olzak, S. 1989. 'Analysis of events in the study of collective action', *Annual Review of Sociology* 15: 119–41.

Omvedt, G. 1994. *Dalits and Democratic Revolution.* Delhi: Sage Publications.

Omvedt, G. 2001. 'Ambedkar and after: the Dalit Movement in India', in G. Shah (ed.), *Dalit Identity and Politics.* New Delhi: Sage.

Omvedt, G. 2003. 'The anti-caste movement and the discourse of power', in N. Gopal Jayal (ed.), *Democracy in India*. Delhi: Oxford University Press.

Otite, O. 1990. *Ethnic Pluralism and Ethnicity in Nigeria*. Ibadan: Shaneson.

Oyugi, W., P. Wanyande and C. Odhiambo-Mbai (eds). 2003. *The Politics of Transition in Kenya: From Kanu to Narc*. Nairobi: Heinrich Böll Foundation.

Pai, S. 2002. *Dalit Assertion and the Unfinished Democratic Revolution*. New Delhi: Sage Publications.

Paley, J. 2002. 'Toward an anthropology of democracy', *Annual Review of Anthropology* 31: 469–96.

Pateman, C. 2003. 'Participation and democracy theory', in R. A. Dahl, I. Shapiro and J. Cheibub (eds), *The Democracy Sourcebook*. Cambridge, MA: MIT Press.

Pélissier, R. 1978. *La colonie du minotaure. Nationalisme et révoltes en Angola 1926–1961*. Orgeval: Editions Pélissier.

Peruzzotti, E. 2008. 'Representative democracy as mediated politics: rethinking the links between representation and participation', unpublished paper prepared for the 'Rethinking Representation' workshop, Bellagio, October.

Pietrowski, M. 1994. 'The one-party state as a threat to civil and political liberalization', in G. W. Shepherd, E. McCarthy-Arnold, D. Penna and C. Sobreperna (eds), *Africa, Human Rights and the Global System: The Political Economy of Human Rights in a Changing World*. Westport, CT: Greenwood Press.

Plattner, M. F. 2004. 'The quality of democracy: a sceptical afterword', *Journal of Democracy* 15(4), October.

Przeworski, A. 1999. 'Minimalist conception of democracy: a defense', in I. Shapiro and C. Hacker-Cordón (eds), *Democracy's Value*. Cambridge: Cambridge University Press.

Putnam, R. 1993a. *Making Democracy Work: Civic Traditions in Modern Italy*. Princeton, NJ: Princeton University Press.

Putnam, R. 1993b. 'The prosperous community: social capital and public life', *American Prospect* 13: 35–42.

Putnam, R. 2003. *Bowling Alone: The Collapse and Revival of American Community*. New York: Simon and Schuster.

Ramos, A. R. 2002. 'Cutting through state and class: sources and strategies of self-representation in Latin America', in K. B. Warren and J. E. Jackson (eds), *Indigenous Movements, Self-Representation, and the State in Latin America*. Austin, TX: University of Texas Press.

Ricardo, C. A. and F. Ricardo (eds). 2006. *Povos Indígenas no Brasil 2001–2005*. São Paulo: ISA.

Robins, S. 2008. *From Revolution to Rights in South Africa: Social Movements, NGOs and Popular Politics*. Oxford and Durban: James Currey Publishers and University of KwaZulu-Natal Press.

Robins, S., A. Cornwall and B. von Lieres. 2008. 'Rethinking "citizenship" in the post-colony', *Third World Quarterly* 29(6): 1069–86.

Robinson, M. 2007. 'Decentralising service delivery? Evidence and policy implications', in *Decentralising Service Delivery?* IDS Bulletin 38(1): 7–17.

Rosenblum, N. 1994. 'Civil societies: liberalism and the moral uses of pluralism', *Social Research* 61(3): 539–61.

Rowe, G. and L. Frewer. 2004. 'Evaluating public-participation exercises', *Science, Technology and Human Values* 29(4): 512–56.

Sacardo, G. A. and I. E. Castro. 2002. *Conselho de Saúde – Observatório dos Direitos do Cidadão 8: acompanhamento e análise das políticas públicas da Cidade de São Paulo.* São Paulo: Institutio Pólis.

Sampson, S. 1996. 'The social life of projects: importing civil society to Albania', in C. Hann and E. Dunn (eds), *Civil Society: Challenging Western Models.* London and New York: Routledge.

Santos, B. and L. Avritzer. 2002. 'Para Ampliar o Cânone Democrático', in B. Santos (ed.) (2005). *Democratizar a Democracia: Os Caminhos da Democracia Participativa.* Rio de Janeiro: Editora Civilização Brasileira.

Satpathy, T. 2006. 'Dalit leadership in local governance', in *Organising Dalits: Experiences from the Grass Roots.* Ahmedabad: Unnati.

Schumpeter, J. 1976. *Capitalism, Socialism and Democracy.* London: Allen and Unwin.

SDI. 2002. Slum Dwellers International Report No. 1, February.

Shah, G. 1994. 'Politics of Dalit Movement: from direct action to pressure group', in S. Pendse (ed.), *At Crossroads: Dalit Movement Today.* Mumbai: Vikas Adhyan Kendra.

Shankland, A. and R. Athias. 2007. 'Decentralisation and difference: indigenous peoples and health system reform in the Brazilian Amazon', in *Decentralising Service Delivery?* IDS Bulletin 38(1): 77–90.

Singer, P. and V. C. Brant (eds). 1983. *São Paulo: o povo em movimento.* São Paulo: CEBRAO and Rio de Janeiro: Vozes.

Skocpol, T. 1979. *Social Revolutions in the Modern World.* Cambridge: Cambridge University Press.

Skocpol, T. 1992. *Protecting Soldiers and Mothers: The Political Origins of Social Policy in the United States.* Cambridge, MA: Harvard University Press.

Skocpol, T. 1994. *States and Social Revolutions.* Cambridge: Cambridge University Press.

Snyder, R. and J. Mahoney. 1999. 'The missing variable: institutions and the study of regime change', *Comparative Politics* 32(1): 103–22.

South African Homeless People's Federation (SAHPF). 2005. Ashoka Full Economic Citizenship Initiative, available at: www.ashoka.org/files/SAHPF.pdf (accessed 4 November 2009).

Sumathi, S. and V. Sudarsen. 2005. 'What does the panchayat system guarantee? A case of Pappapati', *Economic and Political Weekly* 40(34).

Tapscott, C. 2005. *Democracy, Social Capital and Trust Relations in Local Government in South Africa*, Occasional Paper No. 1, University of the Western Cape.

Tapscott, C. 2007. 'The challenge of building participatory local government', in L. Thompson (ed.), *Participatory Governance? Citizens and the State in South Africa.* Belville: University of the Western Cape.

Tarrow, S. 1994. *Power in Movement: Social Movements, Collective Action and Politics.* Cambridge: Cambridge University Press.

Teixeira, A. C., J. Kayano and L. Tatagiba. 2007. *Saúde, Controle Social e Política Pública. Observatório de Direitos do Cidadão*, Observatório dos Direitos do

Cidadão Report No. 29. São Paulo: Institutio Pólis.
Terreblanche, S. 2002. *A History of Inequality in South Africa 1652–2002*. Oxford: Blackwell.
Thompson, L. and T. Matheza. 2005. *Migrants and Service Delivery in the Western Cape: A Gendered Analysis*, Occasional Paper No. 2, University of the Western Cape.
Thompson, L. and N. Nleya. 2008. 'The policy implications of the millennium development goals and service delivery at the national and local levels', *Africanus* 2008/09.
Thompson, L. and N. Nleya. 2009. 'Survey methodology in violence prone Khayelitsha, Cape Town, South Africa', in *Violence, Social Action and Research*, IDS Bulletin 40(3): 50–57.
Thompson, L. and C. Tapscott (eds). 2010. *Citizenship and Social Movements: Perspectives from the Global South*. London: Zed Books.
Thornton, P., J. Devine, P. P. Houtzager, D. Wright and S. Rozario. 2000. *Partners in Development: A Review of Big NGOs in Bangladesh*. Prepared for UK Department for International Development.
Tilly, C. 1998. 'Social movements and (all sorts of) other political interactions – local, national, and international – including identities', *Theory and Society* 27(4): 453–80.
Transition Monitoring Group. 2007. *Do the Votes Count? Final Reports of the 2003 General Elections in Nigeria*. Abuja: Transition Monitoring Group.
UNDP. 2006. *Beyond Scarcity: Power, Poverty and the Global Water Crisis – Human Development Report 2006*. New York: UNDP.
UNI. 2004. 'A União das Nações Indígenas do Acre e Sul do Amazonas e Seus Desafios', *COIAB*, 18 June (accessed 11 November 2005 at: www.coiab.com.br/jornal.php?id=219).
Urbinati, N. and M. Warren. 2008. 'The concept of representation in contemporary democratic theory', *Annual Review of Political Science* 11: 387–412.
Van de Walle, N. 2001. *African Economies and the Politics of Permanent Crises, 1979–1999*. Cambridge: Cambridge University Press.
Verba, S., L. K. Schlozam and H. Brady. 1995. *Voice and Equality: Civic Voluntarism in American Politics*. Cambridge, MA: Harvard University Press.
Verdum, R. 2009. *O Orçamento da Ação Indigenista do Governo Federal em 2008*, Nota Técnica 148. Brasília: INESC.
Vidal, N. and J. P. Andrade (eds). 2006. *O Processo de Transição para o Multipartidarismo em Angola*. Lisbon and Luanda: Firmamento Ediçoes.
Vidal, N. and J. P. Andrade (eds). 2008. *Sociedade Civil e Política em Angola: Enquadramento Regional e Internacional*. Lisbon and Luanda: Firmamento Ediçoes.
Village Study Group. 1975. Working Paper series, Dhaka University.
Virtanen, P. K. 2007. 'Changing Lived Worlds of Contemporary Amazonian Native Young People: Manchineri Youths in the Reserve and the City, Brazil-Acre', PhD dissertation, Latin American Studies/Renvall Institute for Area and Cultural Studies. Helsinki: University of Helsinki.
VKE (Van Niekerk, Kleyn and Edwards Consulting Engineers & Urban Planners). 1985. *Revisions*

to the Draft Structure Plan for Khayelitsha. Cape Town: VKE.

von Lieres, B. 2006. 'Citizen participation in South Africa: land struggles and HIV/AIDS activism', in A. Cornwall and V. S. P. Coelho (eds), *Spaces for Change? The Politics of Citizen Participation in New Democratic Arenas.* London: Zed.

Wampler, B. and L. Avritzer. 2004. 'Públicos participativos: sociedade civil e novas instituições no Brasil democrático', in V. S. Coelho and M. Nobre (eds), *Participação e deliberação: teoria democrática e experiências institucionais no Brasil contemporâneo.* São Paulo: 34 Letras.

Wanjala, S. and L. Mute (eds). 2002. *When the Constitution Begins to Flower: Paradigms for Constitutional Change in Kenya.* Nairobi: Claripress.

Warren, K. B. and J. E. Jackson. 2002. 'Introduction: studying indigenous activism in Latin America', in K. B. Warren and J. E. Jackson (eds), *Indigenous Movements, Self-Representation, and the State in Latin America.* Austin, TX: University of Texas Press.

Warren, M. 1992. 'Democratic theory and self transformation', *American Political Science Review* 86: 8–23.

Warren, M. 2000. *Democracy and Association.* Princeton, NJ: Princeton University Press.

Weber, M. 1946. *From Max Weber: Essays in Sociology.* Oxford: Oxford University Press.

White, G. 1998. 'Constructing a democratic developmental state', in M. Robinson and G. White (eds), *The Democratic Developmental State: Politics and Institutional Design.* Oxford: Oxford University Press.

Williams, M. 1998. *Voice, Trust and Memory: Marginalized Groups and the Failings of Liberal Representation.* Princeton, NJ: Princeton University Press.

World Bank. 2006. *Economics and Governance of Non-Governmental Organisations in Bangladesh,* Bangladesh Development Series No. 11. Dhaka: World Bank.

Young, I. M. 2000. *Inclusion and Democracy.* Oxford: Oxford University Press.

Youngs, R. 2008. 'Trends in democracy assistance: what has Europe been doing?' *Journal of Democracy* 19: 160–69.

Zelliot, E. 2001. *From Untouchable to Dalits: Essays on Ambedkar's Movement.* Delhi: Manohar.

Ziccardi, A. 1994. *Participación ciudadana y políticas sociales en el espacio local.* Mexico City: Universidad Nacional Autónoma de México.

Index

www.ingramcontent.com/pod-product-compliance
Lightning Source LLC
Chambersburg PA
CBHW060150280326
41932CB00012B/1701